{ NEIL YOUNG NATION

: lived and narrated by

NEIL

A QUEST

AN OBSESSION

(AND A TRUE STORY)

as lived and narrated by

KEVIN CHONG

YOUNG
NATION

GRE**Y**STONE BOOKS

Douglas & McIntyre Publishing Group

VANCOUVER/TORONTO/BERKELEY

*This book is dedicated to Mark, Dave, and Geoff, and
all my friends who've come along for the ride.*

Greystone Books
A division of Douglas & McIntyre Ltd.
2323 Quebec Street, Suite 201
Vancouver, British Columbia
Canada V5T 4S7
www.greystonebooks.com

Library and Archives Canada Cataloguing in Publication
Chong, Kevin
Neil Young nation / Kevin Chong.

ISBN-10: 1-55365-116-2 · ISBN-13: 978-1-55365-116-1

1. Young, Neil, 1945– 2. Rock musicians—Canada—Biography.
3. Authors, Canadian (English)—21st century—Travel. I. Title.
ML420.Y75C54 2005   782.42166'092   C2005-903703-2

Library of Congress information is available upon request

Editing by Barbara Pulling
Cover and text design by Peter Cocking
Cover photos: Neil Young: © Henry Diltz/CORBIS; Kevin Chong by Kevin Chong
Map by Stuart Daniel/Starshell Maps
Printed and bound in Canada by Friesens
Printed on acid-free paper that is forest-friendly (100% post-consumer
recycled paper) and has been processed chlorine free.
Distributed in the U.S. by Publishers Group West

The publisher gratefully acknowledges the financial support of the Canada Council for
the Arts, the British Columbia Arts Council, and the Government of Canada through the
Book Publishing Industry Development Program (BPIDP) for its publishing activities.

"Lemme tell you something about Neil Young fans—

the real *fans: They're all a bunch of fuckin' maniacs."*

Jimmy McDonough, *Shakey*

"The thought occurred to me that if men thought me a

little insane they would forgive me if I lit out."

Sherwood Anderson

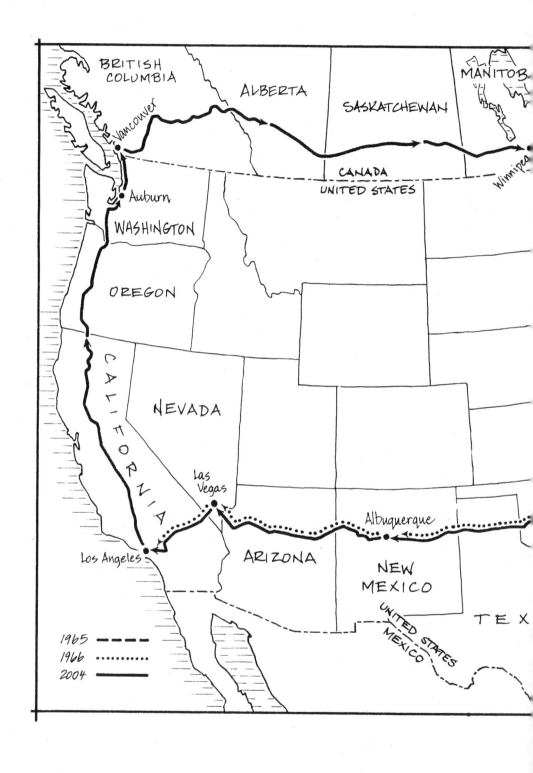

BRITISH COLUMBIA

ALBERTA

SASKATCHEWAN

MANITOB

Vancouver

CANADA

UNITED STATES

Winnipeg

Auburn

WASHINGTON

OREGON

C A L I F O R N I A

NEVADA

Las Vegas

Albuquerque

Los Angeles

ARIZONA

NEW MEXICO

UNITED STATES
MEXICO

T E X

1965 — — —
1966 ·············
2004 ————

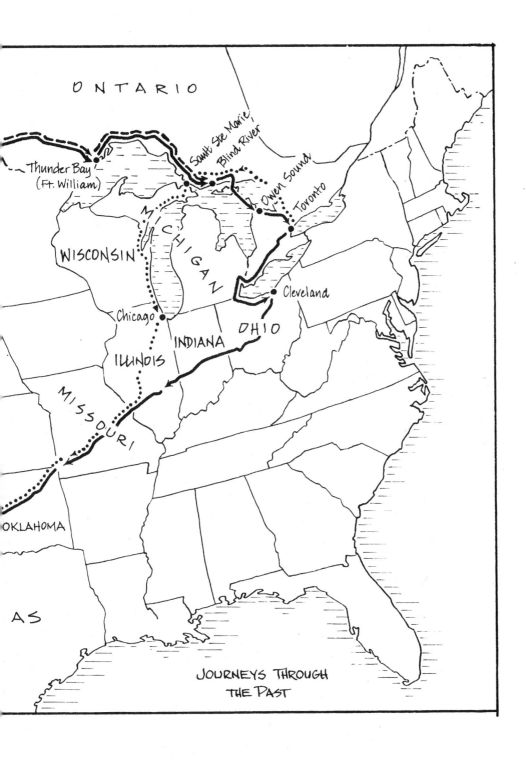

ONTARIO

Thunder Bay
(Ft. William)

Sault Ste Marie

Blind River

Owen Sound

Toronto

WISCONSIN

MICHIGAN

Chicago

Cleveland

OHIO

INDIANA

ILLINOIS

MISSOURI

OKLAHOMA

AS

JOURNEYS THROUGH
THE PAST

INTRODUCTION

IN 1965, a friend asked Neil Young for a ride. Young was a working musician in Fort William, Ontario, and his friend had a show in Sudbury, about 650 kilometers away. On a whim, Neil agreed to drive him there in Mort, his 1948 Buick Roadmaster hearse. Somewhere along the way, the transmission fell out of the car. Neil Young was only nineteen.

Young, who had planned to return to Fort William, took Mort's death as an omen, a sign that he couldn't turn back to either Fort William or Winnipeg, where his mother lived. Heading instead to Toronto, his birthplace, he wrote a bunch of gloomy songs about failure and yearning, was dismissed as clichéd in the local paper, and skulked around various Yorkville coffeehouses. But even at such an early, feckless age, he would do anything to be a rock star. There were a couple of brushes with success, including an audition in a closet at Elektra Records and a stint with Rick James in the most mind-boggling Motown band-that-never-was, the Mynah Birds. Following on his ambition, he decided that he needed to leave.

In March 1966, after hocking some guitars and amplifiers that didn't technically belong to him, and borrowing a sleeping bag, Young took another hearse across America. This time, with Neil driving the whole trip wired on amphetamines, the hearse carried him to fame. He had set out for Los Angeles looking for his friend Stephen Stills, whom he'd met in Fort William. During a traffic jam on Sunset Boulevard, Stills spotted a hearse with Ontario license plates and knew it had to be Young. He was only twenty.

Less than a month after landing in L.A., Young and Stills's new band, Buffalo Springfield, were opening for the Byrds and entertaining record offers. The hearse was abandoned for a limousine, and within a year Young had gone from literally singing for his supper to playing with the Rolling Stones at the Hollywood Bowl.

In the decades that followed, Neil Young would become world-famous as the craggy, cavern-browed hippie in the buckskin jacket, his electric guitar chugging along like a steam engine, his acoustic guitar chopping like paddle strokes in a lake.

But for every idea of Neil Young, there is a counter; for every persona or role, a contradiction. He's the Nixon-bashing hippie and the country singer praising Ronald Reagan. The mellow folkie with his acoustic guitar and the dissolute rocker throttling his out-of-tune 1953 Gold Top, Old Black. The rock 'n' roll Luddite who loathes CDs and the dabbler of electronic music of *Trans*. The patriotic American and the Canadian passport-holder. From these disparate attitudes and guises has come a body of work that is multifaceted, erratic, and original.

THIS MIGHT SOUND FAMILIAR to you. Some bespectacled chubbo walks into a record store. Or some scrawny spaz breaks into his older brother's room. Or some slob sneaks into a party. (Any one of these scenarios can work.)

This guy's life, up to that point, has been a series of unremitting indignities. He can't get his hair right. He can't get with women. His jokes aren't laughed at. He spends his weekends watching videos with his grandmother, who makes him stop movies whenever she hears a curse. He's too tall. He's too short. (Details may vary.)

This is where the album or tape or CD comes in. The music he's heard up until then is too crass, too wimpy, too calculating. It might do for other people, and he has to remind himself that not everyone listens to music the way he does. Not everyone is looking for consolation.

But today he plays this record and it leaves him with his hair standing on end, like in a science-fair disaster. It makes him feel cool; it feels like secret information. He realizes not only that he's a fan of this rock star, but that he's always been his fan. Even before he heard of him, he was a fan. He was a fan from the womb; he just didn't know it at the time.

Maybe this was you. It certainly was me; it certainly is me. Neil Young saved my life.

I was thirteen or fourteen, and the video for "This Note's for You" had just come out. Neil Young was about to emerge, like a Granola Rock phoenix, from the shithole of critical derision and commercial irrelevance. Although music television has never been a haven for normal-looking people, at least in those days people over the age of twenty-two could still occasionally appear onscreen. I knew there had been a stink around the "This Note's for You" video, something to do with Michael Jackson with his hair on fire. MTV had banned the video, which somehow led to it being played endlessly on Canadian television.

"This Note's for You" was followed closely by "Rockin' in the Free World," one of those songs that have since been so overplayed that no one bothers listening to them. A song that assails complacent consumerism and hypocrisy, it has become an anthem for sanctimonious, meathead rage among those who take at face value its mocking anti-slogan of a title. The song gets played at Hard Rock Cafes; boomer politicians belt it out, in shirts and ties, at political fundraisers. Again, there was a memorable video, its humor was more subtle, more self-mocking than that of the video for "This Note's for You." Young played a homeless TV-wielding seer, then a glam rocker with lipstick and hairspray. I was extremely impressed. Here, it seemed, was someone who could also have a good time. I found the song on the album *Freedom* and wore down my cassette copy listening to it again and again.

So I bought his next album, *Ragged Glory*. I had become a fan as Young was experiencing a critical renaissance. He shared a stage with Sonic Youth, recorded with Pearl Jam. His songs were covered by the Pixies and Dinosaur Jr. At that age, I wasn't quite cool enough not to enjoy Led Zeppelin and Jimi Hendrix, just as I liked punk rock and indie rock.

I was taking guitar lessons and I formed a band. The bassist (who is still a musician) brought a copy of "Cinnamon Girl" into my parents' basement. This was my first acquaintance with Young's earlier music, and I loved the opening guitar riff and clapping, the one-note guitar solo, the joyful howls, the minor key–sinister fuzz-guitar lick near the end. Over the next few years, in a number of bands, many hours would be spent noodling through Crazy Horse standards like "Cortez the Killer," "Like a Hurricane," and "Hey Hey, My My (Into the Black)." All of these songs were easy to play—and easy to play *very loud.*

Sometime after my thousandth basement rendition of "Hey Hey, My My," I lost my mind. I started buying Young's older albums: *Everybody Knows This Is Nowhere,* then *Harvest* and *After the Gold Rush,* then *Tonight's the Night* and *Zuma.* I read *Neil and Me* by Neil's father, Scott Young, and John Einarson's *Don't Be Denied,* the essential book on Neil's Winnipeg years. (Young's semi-authorized biography, *Shakey,* by Jimmy McDonough, would appear in 2002. Another major biography, *Zero to Sixty,* by Johnny Rogan, was published in the U.K.) I joined the Neil Young Appreciation Society, and my very first publication was a song-by-song review for the NYAS fanzine, *Broken Arrow,* when I was eighteen. In it, I likened Neil's guitar face to that of someone who's been kicked in the groin.

Why was I such a fan? Let me count the reasons. There was that voice, so unusual—many would say so screechy or alley-cat—that you knew he wasn't skating by on gloss. I remember watching television as a child and seeing a man in a flannel shirt and sunglasses singing on the 1985 all-star famine-relief song "Tears Are Not Enough," Canadian music's answer to "We Are the World." He looked like a lumberjack-pirate among the zipper-clad and poodle-headed Canadian talent, which included Corey Hart, Geddy Lee from Rush, *and* Paul Shaffer. There was something even stranger about his voice. How did *he* ever become famous? When the song's producer, David Foster, told him that his singing was flat, Neil replied, with characteristic assurance, "That's my style, man!" And yet it would take me a few more years to realize that this man wasn't Gordon Lightfoot.

Young, whose idyllic childhood was ruptured by a near-fatal polio attack and his parents' divorce, sang like the child who is the father of the man, in the voice of innocence singed by experience. His lyrics balanced stoner abstraction ("Is it hard to make arrangements with yourself / When you're old enough to repay but young enough to sell?" in "Tell Me Why") with compelling, fragmented imagery ("Big birds flying across the sky" in "Helpless"). Young's trippy songwriting style—which bowled over distinctions between you and me, you and her, now and then, before and after, here and there—was unified by his melancholic vision, his tenuous tenor, his unerring sense of melody.

It was the peculiar, sometimes begrudging way he confessed feelings that made them inevitable, rather than simply a formal requirement of rock songwriting. And yet the off-the-cuff manner in which Young produced his music—songs quickly written while he was laid flat by illness or injury, then recorded with a minimum of rehearsal and studio gimmickry—revealed not only a desire for rawness and immediacy but a fear of equivocation, a fear of his own fear to commit. Even when Young was ambivalent, he wavered fiercely and noisily.

Without idealizing it, he exalted melancholy, which, novelist Thomas Pynchon once mused, "is a far richer and more complex ailment than simple depression. There is a generous amplitude of possibility, chances for productive behavior, even what may be identified as a sense of humor."

Then there was his guitar: the way it shrieked and whinnied sounded *outside* of music, less about melody or hot licks, and more about punishment, more like a stream of anguish.

By the time I finished high school, Young had become something of a role model for me. Looking back, I could have done worse. Young was the embodiment, in his appearance, his singing, his music, of a type of anti-beauty. To an awkward kid, this was appealing. Young sought beauty in frayed edges and worn-out patches. He reveled in bum notes, in buzzing guitar strings. Even his album covers had a rough, unfinished quality. The solarized photo of Young on the cover of *After the Gold Rush* would cost a Fotomat operator his job. Jim Mazzeo's far-out line drawings for

Zuma of a naked woman, a "danger bird," and some pyramids look at first to be found art from a discarded Denny's placemat.

IN AUGUST 2004, I decided to follow the same route Young took from Winnipeg to Fort William (now Thunder Bay), and then from Toronto to Los Angeles. With three pot-smoking buddies and a hatbox's worth of space cakes, I crossed North America in one triangular swoop, traveling 14,000 kilometers and 7,500 miles, through five provinces and fourteen states, in twenty-two days. I visited places that were important to Neil and a few people associated (albeit tangentially) with Neil, and stopped in Auburn, Washington, to see Young play at Farm Aid 2004. It was a trip: in the here-to-there dictionary sense, in the foggy mind-journeying granola sense, in the pratfall sense.

My Wild Neil Chase was cooked up on the fly, and with little premeditation. I had just turned twenty-nine and, like a lot of people approaching thirty, felt as if each birthday was a door being slammed loudly and angrily. Even my twenty-eighth birthday had been a stinging rebuke. For me, it meant I could no longer be a dead rock star who had died at twenty-seven. My chance to choke—gloriously—on my own vomit had come and passed. Now I was a year away from thirty, life's first big speed bump.

Most of my friends were grown-ups. I didn't count myself among them. Grown-ups were those with spouses, mortgages, and car payments, and produce in their refrigerator. Not someone like me, a novelist who stole toilet paper from his parents. People I knew were not so much trying to have children as they were not *not* trying to have them. They'd reached a certain age and succumbed to the inevitable gravity of reproduction. Not me. My mother had so much grandchild-envy that she'd recently encouraged me to find a special *anyone* to knock up.

This is not to say I was some adolescent party-animal, getting loaded on shots of Jägermeister. If anything, I had the lifestyle and income of a septuagenarian pensioner. I played in monthly poker games with my married friends, drank beer at the Legion Hall on Thursday nights, took my dog to the beach.

And this is not to say that I was discontent in my unattached, semi-squalid developmental limbo. The novelist Mordecai Richler once remarked to the effect that no one grows up dreaming of catering the Great American Bar Mitzvah. I've taken his point to mean that some part of a writer, however small, refuses to accept reality. There remained a patina of danger about being a novelist. At least it went over great at parties.

Only a few years earlier, I'd felt ahead of the game. Without ever having had a steady income, I had gone directly from life as an underfunded graduate student to being a working writer. I had published my first novel when I was twenty-five. The book came out and was a very modest non-failure. I would look myself up on Google and find out that a university student in Georgia thought my book sucked compared to *The Nanny Diaries*. Hey, who was I to disagree? I'd bump into someone who'd given me a bad review at a party and fantasize for weeks about taking one of this reviewer's books, smearing it with dog shit, and mailing it to his doorstep. I was now officially a writer. I'd become the person I wanted to be.

Things started going wrong with my second novel. The first thing I noticed was how unbearably hard it had become to write. I was no longer working in a vacuum, and my ambitions had grown larger. It took much longer than my first, years longer. I spent much of 2003 covered in hives; I'd wake up with welts along my arms, my legs, sometimes an eyelid. A blood test showed no food or fabric allergies. I was allergic to my novel.

But I persisted, and after three years cobbling away I had a manuscript that pleased me. And yet it didn't please those big-hearted people who turn piles of manuscript pages into books and give writers money and author tours. It would seem that I'd turned out something like the prose equivalent of anchovies. This wasn't what I'd expected. I decided to put my novel "in the refrigerator." I stopped writing fiction and tried not to think about it. I needed a break. I needed Neil Young, or at least his music, to save me again.

This is strange but true: everything I know about being young I learned from Neil Young, a jowly man approximately twice my age and now hurtling toward senior citizenship. "Well, I keep gettin' younger," he sings in "Crime in the City," "My life's been funny that way." He bristles against expectations; he chooses spontaneity over precision, passion over perfection. This was exactly what I wanted in my life, in my art. What Young called *reckless abandon*. The expressions go *kid at heart* or *old soul,* but these are mere consolations for most people. For Young, old is a choice, a train you can elect not to board. Being young is an awareness of possibility, an unwillingness to stick with what one already knows and lead with one's strengths. And, in my opinion, this frame of mind is much harder to achieve than the physical agelessness exemplified by news readers or yoga instructors.

One can be a rock star at sixty, just as there are teenagers who are already planning to sell life insurance. As a novelist turning thirty, working through the night, searching for the right word to describe a one-note guitar solo, then sleeping into the afternoon, I felt like someone looking for a place in between.

\ | /

CHAPTER

ONE

IT WAS LATE AUGUST, the night before we left Vancouver. The lawns were still scorched, patchy and yellow like scrawny egg noodles, but an autumnal chill had begun dropping over the city. From my days as a schoolboy, I could still track the end of summer by its smell, by the taste of the air. Even now, far past school and as someone self-employed, someone who thinks of the weekend as the days you don't get mail, I still get shivers around this time of year.

My friend Dave Yellowlees had come over from Vancouver Island, by ferry and bus, and arrived at my door early in the evening.

When I decided to go on this trip, Dave, who is a welder in Victoria, was the first person I called. We'd been on half a dozen road trips over the last decade, and of all the grown-ups I knew, he was the one I could count on to shuck everything to eat Taco Bell and share a double bed with another dude. I'd left a voicemail for Dave and got a call back the next day.

"I couldn't sleep the whole night," he'd told me.

"You're coming then?" I asked.

"Of course. I'd quit my job to go on a road trip with you."

(Cue manly sobbing)

Dave is tall and ginger-haired, amiable, an ex–water polo player. Along with our friend Geoff, he and I used to go under-age drinking at wino bars where drinks were a buck a glass and ordered in multiples of two or three; the waitresses gave out change from coin dispensers hanging from their belts. On the subject of Dave's teenage exploits, Miguel, an exchange student from Basque who boarded at Dave's parents' house, wrote this charming quatrain about him:

> *Day-veed Yellow Lees.*
> *Sex mah-sheen.*
> *Day-veed Yellow Lees.*
> *Push ahn squeeze.*

Dave has been with his girlfriend, Lyn, for years, so those days are long past, though he often trots out war stories for my entertainment and is my favorite friend for pervy-old-man conversations about the young starlets we have crushes on. And Dave is not afraid to look or flirt.

Dave came into my apartment to unload his stuff. He'd been laid off and on the dole for the early part of the summer and then been offered back his old job. He stayed only until he'd made enough money for a digital video camera.

"They wouldn't let me have three weeks off for our trip," he said. "So I had to give notice."

"You really did quit your job?"

"Nothing I haven't done before," he told me with a cheerful shrug as he unhitched his backpack. "Lyn's got a friend, a Japanese exchange student, who's living with us for a couple of months. She'll be covering my half of the mortgage."

From his backpack, he brought out the digital camcorder and started showing me its display functions. "I'm going to get a great road documentary out of this," he enthused. By "great road documentary," I was fairly certain he meant a lot of footage of Geoff and his hairy ass in various nondescript motel rooms. I'd enlisted our other old friend to join us on the trip. Dave angled his camera along my bookshelves and out the window, finally settling on the half-dead spider plant hanging from my ceiling.

"Only you could half-kill a spider plant," Dave said, shaking his head. "Why don't you just buy a new one?"

"It's half-dead from *over*watering," I stressed, wrapping my arms around my elbows as though cradling an infant. "I loved it a little too hard." The spider plant would do better in my absence. As usual, my mother would come by once a week to attend to the mail and the plants. My plants preferred my mom to me.

Dave laughed, not so much because I was funny as because I was being typical. I'm his nebbishy writer friend, the hopeless bachelor, the bone-saw ironist, just as Dave is my pot-smoking welder buddy—an accidental hippie. We play up these roles, and yet, because we've known each other so long, we're free to step outside of them; we can take turns being the irresponsible one or the sensible one. There's probably no way Dave and I would be friends if we met now, but still, whenever we hang out, we don't miss a step.

"Let's get a drink," he suggested.

There's a cheesy bar and grill across the back lane from my building, full of men who reek of cologne and women in tight black dresses and boots huddled on the patio smoking. These are the dressy bon vivants whose martini-drenched laughter and piercing declarations of disaffection ring from the back alley at two in the morning. I'd be angry about it if I wasn't normally awake. In the far corner of the establishment, underneath a bank of TV screens showing baseball or hockey games, there's a bar that serves cheap draft. Last year Dave, Geoff, and I got food poisoning there from some bad oyster shooters, but we still come back because, hey, it's cheap.

The place was full. At the short end of the backwards L-shaped bar, two women holding tight to their middle-thirties sat on their stools. One of the women offered us her seat: "We're just about to leave." She was talking on a cell phone while the other woman looked over my long, tall friend. Dave flashed them a smile.

"Let's call Geoff," Dave suggested, after we'd taken our seats and ordered the first round. Seated next to Dave at the bar was a young man scribbling in his notebook. He put down his pen and looked over at us. I ignored him.

"I left Geoff a message," I told Dave. "I doubt he'll come out tonight."

Dave was still as excited about this trip as I was. During the past couple of months I'd kept him up on my preparations. My days as a rabid Neil Young fan—someone who bought everything Young put out on its release date—had long passed. My membership to the NYAS had lapsed. I hadn't bought his last few CDs and I'd skipped the Greendale tour because of boomer-gouging ticket prices. While I still listened to Neil regularly, over the past few years I'd been simply too busy tending to my own work to be the devoted fan of anyone but myself.

That summer, however, I'd reimmersed myself in all things Neil. I'd joined a couple of Neil Young discussion groups, and, introducing myself online, talked to dozens of hardcore fans, known as Rusties. Through Sharry Wilson, one fan I'd befriended, I obtained dozens of bootleg CDs and VCDs, including several rarities compilations, some bootleg live recordings, and her entire collection of *Broken Arrows*, which were full of reviews, Neil sightings, radio interview transcripts, set lists, and weird bits of trivia such as the sighting of an Italian racehorse named "Rust Never Sleeps." Included in Sharry's *Broken Arrow* collection was the issue in which I'd been first published. I looked for the "kicked in the groin" line, and there it was. It was as though I was coming full circle. The more Neil I listened to, the more I read about him, the less time I had to worry about my own problems. His music had the same effect it did when I was younger: it insulated me from my own crapulence. It made me cool by association.

"You should arrange to meet Neil at Farm Aid," Dave was suggesting. "Get that guy who writes his biographies—"

"John Einarson."

Dave nodded. "Yeah. You've been in touch with him, right? Get him to set you up with Neil."

"Uh, I don't think I want that."

"You don't want to meet Neil?"

"No. I'm pretty sure I don't want him to know this book exists, much less have him read it."

In my mind, Neil is fifty feet tall and made of solid gold—even his flannel shirts are gold—and his muttonchop sideburns are bejeweled. I value his music too much to chance any disillusioning encounters, like the time I met Jimmy Page from Led Zeppelin. I was standing outside a Sam the Record Man in downtown Vancouver when a white limousine pulled up. From it first emerged David Coverdale of Whitesnake, whom Page was recording with, and then the scrawny Zep guitarist, clutching a cigarette. I asked if he was Jimmy Page; he replied, "Fuck, no," and walked away from me. It still hurts deep inside.

Dave and I ordered another round, then a couple more. Then a few after that. At some point, I could no longer keep up. Dave started lapping me, ordering only for himself. We discussed in detail the stops we'd be making and the trip's haphazard scheduling.

"I'm not sure what's going on in Thunder Bay," I told him. "The person I want to talk to won't return my calls."

The guy sitting next to Dave at the bar kept looking over at us. I tried to avoid eye contact.

"I'm looking forward to the places I've never been to before," Dave said. "Like Cleveland and Albuquerque."

"I'm not sure how much time we'll have in Albuquerque. We need to get from Cleveland to Vegas in two, two and a half days—tops."

At this point in our conversation, the man sitting next to Dave couldn't help speaking up. He had a thin beaky nose and eyes that bulged slightly, and his hair was in tight blond ringlets. He was at least in his mid-twenties. "Why the hell are you guys driving to Thunder Bay and then Vegas?"

"It's a long story—" I started.

"There's no way you can make it from Cleveland to Vegas in two days."

"We can do it," Dave said.

"You'll need at least four days, and when you're driving through the desert, you should bring a cell phone, two liters of water, and a fan belt. Get an oil change somewhere in the Midwest—"

"It's going to be hard," I said, somewhat forcefully. "But it's doable." I shrugged. Unless otherwise noted, I am always shrugging. In my life, blind optimism has rarely led me astray. Okay, it has, many times, disastrously, but who was he to tell us what to do? This pissant had driven through the desert the year before and was now, without introduction, proceeding to lecture us—two wizened highwaymen—on how to conduct our own kickass road tour? How dare he?

"I mean, why? Why are you going?"

I sighed. "I'm a writer—"

"I'm one, too." He tapped his clothbound notebook. Now I was seriously annoyed. For me, this was like telling someone you're a singer and having him point to his home karaoke machine and say he's one, too. Or you're a fireman, and someone who happens to keep an extinguisher in his basement says he's one, too. Or you're a baker and someone comes up to you with one of those logs of pre-made cookie dough and says he's a baker, too. Or you're a carpet salesman and someone points to an area rug he's trying to sell—you get my point. I could go on and on.

"No," I said, the humor leached from my face. *"I'm a writer."*

"Oh," he nodded. "You make money at writing."

"Well, yeah—sort of."

Most of the time I don't hate people, most of the time I like people, but I don't always feel super comfortable around them. It usually takes me about seven years of acquaintanceship before I feel comfortable around a friend. And around strangers, I have maybe four minutes' worth of small talk before I need to recede back into the darkness. Thankfully, Dave was there. Dave can get along with anyone. Right now Dave was telling the guy with the notebook about the stops on our trip, the people we were planning to meet. He was explaining to the man why his scowling friend was such a pill. My friend Amanda once coined a term to describe her boyfriend's barroom garrulity, and I think it applies to my friend, too: Dave is a *hobo-whisperer.*

\\ | /

CHAPTER

TWO

VANCOUVER IS THE CITY I grew up in, and with the exception of
my infancy in Hong Kong and my graduate schooling in New York, the
only city I've lived in. I love the ocean and the mountains; the year-round
lushness, the tall evergreens and thick bushes whose names I don't know,
but which cover every corner; the breezy summer nights and wet winters.
I can't think of living anywhere else. That said, in some ways I feel the
city is wasted on me. Supposedly Vancouver is a city for leisure lovers. I
love leisure, I like to think of myself as a *lord of leisure*. And yet for many
people here, leisure means doing stuff, like windsurfing and snowboard-
ing. Not for me.

The city also happens to be Canada's capital of crunch. There are
the yuppified hippies in SUVs bought to hold baby seats and Labrador
retrievers. In an entire part of town, Kitsilano, yoga spandex-wear seems
to be a neighborhood dress-code requirement, enforced by punishment of
extended stretching. On the east side, along Commercial Drive, are the
politicized hippies handing out information on the Green Party. There
you'll see more examples of the modern-day hippie: the dreadlock-wear-
ing man or woman who reads Noam Chomsky and Naomi Klein, Richard Brautigan and Georges Bataille.

I have many friends who claim to loathe hippies, but I can't help feeling this to be an expression of self-hatred. In Vancouver one is often granola by default, not a self-identified, by-the-book, tie-dye and microbus hippie but someone perpetuating deracinated tropes of hippie culture. Elderly white women can hold forth on the best way to cook tofu. Punk rockers are caught playing hacky-sack and ultimate Frisbee. Bankers just happen to smoke a lot of pot and listen to Ben Harper. As a first-generation immigrant and, as a teenager, a fan of punk-rock bands like the Ramones and Black Flag I used to think myself insulated from hippiedom, but even I've tried pot and yoga.

What I'm trying to say is that, while I might not be the most likely Neil Young fan, in Vancouver it's possible for anybody to be one. Take, for instance, the provocatively monikered Nardwuar the Human Serviette, whose all-consuming quest to interview Young I see as a cautionary tale. Nardwuar is the leader of a garage-punk band, the Evaporators, known for songs like "I Gotta Rash" and "(I've Got) Icicles on My Testicles." In Canada, Nardwuar is more widely known as the man with the screechy voice and pageboy haircut who prods and taunts musicians and celebrities for MuchMusic, using his brand of campy subversion and punk-rock snottiness to anger, bemuse, and unravel the pretensions of his subjects.

I first encountered Nardwuar when I was eighteen and putting up a poster for my band at the university radio station. In place of our own band photo on the poster was a photocopied picture of Neil Young's teenage garage band, the Squires, whom I had read about but never heard. "How do you know about the Squires?" Nardwuar asked me. Apparently, they were his favorite band. A couple of weeks later, Nardwuar played me a tape dub of the Squires' only official recording, a seven-inch single with the instrumentals "The Sultan" and "Aurora."

When I contacted him earlier that summer, Nardwuar responded to my e-mail with his typical aplomb and exuberance, recalling my band and my crude poster and agreeing to meet for lunch. He suggested bringing along a friend of his, Bev Davies, someone who actually knew Neil Young.

Included on the Evaporators' latest CD, *Ripple Rock,* is Nardwuar's exchange with Mikhail Gorbachev. Nardwuar—who was questioned by the

RCMP (the Mounties, for non-Canadian readers) after the Vancouver press conference with the former Soviet leader—introduced himself by saying "dirgenay rockin' oo slabodnie S'viet": Russian for "Keep on rockin' in the free world." Over the years, "Keep on rockin' in the free world" has become something of a catchphrase for Nardwuar, the way he usually signs off with his interviewees. The one question he was able to ask at the press conference, which stumped Gorbachev, was: "Of all the political figures that Dr. Gorbachev has encountered...who wears the largest pants?"

My experience has convinced me that there are at least as many types of Neil Young fans as there are distinct phases of his career. There are Neil Young fans like Jimmy McDonough who prefer his stuff with Crazy Horse to his solo acoustic work, and others who feel the opposite way. Many music fans love Young's work with the 1970s supergroup Crosby, Stills, Nash, & Young. Some people prefer Young's work with Buffalo Springfield and the handful of songs he sang with them. But Nardwuar is probably the only fan whose favorite era in Young's music is the stuff he did *before* 1966.

"I know nothing of Neil Young's later work," Nardwuar told me over lunch. A dubious claim given his "rockin' in the free world" tagline. "I'm like one of those dudes who think the Rolling Stones ended after Brian Jones left the band." Nardwuar has never had time for what he calls "lame fat folk-assed shit." He first learned of Young's garage roots when reading the British music magazine *Select:* "There was a review of a fanzine from the Neil Young Appreciation Society. I became obsessed with the Squires."

The Evaporators celebrate this period of Young's life in their song "Winnipeg 64": "On the Great Canadian Shield, where the Bear and Bison Blow / There once was a man, Neil, he used to be a Squire / 'Aurora' backed with 'The Sultan' was such a great song / Better than anything Dinosaur Jr ever covered!"

Having interviewed Gorbachev and Kurt Cobain (Nardwuar had been allowed access to him backstage by Courtney Love, whom Nardwuar knew from an earlier interview), Nardwuar's next target was Neil Young, who became the white whale to his Ahab. With Young set to play a solo show in Vancouver in 1999, Nardwuar decided it was time to actively pursue an interview. His attempts to gain access through official channels fell flat. Bob Merlis, head of publicity at Warner, Young's record label, was unequivocal: "Let me give you the standard Neil Young speech. It will never, ever happen."

Nardwuar enlisted music journalist Kerry Gold, and an article detailing his quest to find Young was published in the *Vancouver Sun*. He faxed the article to Merlis and to Young's manager, Elliot Roberts, but as the concert date approached, there was no response. Then a local music writer spotted Young having lunch downtown the day before the concert and immediately phoned Nardwuar.

Nardwuar phoned Bev Davies, the woman with the Neil Young connection. Bev, who was now sitting across the table from me, took up the story. "Nardwuar called me on my day off and I was asleep. I grabbed my camera and was standing outside my door. And I thought, 'What if I dreamt this? What if the whole thing is a dream, and Nardwuar is not on his way here and Neil Young is not having lunch?'"

"How did I know that you knew something about Neil Young?" Nardwuar asked, commandeering the interview. "How did I meet you? And who are you, Bev Davies, just to clarify for the people out there?" He gently nudged the microphone of my MiniDisc recorder toward Bev.

"I'm just this person who knew Neil from the sixties—" Bev began.

"Bev is downplaying herself a tiny bit," Nardwuar bragged. "Bev Davies is an integral part of the Neil Young story, a side note that should be perhaps a bigger note."

Nardwuar and Bev met in 1998 at local punk legend Joey Shithead's garage sale. Bev had been a photographer for the *Georgia Straight,* a Vancouver free weekly and one-time counterculture organ, and had snapped photos of the Dead Kennedys, the Modernettes, and Billy Idol. Nardwuar was duly impressed, but as their friendship progressed, Bev played her "little ace-in-the-hole thing," where she mentioned that *"she knew the Neilster."*

"Me and Bev," Nardwuar continued, "wanted to ask Neil Young about *the sleeping bag.* What is the sleeping bag, Bev Davies?"

"It was one of those sleeping bags that had Indians and teepees and trains on the inside, one of those kids' ones. It belonged to me, and Neil took it to California in his hearse. I was supposed to go, and Tannis"—Neiman, Bev's friend—"and Jeanine"—Hollingshead, another friend—"went, and Brucey Bassey"—reclusive Buffalo Springfield bassist Bruce Palmer.

"Let's just go back and think here for a second, Kevin," Nardwuar interrupted, though I was already reeling as I thought about Bev's part in the hearse story. This was exactly the kind of thing I was looking for. "This was a defining moment. Remember the movie *The Gods Must Be Crazy*? A Coke bottle dropped out of the sky—what would have happened if that Coke bottle didn't drop out of the sky? There would have been no movie. Now, this is an amazing moment. Here's Neil Young getting in his hearse to drive to California. And the one person who wasn't allowed in that hearse was—"

"Bev Davies," I answered, turning to her. "Why weren't you allowed to go?"

"I didn't have any money. There were other dynamics; I don't think Tannis wanted me to go. So, he just took my sleeping bag."

"So Bev stayed in Toronto," Nardwuar interjected, resuming his narration, "and the hearse"—I think he meant Neil Young—"went on to write the songs that you love. Although, let's not forget about the Squires. Forget all that stuff about how Neil was great after 1966. Let's not forget Winnipeg, sixty-four."

On their way to ambush Young in Vancouver, Nardwuar and Bev decided to confront him about the sleeping bag. "We waited outside the door of the restaurant, where his car was. They sent somebody to look at us, and they went back with word that we didn't look that dangerous. So then Neil came out, and he went walking right past us. And I said, 'Neil, it's Bev.'"

Bev had reacquainted herself with Young a few years before, backstage at a concert. She'd been taking photos of Young and a relative of his from the Prairies when Neil started looking at her. "Don't I know you from somewhere?" he'd asked her. Bev reminded him of their connection. "And Neil said, 'Oh, Bev. It's all coming back now.' And I said, 'Please, be very selective. Only have certain parts come back.' " Bev has no photos of Neil from their time in Toronto, she says, because, living in the age of communal property, she would share her cameras with people who didn't share back.

Anyway, Bev and Nardwuar were outside the restaurant with Neil Young: "And he turned around and came back and gave me a hug. I said, 'This is my friend Nardwuar, and he wants to interview you.' "

Nardwuar continued: "He said, 'No interviews, but you can have a photo.' And I was like, *'Uhhhhhh.'* So Neil basically sped off, and we didn't get a chance to ask him about the sleeping bag."

"But you gave him that present," Bev reminded him, "that he remembered."

Nardwuar had seen a picture of the drumhead used by the Squires in one of John Einarson's books and got a friend to re-create the drumhead logo on a piece of wood. "I brought it with me and I said to Neil, 'Hey, Neil—look what I found at a garage sale in Winnipeg.' I was totally lying."

Young recognized the sign: "It looks like our old drumhead." According to Nardwuar, a friend watching a Neil Young concert DVD saw that Squires replica drumhead on footage shot in Neil's bus.

A few years later, Nardwuar and Bev made another attempt to locate the sleeping bag. "It was February 19, 2004," Nardwuar recalled, "at the Queen Elizabeth Theatre. I think he was doing his *Greendale* thing. We showed up there at sound check." He turned to Bev. "And sure enough, what happened?"

"Neil pulled up, and I called out for him, got the hug—"

When Nardwuar advanced, Young's handlers moved to intercept him. In the confusion, he forgot to ask for an interview. "The next thing I knew I was being herded out of there."

"Didn't we mention the sleeping bag that time?" Bev prompted Nardwuar.

"He said it was a *well-used* sleeping bag," Nardwuar remembered, "it got a lot of use, and he didn't have it anymore." He thought for a moment: "That's kind of gross."

Bev laughed. "Kind of—yeah."

Nardwuar's quest was continuing, even as mine was just starting. "I'm not sure if this is the end of my story," he said. "I'm still hoping I get to talk to him. I'd also love to interview Bill Clinton. I hear he's on a book tour. Maybe you can set something up, Kevin."

"I'll, uh, see what I can do."

\\|/

CHAPTER

THREE

THE CAR I normally drive is a 1986 BMW with at least 229,544 kilometers on it (that's when the odometer broke), handed down from my mother to my father to me, and when I was in grad school, it went to my brother, before I took possession of it again. It's the same car that I've driven since high school, and I've witnessed it go through a couple of phases. In the late 1980s, it was clearly a status symbol. During that time, immigration from Hong Kong was peaking in Vancouver and affluent Chinese began acquiring huge houses in nice parts of town. It became an unsavory stereotype that all Chinese people owned flashy German cars. As it's aged, and the mud flaps have begun falling off one at a time, it's become a gauge of my decline in prosperity.

I like to think I keep my car for the sake of continuity, for the trunk of memories it holds, but a less flattering interpretation might be that it represents my inability to grow up. I continue to throw money at this car—tires, brakes, speakers, timing belts—because I can't conceive of owning another one.

But symbolic as my car was for me, I needed a hearse for my trip. The hearse breaks down—*adventure!* Goth girls find the car and molest us—*adventure!* We get strip-probed at the border—*harrowing trauma,* er, *adventure!* It wouldn't be the same without a hearse.

Neil Young *is* a car. According to his many biographies, Young collects vintage automobiles and stores his fleet of cars—sixteen-cylinder Cadillacs, a Rolls-Royce with bulletproof mirrors owned by a dictator, a Packard he drove while living in Santa Cruz and playing as a member of the Ducks—in a specially built barn on his California ranch.

Young often writes his songs on the road, scribbling lyrics on newspapers in his customized bus. And even if cars and driving are common tropes for rock 'n' rollers, the road metaphors in Young's lyrics are remarkable for their abundance, their strange tenderness, and their continuing presence in a career spanning four decades.

Going by his songs, you might even think Young confuses his cars for people. Many casual fans are surprised, some dismayed, to learn that "Long May You Run," a song infused with the ache of lost love and nostalgia for journeys past, is actually an ode to Young's first hearse, Mort: "With your chrome heart shining in the sun / Long may you run."

Elsewhere, Young has used his cars-as-people metaphor to describe his long, switchbacking career. "When I came out I was a very cool car," he told the *London Times*. "[Then] I got a bit used and there were all these newer models, and pretty soon it was time to put me in the junkyard and use me for parts—maybe some other bands would take a bit from here, piece from there. Then for a long time it seemed like I must be falling apart, although that didn't bother me because inside I felt good about what I was doing. And finally people started going, 'Hey look at that over there, that's a classic. And it's in pretty good shape.' "

Or, as Young sings in "I'm the Ocean," "I'm an Aerostar / I'm a Cutlass Supreme / In the wrong lane / Trying to turn against the flow."

It's also worth mentioning the two Young songs that link cars with death. There's the line in "Long May You Run" about how "It was back in Blind River in 1962 / When I last saw you alive." The song "Driveby" was inspired by the murder of a classmate of Young's daughter, Amber: "I can't believe a machine gun sings / Driveby, driveby, driveby, driveby."

"Tired Eyes," a caterwauling lament from *Tonight's the Night,* is Young's account of a botched drug bust that leads to a shooting. "Well he shot four men in a cocaine deal," Young sings, half-speaking, in the opening chorus. "And he left them lyin' in an open field / Full of old cars with bullet holes in the mirrors / He tried to do his best but he could not."

Later in the song, Young repeats the line about the bullet holes in the mirrors, probably because it's so good. It's one of those full-bodied images that tether his sometimes free-floating narratives to common experience. It's been noted that many of Young's songs written following *Harvest,* including "Revolution Blues" and "Tonight's the Night," deal with the brutal aftermath of good times and free love. The old cars in "Tired Eyes" are like the sunken galleons in underwater sea documentaries: they're gravestones, markers for over-reaching greed and bottomless rapacity.

In addition to "Long May You Run," references to the first Mort appear in two other songs, the unreleased "Hitchhiker" and *Lucky Thirteen*'s "Get Gone," in which Neil sings: "I had me a Buick, was a '48 / Yeah, tons and tons of rollin' steel / With a long black hood and four big wheels." His second hearse, Mort Two, is mentioned in a more recent song, "Big Time": "Gettin' in an old black car / Gonna take a ride so far / To the land of sun-tan lotion."

Over the summer, I checked for hearses on eBay and in the classifieds. On Vancouver Island, Dave inquired about a souped-up hearse with, in his words, "half the engine sticking out of the fucken hood." A friend was driving to work when she saw Jim Fitzgerald's vintage funeral car barreling down the road. Aware of the hearse hunt I'd been conducting, she followed the death wagon until it stopped and asked Jim if he'd consider lending it to us. For no other reason than his general coolness, Jim agreed to help me out.

After a couple of weeks of phone-wrangling, Jim and I arranged to meet. I arrived at the pub early and waited outside. Five minutes later, the hearse appeared. It would be an understatement to say that the blue 1977 Cadillac stood out in traffic. It came up the hill like an antique, lovingly attended battleship.

The tattoos streaming down Jim's arms fit the profile of the stereotypical hearse owner, but he had a self-effacing demeanor and a gentle spirit that was far from intimidating. Jim didn't worship the devil, either, as a lot of people who see him in his car expect. Someone who owns a hearse is likely to be a little eccentric, though, and Jim obviously had an appreciation for the unusual. Before he got his current job with the City of North Vancouver, where he works on the roads, he was employed at a funeral home as a gravedigger. For a few weeks after one break-up, he actually lived in the offices of the funeral home. Every night, before going to sleep, he'd walk through the entire place, making sure everything was where it should be. And at one time, Jim told me, he had a mahogany casket for a coffee table. He now regretted having sold it so cheaply.

Jim owned three cars and worked on them in his spare time. For his beloved hearse, he'd spray-painted blue flames on the hood and added speakers and two seats in the back. It hadn't even occurred to me that a hearse wouldn't have rear seats.

He'd bought his hearse two years before, he told me, from a tattoo artist on Vancouver Island. A few weeks after our meeting, I got a call from a friend I hadn't talked to in a while. He was a drummer and we'd been in a high-school band called Fetal Pig with a bassist named Nate. My friend and I were catching up, and when I mentioned my hearse trip, he remarked, "Do you know who else owned a hearse? Nate." Nate was now a tattoo artist in Nanaimo, and Jim later confirmed the connection. That sealed it: this hearse and I were meant to be.

At least I thought so. Two weeks before I was set to leave, I got a phone call from Jim Fitzgerald. His left rear wheel had flown off on the highway. "Funny it should happen today," he added. I'd forgotten it was Friday the thirteenth. So after all that trouble, I couldn't travel in a hearse—it killed me.

ON THE CLOUDY MORNING after Dave arrived in town, the two of us spent a good half hour cramming the back of my brother's late-model Suzuki Grand Vitara with my junk. I usually packed light. On past trips, I'd sometimes left for a week without remembering to bring socks. On other trips, we'd have to pull over so I could buy a toothbrush, a copy of *Sassy* magazine, and a change of underwear. This time around, things were different. Not only did I remember to pack my unmentionables, but I brought my laptop, a stack of Neil Young books and three dozen CDs of his music, a tent, and a suitcase on wheels that was much larger than I'd thought it was.

"Look at you. You've turned into a princess," Dave said with disgust. "Where did you pack your tiara?" He shuffled bags and camping gear around like puzzle blocks until he found room for one last item.

Standing by the side of the road, I cracked open the huge cookie tin Dave had brought. He'd made space cakes using two boxes of brownie mix, chocolate chips, some silver ball-bearing sprinkles, and a quarter of shake. (Please be aware that, as a non-smoker, I use terms like "shake" and measurements like "a quarter" without any sense of what they mean.) I looked at Dave. "Uhhhhh, this is overkill, don't you think?"

Dave shook his head with characteristic insouciance. "It won't be hard to give them away as gifts. They're really tasty. Lyn was pissed I used all the butter and chocolate chips in the house, but I like my space cakes to taste good. It's not just about getting high. Some people don't understand that."

I tried to reason with him. "This is a road trip, not an Amsterdam hash bar. We'll be crossing the border in a week and a half."

He sighed as he wedged the cookie tin into the car. "Usually, you don't start nagging until we're at the border." He started patting my head. I turned away from him and climbed behind the wheel.

Dave and I headed to Geoff's place, which was en route to the highway. Dave, Geoff, and I went back to high school, to our days as pink leather clip-on necktie–wearing Catholic middle-schoolers who'd cross a room to smell a fart.

Geoff had only two weeks off, and at some point we'd have to put him on a plane back to Vancouver. "He could leave from Vegas," Dave said. "If he bought a ticket right now, he could get it cheap."

I looked at him. "Do you really think Geoff will do that?"

Dave rolled his eyes and laughed. The thing with Geoff is, he does things his own way, at his own speed, on his own schedule. Invariably, he does what he needs to do, he's reliable and hard-working, but he proceeds in such a deliberately offhanded way that Dave and I fret over him, even though we are hardly upstanding overachievers ourselves.

"He should quit his job, anyway," Dave said. Geoff drives a truck for an organic grocer. "I keep telling him that he needs to go back to school and get a trade. We should kidnap him."

At the time, Geoff lived with his girlfriend, Sarah, and their one-year-old, Sullivan, on the ground floor of a house owned by a friend. Their apartment had a makeshift stylishness that reminded me of the kind of apartment friends from grad school would rent in Brooklyn. There were no walls, so a few curtains hung where bedroom walls might have stood; music equipment and baby paraphernalia cluttered the floor.

"Hello, gentlemen," Geoff said with big-spirited irony, standing on the porch with a guitar amplifier in one hand and a cup of coffee in the other. Under a gray railroad-conductor hat, his dark hair, tendriled and tousled, fell past his ears, and he wore a caramel-colored leather jacket over a T-shirt and jeans. There's a sort of self-aware elasticity in his face, a playful bounce to his head, a winking rubberiness in his limbs that comes out when he's amiable—it's as though he has a slow, degenerative disease that will, years down the road, transform him into the lounge singer character Bill Murray played on *Saturday Night Live*. Sarah's dog, Trey, yapped at us as we stepped inside. "You had a late night?"

"Sort of," Dave said, taking Geoff's bag.

"I couldn't sleep," I told him.

"I wish I could have joined you guys, but I figured we'll be spending enough time together."

Geoff is my oldest friend. Our first conversation ever, at a high-school dance, had involved Jethro Tull: if I recall correctly, Geoff was a fan. He used to wear tie-dyes and come down the street in a slow lope, six feet tall and hunched over, hair down past his ears, hands in his pockets, his bass slung over his shoulder in a black traveling bag. Even at that age, Geoff could grow sideburns in half a week.

Geoff and I had been in a couple of bands together in high school, playing under-age at bars around town. We were pretty bad, but in a young, good-hearted way. After one show, a weasely-looking sound guy with a greasy ponytail and a black leather fanny pack snickered that we should rename our band "Fire Drill." But Geoff had kept at it, and I admired that. I'd played an early gig with his current band, Notes from Underground, right before I gave up my guitar dreams for writing.

I definitely don't miss lugging equipment around to bars and rehearsal spaces, but I do miss the bond that non-related heterosexual men can forge only by being in a rock band. (Or in extreme circumstances, as when sharing a sleeping bag under threat of hypothermia.) Over the summer, I'd often burned copies of the bootlegs and rarities collections I'd received and taken them across town to Geoff's house. Neil Young is a musical hero we have in common—along with Iggy Pop, the Velvet Underground, Jonathan Richman, and early Dinosaur Jr—and I must have thrashed through "Hey Hey, My My" at least nine hundred times with Geoff. Music is better when it's shared, it becomes more real, and there's no one else I can share music with. It's safe to say that, when I rushed over to Geoff's house with a 1970 Crazy Horse recording, it was more about me than him.

Geoff is an exceptional friend, good-natured but also fiercely introspective. Around him you soon sense his stubbornness, a self-possession that extends beyond independence into a kind of impregnability. If I were to trust a secret to anyone in the world, it would be him. On the other hand, it can be hard to wring any of his deep thoughts from his head. Which is, perhaps, understandable because: (a) guys don't share deep thoughts, (b) I'm a blabbermouth, (c) I'm a writer.

We took Geoff's guitar and amp and somehow found room for them in the car. Due to money and scheduling, his band hadn't toured past Alberta, and he was eager to branch out. He'd booked a couple of solo shows in Toronto and was threatening to busk in other cities.

Sarah sat on a wicker chair on the porch holding Sullivan, a big boy with sandy hair, milky skin, and his father's blue eyes.

"He's been taking a step or two, then falling down," Geoff told us, finishing his coffee. "I've been working him out in the past week, leading him around the house. I was hoping he'd walk before we hit the road."

"You'll see him in a couple of weeks," I said.

"Unless you quit your job," Dave said, his prodding subtle but noticeable. "This might be your chance."

Geoff laughed, maybe a little uncomfortably. "Yeah, we'll see about that."

"Dave wants everyone to quit his job," I interjected. "He wants me to *get* a job, just so I can quit it."

Geoff kissed his girlfriend, he kissed his boy. I felt a little guilty to be stealing him away. As an unmarried, childless man without any attachments, there was a part of me that was annoyed at how my grown-up friends' obligations and families kept them from staying out late or having that last round. I knew Geoff had wanderlust in him. I knew he loved driving, and as much as he loved his family, I knew he loved being with us. Was I the little devil on his shoulder? I just wanted to have fun.

"We'll take good care of him," I told Sarah. "We'll get him back home on time. I give you my guarantee."

"You guys have fun," Sarah told us, as if to assuage my guilty feeling. We were all good boys, she knew that.

It was about ten minutes before we hit the highway. It was like the beginning of every road trip I'd taken with these guys, everything chatty and chummy. As Geoff and Dave sparked up, I realized things wouldn't be much different from before. We were a great road team. Dave was the opener, easily the least moody of us three. Geoff was more aloof at the outset, but became gregarious and high-spirited on barstools. I was the most responsible one. I usually faded the earliest. I filled out motel forms while they hid in the back seat. I loved these guys without reservation.

As I drove, I thought about a trip to the Grand Canyon I'd taken seven years earlier with another set of friends. One friend brought along a tape recorder. He told people he met at gas stations or outside supermarkets that he was an anthropology student (which he was) working on a project (which he wasn't) in which he asked people about The Meaning of Life. The answers he got ranged from sincere, mulled-over responses about personal belief in God to glib one-word answers like "Darwin" or "adrenaline."

When that friend moved with his wife and two young children to do computer stuff for an online casino in Gibraltar, I borrowed his tent. On this trip, it would be a reminder of his presence. I had my own tape recorder and was on a quest for something equally lofty and absurd. I was looking for the meaning of Neil Young.

CHAPTER

FOUR

THE DRIVE through British Columbia was wet, winding, and uphill. The rain fell in a spray-nozzle mist, then in wavy streaks down the windshield, and as we traveled along the Trans-Canada Highway, through hillsides carpeted in green, over rocky escarpments, past silvery, dimpled lakes, it felt as though the bad weather was dogging us, like a swarm of gnats. The scenery was beautiful, and yet it was too familiar. I saw mountains and fir trees every day. I wanted something new. Looking out into the grayness, I drove, steeping in sentiments best reserved for power ballads. We're running away from the rain. Running from the tears and the pain. *Fist grip, pick scrape, drum fill.* Around this time, my mom called my cell phone to say I should drive safely.

At the gas station, I let Geoff take over the driving and moved to the back seat. On either side of the road, recently planted trees occupied landscape that had been emptied out by forest fires. I decided to interview Dave and Geoff.

"I have a question," I asked Dave. "What the hell is this book going to be about? Please help me."

Before answering, Dave rolled down the window and lit a cigarette; he told me he was going to quit when he got home. "It's about our travels and our love of Neil."

"Do you love Neil?"

Dave let out streams of blue smoke from his nostrils as he measured the depth of his feelings: "I do, I do."

"Do you remember the first time you heard Neil?"

"I think it was *Tonight's the Night.* I remember the old man playing it."

"Favorite song?"

"Uh... 'Cortez the Killer.'"

"Who do you think is better: Bob Seger or Neil Young?"

"Neil Young."

"Steve Miller or Neil Young?"

"Neil Young."

"Jimmy Buffett or Neil Young?"

"Ooh—that's hard."

"Do you remember that time we went to see Neil play in Washington State and we did a lot of drugs?"

"Very fondly. It was a great show."

That was our first Neil Young–related road trip, back in 1992. We'd bought acid in the parking lot and were soon fried. I remember Geoff's mom had made sandwiches, which, fueled with psychedelics, we ate ravenously.

"We got into our seats," I recalled, "and before the warm-up band came on they were playing a live album by someone on the concert speakers and we kept looking around for people onstage. We were really tripped out."

Dave laughed. "I remember thinking, *These drugs are really good.*"

"What's the most memorable place we've been to in a car?" I asked.

"I would have to say Berkeley,"—the three of us drove down in 1993—"because we had a really good time there. We were young, we were eighteen, and we were buying booze for people who were twenty, and that was fun."

"We had some guy's driver's license," I remembered.

"That's when I worked at a golf course," Geoff jumped in, "and a guy had to leave his driver's license as a deposit for some rental and he never picked it up. It was sitting in the desk there, under the till, for the longest time, and when it came time to go on the road trip, I scoped it out and said, *Ah, this is coming along with me.*" Dave and Geoff later traded the license for some weed. I think I was asleep at the time, which happened often; I didn't have their stamina or bottomless appetite for partying.

I asked Dave: "Are you disappointed I'm not wearing a buckskin jacket on this trip? Like the one Neil wore in Buffalo Springfield?"

"Slightly. But I'm actually kind of happy, because I wouldn't be able to take you seriously at all."

"I'm saving that jacket for my book on the Counting Crows—"

"That's going to be a sweet road trip," Geoff jumped in again.

"Yeah, I'm going to drive down to the Wal-Mart and get myself a Frappuccino."

"—and watch *Friends.*"

I turned to Geoff. "What do you think this book is about?"

"It's about funding."

"What do you think of Neil Young?"

"I think he's a great singer and songwriter."

"Do you have a favorite Neil Young album, period, or phase?"

"I think my favorite album is *On the Beach.*"

"That's pretty *down.*"

"Yeah, it is, and it's pretty bitter, too. But there's something about it, because if you're feeling kind of despondent *On the Beach* is the perfect album, more so than *Tonight's the Night,* because it's also kind of upbeat."

"You're a driver by profession. How do you like driving as a vacation from driving?"

"It's good to keep my skills up. Maybe I can write this off as a work retreat." Actually, most of Geoff's driving was in the downtown area, with lots of stopping. No highways run through Vancouver city limits, and I went months without traveling on one.

"The road is a source of renewal in Neil's songs," I said. "What do you find in being on the road?"

"I guess for me, because I'm a broke musician who hasn't toured nearly as much as anyone else would by my age"—twenty-eight, like Dave—"the road is like the promised land of fully living the dream of being a musician. Even Tom Cochrane has that song, 'Life is a Highway.' It's a pretty tried-and-true metaphor. I'd agree it pops up in Neil Young's songs as well. He's a motorhead, so it all makes sense."

The year before, I had taken Dave and Geoff along as I drove down to Northern California for a bookstore reading that only one person turned out for. (The woman who ran the bookstore developed an obvious crush on Dave. When we went for drinks after the event, she kept turning away from Geoff or me or the one woman who'd come to the reading so she could chat with Dave. She even followed him outside to smoke the lung-scorching, bargain-brand cigarettes he always buys in the States.) It was a few months before Geoff's boy was due, and I remember thinking it might be our final trip together.

I asked Geoff: "Do you think our trips are haunted by other journeys and past selves? Are we were getting too old for this?"

Geoff shook his head. "We're going away for longer now. We're able to go farther, and with more purpose than we had when we were twenty or nineteen. For myself, I can't remember ever being able to scrape together more than a few days for something like this before."

"But our trips are no longer as spontaneous," I said. "This one required months of planning. Babysitters needed to be located. This is the first road trip I've ever bought travel insurance for. I just feel I'm more *responsible*." I spat it out like a cuss word.

"Yeah, yeah—but maybe, as Bon Jovi says, 'We're not old, just older.'"

"You have a one-year-old son named Sullivan. I hear he really likes OutKast."

"Yeah, he does. He really likes bananas, too."

"And he likes your guitar-playing."

"Yeah, he likes to play guitar and a lot of instruments himself, too. And he's really good at telling you when to stop playing. With any instrument you're playing, he'll come up to you and put his hands on your hands. Or he'll mute the strings in a way. Sometimes it's at the perfect moment when you should stop playing."

"Is he saying *Daddy, you suck*?"

"He's probably saying *I pooped my pants. Pay attention to me.* That's one thing about being a parent. Say, if you're trying to work all the time and trying to take care of a kid, where do you draw the line? It's good that he can communicate with me in small ways."

"How do you think being a father has affected your outlook on life and your maturity?"

"Uh, I don't know. Looking at the short time I've been a father so far, I feel younger, I think, than I did for a while before I became a parent. But there's the responsibility factor and the basic energy level. I'm too tired to be a total idiot all the time."

Nowadays, Geoff told me, he usually woke up with the baby early in the morning and watched the yoga and tai chi shows on TV. Maybe it was all that stretching that contributed to his youthfulness. And in the last few months Geoff, who could drink until sunrise and had a cast-iron stomach, had pretty much stopped drinking; he claimed he'd become "allergic" to beer. This was the same guy, who, a few years earlier, when I'd invited him over to my parents' house for a holiday party, was coerced by my father to down three or four consecutive shots of Moutai, a Chinese firewater, to the amazement of my father's friends. Geoff had been a good sport about being the night's entertainment.

I asked Dave to hand me the CD wallet with all my Neil Young albums. I'd thought about listening to Young's albums in sequence on our trip, from his Buffalo Springfield work to his most recent album, *Greendale,* or about proceeding thematically, playing songs about Winnipeg or Toronto or California when we got there, but both strategies felt too contrived, too counterintuitive. I'm not someone who alphabetizes his record collection: I keep my CDs in piles on the floor.

It seemed appropriate to put on *Everybody Knows This Is Nowhere* while we whizzed through highway towns distinguished by the quantity and arrangement of their outlet stores and fast-food stops: "Every time I think about back home, it's cool and breezy / I wish that I could be there right now, just passing time." Of course, the album's title song is actually an ode to the simple life: "Nowhere," a place full of "day-to-day running around," would be a city. That's how it is with a lot of Neil Young songs.

You think it's about one thing, but it's really about the other. Or both. Or about the thing you originally thought it was. In any event, you get to decide. The title track is easily my favorite on the album: loose, spirited yet melancholic, *cool and breezy.* I love the fuzzy guitar lick that opens the song, then the jangling chords of the chorus. And you can't help but join in on the "lalala-*la*-la-lala" background vocal.

When we got to "Down by the River," Geoff turned to me: "Listen to that."

It was that moment in the middle of the final chorus in which the band seems to speed up. It was something I'd noticed without ever really noticing.

"I don't know if it's the tape or the band," Geoff said.

With Crazy Horse, a band originally known as the Rockets that he adopted and rechristened, Young had found a group of imperfectionists who perfectly suited his aims. *Everybody Knows This Is Nowhere,* Young's second album, was released only six months after his self-titled debut, but the change in direction was startling. *Neil Young* has its moments of charm: Young's hesitant melodies grow on you and the songwriting has glimmers of brilliance. Unlike his later albums, Young's debut is meticulously multitracked and overdubbed, a china cabinet of ornate sounds and pristine tones that pin it to a specific time in rock 'n' roll: namely, the years following the Beatles' *Sgt. Pepper,* when the rock 'n' roll album aspired to become a studio-incubated art form.

Everybody Knows This Is Nowhere, by contrast, is raw and lively, the first album to exemplify the Neil Young sound as we know it today. Unlike his debut album, it doesn't feel dated; it's a work that's familiar without being tired. On side one are celebrated rockers like "Cinnamon Girl," with its infamous one-note (played on two strings) guitar solo, and "Down by the River," with the hypno-telepathic riffing and counter-riffing between Young and original Crazy Horse guitarist Danny Whitten. Both songs continue to get heavy rotation on classic-rock stations.

On the flip side, there's "Cowgirl in the Sand," in which the image of rust, an enduring metaphor in Young's work, first appears. Like a lot of Neil Young songs from around this time, "Cowgirl in the Sand" is filled with lyrics that immediately sound vivid ("Hello, ruby in the dust"), but which upon close listening become enigmatic and double-crossed, as though we're tuned between two radio stations in someone's head.

Initially, "Cowgirl in the Sand" seems to be about a femme fatale: "It's the woman in you that makes you want to play this game." But then it seems as if the woman might be a mirage, and then as if it's Young's own desire that he calls into question. Midway through, he turns the song on himself, throwing in the line "Has your band begun to rust?" Already, in his early twenties, Young was afraid of creative decay. "The longer I keep going the more I have to fight corrosion," Young would later tell journalist Mary Turner. The refrain "When so many love you is it the same?" becomes a self-accusation, a comment on stardom's toll on his music.

Dave had finished his cigarette and rolled up the window. It was a couple of minutes before I could smell it.

"Dave, did you cut one?"

"Uh-huh."

"Why don't you roll down the window?"

"Because I'm an asshole."

IT'S A STRANGE and unproven fact, and yet it's thoroughly incontestable: many Canadians have a connection, however brief or tangential, with Neil Young. To search for an explanation is to unravel your mind. Maybe the same thing happens with other Canadian celebrities. Maybe I'm not paying attention when someone mentions going to high school with Neil Peart from Rush. And yet Young is someone who hasn't lived in Canada in forty years but was recently voted number fourteen on a poll of greatest Canadians.

I have a friend whose ex-landlady remembers Neil as the guy in Yorkville who left a cigarette burn on her couch. There's the books editor who knew him from Winnipeg and moved to Yorkville around the same time. I've met several people who claim to have an aunt or a grandmother who babysat Neil: he must have been passed around more than a high-school basketball.

Another friend, novelist Claudia Casper, was winked at by Neil. "When I was fifteen," she confided in me, "I went to the Mariposa Folk Festival on Toronto Island. It was 1972. I went to listen to Neil at one of the small stages, and I was sitting in the audience, probably looking starry-eyed. Toward the end of the concert, he winked at me. I was both thrilled and terrified, because back then, people with long hair were extremely unusual and, for a young girl, a little scary. And I thought somebody was going to come up to me and ask for my phone number."

Dave's Neil Young connection (and through Dave, mine) is his father, John Yellowlees, who shared a high-school girlfriend with Neil in Winnipeg. John had long since moved to the west coast, where he worked for the British Columbia liquor board until a year ago, when he took early retirement. In search of dry, hot weather, he and Dave's mother, Barb, sold their house in West Vancouver and moved to a property outside Merritt, three hours inland from Vancouver.

In the thick of boots and cowboy-hat country, we stopped to visit John and Barb at Burnt Stump Ranch, their fifty acres of hillside property in the Nicola Valley. There had been a fire years earlier, and young pine trees now dotted the property, in between the stumps. Their house was the first one on their road with a numbered address: the other homes had lot numbers, but the Yellowlees were told that police cars and ambulances would only come to homes with proper street addresses. On the property, John and Barb have built a space-age-sleek house with a corrugated aluminum exterior, wide verandas, and a covered boardwalk leading from the driveway.

Dave's mother answered the door on crutches. Her hip had recently been operated on. "What are you doing here?"

"I called you on Wednesday," Dave said. "I told you."

"Your father and I thought you were coming on Labor Day weekend. We had a whole meal planned out for you." Barb shook her head, disconsolate. "Your father's out running errands. We were not expecting you at all."

"Do you want us to leave?" Dave asked.

"Of course not." Barb welcomed us in, moving into the kitchen on her crutches. She opened the refrigerator. "I can make salmon sandwiches."

"That's great," Geoff said.

Barb removed some salmon and mayonnaise from the refrigerator and pulled a loaf of bread from a cupboard. She sighed again at this improvised hospitality. "The lunch we'd planned was going to be so nice—satay chicken, a salad, some good wine."

I turned to Geoff and said in a low, glum voice: "I really like satay chicken." Geoff snickered.

John returned a little while later, his pick-up truck throwing up dust as he pulled into the driveway.

"What are you guys doing here?" he asked us. "When did you change your schedule? And why didn't you tell us?"

"*I told you*," Dave was saying. "The last Saturday of August."

John smacked his forehead with the heel of his hand. "I thought it was the first Saturday of September." He turned to us and explained: "We're retirees. We have no use for time."

John is tall, like Dave, with the same reddish complexion but a shaved head. The first time I met him was before a Neil Young concert in 1993, when Dave, Geoff, and I abandoned him to head for the floor, something John is still sore about. He laughed when I first asked if I could interview him. "I don't have a lot to tell you."

"That's okay."

"I didn't know Neil Young."

"No worries."

"I never even met him."

"I'm not writing that kind of Neil Young book."

"You mean the kind where the author speaks with people who actually knew Neil Young?"

"Exactly. That would be too obvious."

John once met someone at a party who was into numerology. When John's hometown was mentioned, she told him that it had a "real strong" number combination: "She said it was so strong that if in a group of people there were two Winnipeg people—it doesn't matter if it's twenty or two hundred—they would gravitate toward each other. You know, it's almost true. Inevitably, you bump into someone from Winnipeg. And because Winnipeg's such a small city you inevitably know someone that they know." Maybe this is why everyone seems to know Neil Young.

"You could call your book *Six Degrees of Neil Young*," John suggested.

"I could," I said, tossing my head as I pretended to deliberate, "but I won't."

John and Neil were both born in 1945, and they dated a girl named Fran Gebhard who attended St. Mary's Academy, a Catholic girls school in Winnipeg. According to John, an extremely attractive nun brought Fran and John together. "I used to make a lot of headway," he told me, "out of the fact that a relative of mine, Sister Rose Terese, was a nun at St. Mary's. She had a folklore surrounding her that she was a model from New York, because apparently she used to be a very good-looking nun. All the girls at St. Mary's Academy thought it was pretty cool. It was always a good opener."

While John never met Neil, he'd been aware of the Squires. "The Squires were an up-and-coming group, not of the same caliber as Chad Allan and the Reflections, but they were there." And he remembered that Fran went back and forth between the two of them: "Two weeks with me, two weeks with Neil. Back to me, back to Neil." John attended Miles Macdonell high school in East Kildonan, but he went to the River Heights neighborhood often to hang out with the crowd at Kelvin, Neil's high school. John lived near another of Neil's high-school girlfriends, Pam Smith, and says he vaguely recalls Neil and Pam riding up and down Green Avenue in a convertible.

As we talked, John flipped through the pictures of 1960s Winnipeg in John Einarson's biography of Neil. His nostalgia for those days, it seemed, was tempered by how long ago it had been. He pointed to one picture of the teenaged Neiler: "You'd swear, if you saw a picture of me from the same time, we were brothers."

Geoff and I liked having fun with John. Even while he somberly instructed his son not to get too drunk or high on our trip, we felt we knew better about him. Dave is his spawn, after all, and father and son have the same round brown eyes—boyish, mischievous, horndog. "So, if you and Neil looked exactly the same," I asked, "what was the point in her dating both of you?"

John's mouth was half-cocked in a smile; he knew I was shining him. "I don't know," he said. "I guess it was fun at the time."

"What was Fran like?"

"She was a wacky little blonde-haired girl who yakked a lot. She had a really good personality."

I raised an eyebrow, nodding suggestively. Unless otherwise noted, I always nod suggestively. "So you like women with *nice personalities*."

"Yeah," John replied, defensively. "It helps."

I studied Young's yearbook photo in the Einarson book. "You guys don't look alike anymore."

John sighed in relief. "Sex, drugs, and rock 'n' roll have aged him dramatically, unlike me."

"You could be Dave's slightly older, better-looking brother."

John nodded. This was maybe an exaggeration, but he had spent much of the summer fireproofing the property and building a flagstone walkway, and he looked enviably fit. Retirement suited him. After our interview, John took us to the guest suite above the garage, where he works on his pottery. To the extent of keeping a copy of *Modern Cowboy* magazine on his coffee table and volunteering at the local country-music festival, John has gone native, adapting to his new community. And yet, with Barb, he still collects art and haggles over antique chandeliers. He's apprenticing, via e-mail, with a Dutch potter whose work he admires.

"So," Geoff said, his head bobbing with good humor, "do you and Barb ever start up that potter's wheel and re-enact that scene from *Ghost*?"

"Yeah," I chimed in. "Demi Moore in a white cut-off shirt, Patrick Swayze, 'Unchained Melody'—"

Geoff and I doubled over with laughter. Dave rolled his eyes at us, unnerved by the image of his parents doing it. To Geoff and me, John's silence said it all.

JOHN HAD LOST TRACK of Fran Gebhard since a party in Winnipeg, on Wellington Crescent, in 1965 or 1966. A week before leaving Vancouver I started looking online for Gebhards listed in Winnipeg. After searching one hard minute, I found Fran. It turned out she was now living in Vancouver, about twenty blocks west of my apartment, in a one-bedroom condo with a patio garden.

THE DESCRIPTION JOHN GAVE later, of Fran as a lively personality, rang true. When I met with her, she was moving to Vancouver Island to teach acting and directing at the University of Victoria. Boxes were stacked on the kitchen table; her bookshelves had been emptied. Two spaniels, one she was looking after for a friend, ran around her feet. As an actor, she'd recently guest-starred on episodes of *The Chris Isaak Show,* she told me, and was appearing in a play in which she was supposed to sing like Kitty Wells. Before moving to Vancouver, she had lived in Toronto, Stratford, and Banff and worked briefly as a realtor in Kelowna, B.C.

"I have no sense of time," she claimed. "When I see him on TV, Neil still looks like the same guy, 120 pounds of young man, I knew back in Winnipeg." Fran had last seen Neil perform a few years earlier. "I didn't see him as having aged at all."

In *Don't Be Denied,* Fran Gebhard is quoted by John Einarson as saying, "You knew that when you went out with Neil that you had to bring money. He never had any money. And you had to carry his equipment, too." Gebhard didn't recall the interview with Einarson, she told me, but when I reminded her of this comment, she said that it was "*so* not what comes to mind when I think of Neil. Because money was not a big thing for me. Dating Neil Young was huge. Being in his presence, I always knew I was with a genius. The guy was unbelievable right from the beginning, when we first met. He had such a unique quality. First of all, he was really nice. He was a caring, considerate human being. And all he wanted in life was to make a living with his music."

Fran had felt apprehensive about speaking with Einarson, and only later, when looking over her diaries from the time, did she realize it was because of the huge impression Young had made on her life. "The stuff I wrote about him—it's almost still painful. I was really, really mad for him."

Fran continued: "I can remember having conversations about whether or not Neil should stay in school. And I can remember saying to him that with the amount of talent he had, school was completely irrelevant. He was a cut above. We ran with the music scene, Randy Bachman and Chad Allan and the Reflections. I always felt that Neil had the biggest social conscience. He was about changing the world."

Fran recalls first meeting Young at a Catholic Youth Organization (CYO) dance. "I was just staggered," she told me. "He was so handsome—

just tall and gorgeous. I immediately fell in love with him. This was the guy for me. And I started going to dances where he was playing. I was like every groupie in the world, up front there, shaking my money-maker as fast as I could to get his attention."

At St. Mary's Academy, Fran was a dutiful student. "You're taught there that one of the things you need to do in life is pray. I went to Mass every morning for about ninety, maybe ninety-five days, on my bended knee praying that Neil Young would notice me. And it worked."

Neil Young finally asked her to dance at a CYO party. "He put his hand down at the side, he didn't hold my hand up in the air, like a seven. It was terribly sexy. He was a giant, about six-five." (A not-quite-accurate recollection.) They only dated for a few months, but she "carried a torch for him for so long it would seem longer."

I asked her if John Yellowlees had been a rebound fling. I wanted something to tease John with, but Fran wouldn't bite. "I was a passionate kid. John was intelligent, sincere. A nice person, a warm person. A catch. I did *not* date him long enough." Fran was single and added: "I wish I could meet these guys all over. Now the people I meet who are my age are boring. They're way too old for me."

I looked at Fran, who was beaming down at her spaniel, and in that moment I could see the fiery, wacky teenager who caught the eye of both Neil Young and my friend's dad. I could imagine in her the girl who went to church and prayed to meet certain guys. For that instant I could see how it might be possible to lose one's grip of the decades. As I left through the garden gate, Fran's smaller spaniel squirted out. I picked up the dog, handed her to Fran, and wished them well in Victoria.

1

2

3

4

1, 2, & 3 *These previously unpublished photos were taken by Stephen Lang and show Neil Young with Billy Talbot and Danny Whitten of Crazy Horse in March 1970, at the Fillmore East in New York City. Whitten died of a heroin overdose in 1972. These rare photos came to me via Rustie Bill Neuschulz, who's seen Neil play 150 times. Thanks, Bill.*

4 *This photo of Neil performing in Hampton, Virginia, on September 12, 1985, was taken by Rustie Stephen Cross. In my opinion, Steve has the coolest piece of Neil Young memorabilia: a chunk of Young's hair. And no, he didn't tear it off Neil's head.*

\\|/

CHAPTER

SIX

WE LEFT Burnt Stump Ranch that afternoon and headed for the Rock-
ies, the car's automatic transmission lurching capably. Who knows if
an old hearse would have made it through the mountains? On the other
hand, an old hearse wouldn't have a car alarm that went off every time
we breathed on it. Dave, Geoff, and I set off the car alarm five times, no
kidding, before we'd even left B.C.

Along the mountainside we could see trains pulling freight across the
country. It felt as if we were part of a huge model train set, an image
appropriate enough for a book about Neil Young, who is a part-owner
of the Lionel train company. Highway signs pleaded for us to stop, their
billboards for Go-Karts and Miniature Worlds and Enchanted Forests
like siren calls.

Geoff was still behind the wheel and I was riding shotgun, fiddling
with the heat and air valves. Somewhere around Salmon Arm, the rain
turned into a fine mist. Outside of Sicamous, we passed a tractor trailer
that had tumbled and sat smacked and crushed along the side of the road.
I knew people in Vancouver from places like these. Every so often, they'd
talk about going home for Christmas or back to some lake in July. I'd
hmm without interest, and they'd trail off into a polite, grinning ellipsis.

By nightfall we were driving through the Kicking Horse Pass, which is on the Alberta border and the continental divide, and is the highest point on the Trans-Canada at an elevation of 1643 meters. The moon was nearly full as we entered Banff. Strands of clouds were shot through with its porcelain light, given a satiny texture.

Around midnight we arrived in Calgary, where we had arranged to pick up the fourth person on our trip: Mark Latham, Dave's ex-roommate. Dave had met him years before when Mark passed out on Dave's patio; Mark had thought he was indoors. A couple of weeks later, Mark had asked Dave if he could move in. Dave grew up around the exchange students his parents housed and fed, and has a knack for taking strangers into his home.

I'd met Mark a few times, and while I didn't know him as well as I knew my other two traveling companions, Dave had sold me on him months earlier. "Mark's an easygoing guy," he said. "Plus, he's got a great hibachi. When he lived at my place we used to eat so well. Man, I miss that hibachi."

When we got to the house where Mark was staying, Dave shrieked like a little girl at the sight of Mark's small brown hibachi. Dave was also happy to see Mark. Mark had finished tree-planting for the summer and was back living in the interior of British Columbia—several hours south of the Trans-Canada—with his girlfriend, Sophia, who was studying to be a park ranger. In the winters, he volunteered for the local search and rescue team. He has curly hair and a goatee and is not only as tall as Dave but also fairly big. With Mark in our car, we wouldn't get muscled around. We found space in the car for his hibachi, but Mark had to strap his bag, laden with camping gear, to the roof. Then we set off the car alarm—again. Before leaving Calgary, we went for beer and chicken wings at Boston Pizza.

"Welcome aboard," Dave said, hoisting his pint. "Welcome to our holy road trip triumvirate."

Mark laughed a little nervously into his Coke. "Uh, thanks."

"I think we need to initiate Mark," I said.

"What initiation?" Mark asked in his sleepy baritone.

"Have you heard," Geoff asked, "of a Rusty Trombone?"

Despite our threats of hazing and sexual humiliation, Mark was keen to hit the road. He took the graveyard shift into the Prairies. I nodded off in the back seat as Mark and Dave updated each other on their lives. Dave would turn on the ceiling light periodically to look at the map book. Every once in a while, I'd wake up long enough to use a gas station washroom or to glance at a road sign in the glare of our headlights. This was my impression of Alberta—dark. Driving at night was like running on a treadmill. You didn't feel you were going anywhere.

I woke up at sunrise. The roads were straight, if patchy from icy winters. At seven in the morning, after twenty hours of driving, we stopped at a campground in Swift Current, Saskatchewan—"Where Life Makes Sense," according to the town motto. We slept until eleven, when the tent started baking in the midday heat, and then had coin-operated showers and a diner breakfast. We bought groceries in a Swift Current supermarket where a Muzak version of John Lennon's "#9 Dream" played. We hit the road again.

Saskatchewan was enjoyable because it had nothing to do with Neil Young. We were on the non-canonical leg of our journey, and I didn't have to start paying attention and taking notes until I got to Winnipeg. There was something soothing about the flat, unbroken landscape: a transparency, a kind of truth. There was nowhere to hide. The road was like a straw sucking us up into the endless sky. To either side were fields of wheat and corn. The strip of highway median was dotted with hay bales. When Dave rolled a number, I decided to spark up. Marijuana usually makes me light-headed and sometimes paranoid, and I got the same effect here. I was twitchy and anxious.

We stopped in Moose Jaw, a dusty town with a strip lined with old brick hotels that date from the Prohibition era, so that Geoff could visit his grandmother. Except that Geoff hadn't remembered to bring her phone number with him. At the gas station, he went through the phone book, but no one with his nan's surname and first initial picked up. We got a couple of beers at a bar next to Capone's Hideaway, a theme motel.

"Typical Geoff," Dave sneered into his drink. "Just like him to come to Moose Jaw without his nan's number." Geoff had gone to a pay phone outside to call Sarah and get it. "I don't know how he's going to get home."

"Any luck?" I asked, when Geoff returned.

Geoff shook his head. "Maybe next time I'm passing through Moose Jaw."

Dave laughed.

"Better luck next time," I told him. We had a couple more beers, relishing not being in a car, watching people play pool. I bought some pornographic playing cards, which were raunchier than I'd expected. We listened to the classic rock on the jukebox. A familiar-sounding song started playing.

"I wrote this song for you," Geoff said, pointing at me with a snicker. It was kind of a recurring joke for the two of us. The song was "Born to Run" by Bruce Springsteen.

By acclamation, it was decided that I would drive to Manitoba; everyone else had eaten pieces of Dave's space cake, which hit them slowly, then very hard. The sun began to set as we approached Regina, the light turning the color of sweetened apple juice, and the full moon rose to fill a third of the huge sky. In the twenty-nine years of my otherwise-privileged life, I'd never seen the moon so large. It grew so fat and ripe that I half-thought it would fall from the sky. This was what a mother's breast must look like to an infant. I nodded suggestively at the moon.

We were listening to *Harvest*. Much of Young's fourth solo album was recorded after an appearance on a television variety show hosted by Johnny Cash. Young was already an emerging star through his association with Crosby, Stills, Nash, & Young and his most recent work, *After the Gold Rush*. For many people, *Harvest* is the only album with which they're familiar. Before *Harvest* came out, music journalist (and later filmmaker) Cameron Crowe wrote, he was constantly defending Neil Young to his family: "There was a time, sure, when I tried to explain to them what it was to be a Neil Young fan." He'd say "How important is an in-tune vocal?" or "But it's great when he hits the same note 38 times in 'Down by the River.'" This would all change with *Harvest:* "In 1972, my parents would hear 'Heart of Gold' played in the supermarket, find it tuneful, and begin to see things differently."

Yet of all the diehard Neil fans I've talked to, no one claims *Harvest* as their favorite album. Maybe because it's so popular; it belongs to too many people. In any event, I still have a soft spot for it. The album begins with "Out on the Weekend," which sets the pastoral, retiring tone of the rest of the songs. First comes a lazy drumbeat and the acoustic guitar, then the purr of a harmonica followed by a sweetly reassuring lap steel guitar. "Think I'll pack it in and buy a pick-up," Young starts singing, his affected weariness disarmed by the image of the humble pick-up, "take it down to L.A." An unnamed woman is mentioned before the crypto-hippie refrain: "See the lonely boy, out on the weekend / Trying to make it pay / Can't relate to joy, he tries to speak and / Can't begin to say."

What the hell is he singing about? I can't begin to say. When I sing along to this song in the car, I always hum through the "lonely boy" refrain. With his fragmentary style of songwriting, Young seems to have an intuitive grasp of the absentminded way people normally listen to lyr-ics, singing along before drifting off with the melody or the guitar lick. He's also canny enough to know how to regain your attention. The second verse, for instance, plants you back in the world of bodies and objects: "She got pictures on the wall, they make me look up / From her big brass bed." The big brass bed reminds me of the bathtub that John Lennon falls asleep in in "Norwegian Wood," a kind of painterly detail used sparingly and precisely at the right moment. It's enough to keep you interested in the next couplet: "Now I'm running down the road trying to stay up / Somewhere in her head."

The desire to seek refuge from romantic love appears again in "A Man Needs a Maid," a quiet song despite an orchestral accompaniment that gives it a soap-operatic bombast. (Unlike in "There's a World," the other song Young recorded with the London Symphony Orchestra, I think here the orchestral score works by inflating the feelings in the song to the point of italicized irony.) The self-portrait of the artist is of someone wounded and made distrustful by both sudden fame and romantic love.

Like the new millionaire that he is, Young seeks out domestic help: "I was thinking that maybe I'd get a maid / Find a place nearby for her to stay / Just someone to keep my house clean / Fix my meals and go away." Yet midway through the song he softens up and reverses his atti-tude: "To give a love, you gotta live a love / To live a love, you gotta be 'part of,'" he sings, addressing himself before addressing someone else: "When will I see you again?" Young's contradictions form a larger truth, a more capacious understanding, not so much a cognitive dissonance as what John Keats termed "negative capability" in describing a mind able to hold contrary thoughts "without any irritable reaching after fact and reason."

Young emerges in *Harvest* as a comfortably eclectic songwriter: there are the ballads like "Out on the Weekend" and "Old Man," the playful honky-tonk of "Are You Ready for the Country?," the anti-drug message of "The Needle and the Damage Done," and the socially conscious guitar rock of "Words (Between the Lines of Age)" and "Alabama." These songs are unified—ruthlessly self-engineered, some would say—by Young's persona as a wounded troubadour in a ruffly white shirt. How is it that someone's solipsism can be so universal? Whatever skill this required, whatever alchemy or rock 'n' roll voodoo is involved, Young had mastered it by the time of his only number-one hit, "Heart of Gold," yet another song about yearning and incompletion.

In his *Rolling Stone* review of *Harvest,* John Mendelssohn concluded: "Neil Young is not one of those folks whom superstardom becomes artistically." For once an artist would publicly agree with a critic. "This song put me in the middle of the road," Young said about "Heart of Gold" in the liner notes to his greatest-hits compilation *Decade.* "Traveling there soon became a bore so I headed for the ditch. A rougher ride but I met more interesting people there."

(Ironically, Young's only chart-topper would be displaced by America's "A Horse with No Name," a song that apes his sound so well that for many casual listeners it is their favorite Neil Young song. According to *Shakey,* when Scott Young heard "A Horse With No Name," he actually called to congratulate his son on his newest hit. And when the members of America were brought to Young's ranch to meet him, Young made a point of fleeing. During the writing of this book, friends would play the song on my answering machine to piss me off. They succeeded.)

In *Harvest*'s aftermath, Young would thwart his established image not only by being a wino onstage, with cocaine boogers dangling from his nose, but being a wino who refused to play "Heart of Gold." Instead he sang from gloriously off-key albums like *Tonight's the Night,* part of the post-*Harvest* "Ditch" (or "Doom") Trilogy that also included *Time Fades Away* and *On the Beach.* Young became a musician who thrived on his ambivalence, who changed his opinions and attitudes from song to song like an actor from role to role.

Cameron Crowe recalled a family outing to see Young perform. Young was in confrontational mode, refusing to behave like a Wurlitzer and playing only new material. "A few minutes later, the houselights were turned on and the hall was filled with an eerie silence," wrote Crowe. " 'He acts like a drunken monkey,' said one of my cousins. The rest of the family didn't say much. We didn't talk about Neil Young for the next few years." Young's journey to the ditch was well underway.

In the eighties, Young's shape-shifting would lead him to court. After signing a five-album deal with Geffen Records in 1982, he proceeded to release three albums in three different genres: the electronica of *Trans,* the rockabilly of *Everybody's Rockin',* and the country of *Old Ways,* an earlier version of which had been rejected by the label. Biographers have suggested that the personae he adopted for these albums were a way of masking the anguish Young felt over the cerebral palsy that severely afflicted his second son, Ben. (Young's first son, Zeke, also has cerebral palsy, though there's no hereditary cause.) The vocoder obscuring Young's voice on *Trans* represents his inability to communicate with Ben. A song like "Transformer Man" gathers poignancy when you understand it's about his son's efforts to communicate: "Unlock the secrets," Young implores in his robot voice. "Let us throw off the chains that hold you down."

Young chose not to publicize his private life, and record company head David Geffen, who'd originally persuaded Young to take less money in exchange for artistic control, sued him for producing music that was "not commercial in nature" and was "musically uncharacteristic of Young's previous recordings." Young countersued. Both groups eventually backed down, the lawsuits eventually withdrawn, with Young completing his deal with Geffen and voluntarily renegotiating his contract, reducing his fee by half. Eventually, Geffen would come to regret his lawsuit. He'd claim he'd been trying to save Young from himself—whoever that was. "They said, 'We don't know what you're doing,'" Young explained at the time. "'We're scared. You did a *Trans* and then you did *Everybody's Rockin'* and now you want to do a country album. We want Neil Young.' That was confusing to me because I'd always thought I was Neil Young."

Young's last album for Geffen was *Life,* which featured his most spirited song of that period, "Prisoners of Rock 'n' Roll." "People tell us that we play too loud, but they don't know what our music's about," Young screams. "We never listen to the record company man, they try to change us and ruin our band." Crazy Horse adds their gang vocal to the defiantly obnoxious chorus: "That's why we don't wanna be good / Oh, oh, oh, oh-oh, we're prisoners of rock 'n' roll."

As we left Saskatchewan, *Harvest* played out. Long stretches of the highway were only two lanes wide as we crossed into Manitoba. My grip tightened every time a big rig passed us in the opposite lane, and I got stuck behind one truck because I was afraid of passing it. We spent the night in a motel in Brandon, Manitoba, only two hours from Winnipeg. The next morning, we stopped to fill up at a gas station, where I bought the fifteenth pepperoni stick of the journey and another bottle of v8. Getting back into the car, we set off its alarm again. Now we were triggering it even when the doors were unlocked. We surmised that the trick to keeping the alarm from sounding was to leave at least one door open a little bit.

On the CD deck, Iggy Pop was singing his version of "China Girl."

"This is the song," I said, "that I listen to when I dance around naked, with my penis tucked between my legs." I was joking—really.

"What are you going to do if you meet Neil?" Geoff asked.

"It won't happen."

"Would you interview him?"

"Possibly," I said. "Sure. Of course."

"What would you say?" he asked me.

"I don't know. What is there to say?"

"If I were you, I'd run up to him at Farm Aid—naked, with your penis between your legs—and scream, *Give me back my life!*"

"It would be like *Heart of Darkness*."

"*Heart of Darkness* meets *Almost Famous*."

"Shut up," I said.

"Whatever you say, boss."

Between CDs, I'd been looking for radio stations. Commercial rock radio seems to be a lost cause, though. Such shit. The stuff on the air manages to expose the worst aspects of recent genres: chugging metal riffs, hard-rock bombast, the self-conscious brooding of alternative music, and all those interchangeably terrible singers with Eddie Vedder baritones.

I found a classic-rock station and waited to see how long it took until I heard a Neil Young song. After an hour, I got "Southern Man." That's the thing about these classic-rock stations: they always select the most overplayed, recognizable hits of any artist. I love the Rolling Stones, especially *Exile on Main Street* and *Some Girls,* but I cannot bear to listen to "Brown Sugar" or "Ruby Tuesday" or "Start Me Up." I love the Beatles, but I don't like "Let It Be" or "Come Together." And of course I love Neil Young, but I wouldn't be heartbroken never to hear again "Down by the River" or "Cinnamon Girl" or "Rockin' in the Free World."

The problem is, if you play any song enough, it becomes a jingle. And there are enough jingles to listen to these days, many of which are catchy or come with a great video, but little music I want to own or claim as my own. There's plenty of music worth burning to CD or making spaghetti to, but very little music that I love. Was it different with the granola rock of the sixties or the singer-songwriter suicide-soundtrack and riff rock of the seventies? Apparently, FM radio was more freewheeling then, and record companies were slightly more patient. There were no music television networks, no movie soundtrack tie-ins, no cell-phone ring tones. But I can't remember a time when music wasn't a commodity.

Fifteen years after Young's "This Note's for You" attempted to shame musicians away from shilling cola, bands like the Clash, the Rolling Stones, and Young's favorite, Devo, have willingly licensed their songs as they approach or pass retirement age. Some musicians argue that commercial licensing makes up for income lost through illegal music downloading. The economy that kept Neil Young in model trains and vintage cars without selling any Jell-O Pops is, if not extinct, then under siege. New performers can point to the whitewashed, over-formatted, cash-lubricated radio playlists and legitimately argue that car commercials help get their music played.

Notions of "authenticity" and "artistic integrity" are dismissed by younger critics as "rockism," a romanticized elevation of the baby-boomer soundtrack by middle-aged critics. Maybe this explains why Bob Dylan appeared in a Victoria's Secret ad. Some have convincingly argued that the concept of the rock star is itself obsolete. Critic Stephen Metcalf, for instance, deems rock music a marginalized "niche product": "In pop music, albums still triumph commercially, and albums still triumph artistically. But they're almost never the same albums." The best artists of the past decade have been those who "embraced this marginalization by cheerfully casting off all of rock's old pretence to grandiosity." Metcalf cites low-fi indie-rock favorites like Stephin Merritt of the Magnetic Fields, Elliott Smith, and Chan Marshall (a.k.a. Cat Power) as artists who "hide behind aliases or their fellow band-mates, or record out of their own bedrooms."

Mostly we'd been listening to CDs since we left Vancouver. Besides Neil, we'd been playing Lou Reed, Frank Zappa, the Eagles of Death Metal, Iron and Wine, Television, Richard Hell and the Voidoids, the Streets, Franz Ferdinand, Joanna Newsom, *Exile on Main Street*. Some of the music I'd brought along I've listened to since high school, alt-rock bands like Dinosaur Jr and the Pixies. Grasping for obscurity, I'd chosen as my favorites groups that belonged to the second tier of popularity, like the Archers of Loaf or My Morning Jacket. Music, for me, was about fragile, secret loves that wilted when exposed to crowds. There are still bands like this, but not enough of them.

Maybe the trouble wasn't the music, I thought morosely, but the person listening to it, someone staring down the feeling that it was a precipitous decline from here. Several times on the trip I'd had to remind myself to be in a good mood, to try not to pick at the scabs of my doomed novel and feelings of obsolescence. Such a waste, I kept thinking to myself. I've wasted so much of my life already. I wished I had another chance at being nineteen or twenty-one or twenty-six; if I'd known that would be it, I'd have done a better job, I swear. I'd have spent less time moping, less time worrying about the future. I'd have spoken up, I'd have acted instead of speaking, I'd have kept my mouth shut.

What's worse was how jaded I'd become. Maybe that was really why I was worked up. It was less about friends having kids and buying homes—things I've never really, actively wanted or sought—than the fear that growing older meant it was getting harder to fall in love. It was getting harder to get excited about stuff, harder not to fall into ruts. It was getting too easy to keep everything—and everyone—at hand-shaking distance, to be gracious, polite, friendly, and decent without bringing people any closer, without bickering with them, without taking them to heart. The *same old same old:* that was the kind of death I feared as I approached thirty. I wanted to know how Neil Young did it, how someone nearing sixty seemed to peel off old skins in search of something new.

\\|/

CHAPTER

SEVEN

BOTH OF NEIL YOUNG'S PARENTS were from Winnipeg, and after his parents divorced in 1960, his mother, Rassy Ragland Young, brought Neil and his brother Bob (who would eventually return to Toronto to pursue a golfing career) back to Manitoba to be closer to her family. Young's most nakedly autobiographical song, "Don't Be Denied," begins: "When I was a young boy, my mama said to me / Your daddy's leavin' home today, I think he's gone to stay / We packed up all our bags, and drove out to Winnipeg." As recently as 1989, Neil seemed to allude to the pain of his family's dissolution in "Crime in the City (Sixty to Zero, Part One)," his panoramic opus of urban desperation: "Sometimes I talk to Daddy / On the telephone / When he says that he loves me / I know that he does / But I wish I could see him / I wish I knew where he was."

Yet in spite of this buried pain and the stigma that surrounded children of divorced parents at that time, the Neiler seemed to have made friends fairly easily. He was coeditor of the yearbook, went to parties, and hung out at the local Salisbury House (one of a chain of local restaurants, still thriving, whose owners now include Burton Cummings from the Guess Who).

Neil was a tall, skinny teenager with a damaged left-front tooth that had turned blue and would later be capped. He wore a black felt fedora and, in one photo, a jacket with "Canadian Freeloaders Society" emblazoned on its back. He was admired by girls for being sensitive and well-mannered, but he also had a prankish sense of humor that would land him in detention. His grade nine yearbook write-up from Earl Grey Junior High read: "Neil is the 'happy-go-lucky' guy of our room. He's often seen at Earl Grey Canteen on Friday nights. He is active in the instrumental group called the 'Esquires.'"

The yearbook mention of his band hints at Young's early resolve to make his life as a musician (note the "Canadian Freeloaders Society" jacket), a hand-to-mooch proposition for all but very few. In Ontario, an appearance by Elvis on *The Ed Sullivan Show* had caught Young's attention. He played ukulele and had just picked up a Harmony Monterey acoustic guitar before arriving in Winnipeg. "I knew when I was thirteen or fourteen that that was what I wanted to do," he told John Einarson. "There was nothing else that interested me."

Winnipeg's thriving rock 'n' roll scene was centered around the community clubs. These clubs began hosting teen dances in 1960, playing the latest hits on 45s before local bands began appearing onstage. Einarson evokes the scene in wistful detail in *Don't Be Denied:* "Invariably the girls sat on one side of the tiny hall and the boys on the other... Once that first brave male crossed the floor, the floodgates opened, and before the song had ended, the creaky wood dance floor was full... Parent chaperones went around the floor, ever vigilant for young couples dancing too close. Spot dances and lady's choice added to the fun. For a break, kids went to the canteen to buy six cent bottles of Coke, with a straw, of course. At the end of the evening the lights went on, and with parents waiting at the door and the car warming up outside, newly kindled romances were suspended until the following week when it would all start again."

By 1964, there were about seventy-five community clubs in Winnipeg. "It was music at a grassroots level," Einarson would later tell me. "The community club next door was where you'd play all your sports—baseball, football, hockey. There'd be a couple of outdoor hockey rinks. That was the hub of the community. If you weren't playing any sports, you went to the canteen. It made sense to have teen dances there. The local guys who had guitars would rehearse in basements; it was too cold to rehearse in the garage. The guy across the street was the one who booked the dances. You'd play your local community club, and all your friends would come out and cheer you on or razz you. And that's how everything started. The Squires were no different."

Neil, who came from a family of golfers, swapped golf lessons with a friend, John Daniel, in exchange for guitar lessons. The two of them, plus a couple of bongo-playing classmates, formed Young's first band, the Jades. The Jades played their repertoire of guitar instrumentals at their first show at the Earl Grey Community Club. The group disbanded when rehearsal—and Neil's all-consuming passion for music—conflicted with Daniel's hockey practice. Neil forced him to choose between hockey and music. "I guess I wanted to play hockey," Daniel told Einarson.

Young would play briefly with bands like the Esquires, which he was kicked out of; the Stardusters, with whom he'd play at a Kelvin alumni basketball game, and the Thunderstorms. "Neiler would play with anyone back then," Rassy Ragland Young told Einarson. At Kelvin Technical High, he spent most of his time "drawing amplifiers and stage setups." Such studious attention meant that Neil failed grade ten.

With Ken Koblun, a friend he made at Earl Grey Junior High, Neil played six live shows with the Classics, in 1962, before the group disbanded. Around this time, Young began writing his first songs, guitar instrumentals inspired by the Shadows. By the end of that year, Neil and Koblun had recruited drummer Jack Harper and guitarist Allan Bates to form the first incarnation of Young's longest-lasting Winnipeg band, the Squires. Neil ran the band, choosing rehearsal times and songs for set lists, which included popular instrumentals like "Walk, Don't Run," "Tequila," and "Wipe Out." The Squires, already with the first of many replacement drummers, Ken Smyth, played their first show at the Riverview Community Club in February 1963. They were paid five dollars. For their next show at Neil's community club, Crescentwood, they earned thirty-five bucks.

From Toronto, Scott Young implored Neil to improve his grades. "Exams must be upon you, and every hour at the books counts," he wrote in response to Neil's request for six hundred dollars to buy an amplifier.

"Now would be a good time to show what you are made of." Neil's mother supported her son's musical aspirations. By all accounts, Rassy was an outspoken and sharp-witted woman who fought fiercely for loved ones. "If she was dealing with one of her sons or a relative," Scott Young told biographer Johnny Rogan, "she was like General Eisenhower." Perhaps to spite her ex-husband, it was Rassy who found the money for the amplifier.

By 1963, the best neighborhood band in Winnipeg was Chad Allan and the Reflections (later renamed the Guess Who), featuring Randy Bachman on lead. Young would replace his Les Paul Junior, a guitar that gave him shocks, with an orange Gretsch to emulate Bachman, who shared with Young an appreciation for guitarist Hank Marvin of the Shadows. The Squires never became a top-tier band in Winnipeg but were well-known enough to play the River Heights Community Club—as Einarson told me, it was "the pinnacle of success for local bands."

The Squires found a fan in local deejay Bob Bradburn, who mentioned their shows on-air at CKRC and hosted their community-club appearances. Bradburn arranged for the Squires to record two of Neil's instrumentals at CKRC with engineer Harry Taylor on July 23, 1963. Two months later, those two songs—"The Sultan," on which Ken Smyth played a gong, and "Aurora"—were released by V Records as a 45. Both numbers highlighted Young's gift for melody, which would reappear in his later songs and his more scorching guitar solos.

(The "The Sultan/Aurora" seven-inch is considered by many to be the Holy Grail of Canadian rock 'n' roll. Winnipeg's V Records had scored a big hit with a song entitled "Lovesick Polka" by Mickey and Bonnie. Another group on V Records were the D-Drifters Five, who recorded Beatles songs in Ukrainian. One copy of the Squires' single recently sold for three thousand dollars on eBay. A friend of Nardwuar's, on the other hand, found it at a Calgary thrift store for twenty-five cents.)

"They would do a polka song, country, Beatles pop, fifties rock, instrumentals," Einarson later told me. "You'd have to be an everyman band, in the sense that you had to provide music that appealed to everyone. The Squires' set lists would include sixties songs. They'd do four forty-five-minute sets."

Inspired again by Chad Allan and the Reflections, who had noticed the hysteria the Beatles were creating across the Atlantic, the Squires began to play songs with vocals in 1964. Young grew out his hair and would first sing in public—two Beatles covers, "Money" and "It Won't Be Long"—in the Kelvin cafeteria. After he sang again in the St. Ignatius club basement, a smartass in the audience yelled: "Stick to instrumentals." Even among friends, Young was needled mercilessly about his singing. Ken Smyth's mother kicked the Squires out of her basement because of it. But, thankfully, Young was determined: "People told me I couldn't sing but I just kept at it."

THREE YEARS EARLIER, on my first visit to Winnipeg, I'd felt as though I were visiting the city equivalent of an emptied-out aquarium. I'd been sent on my first book tour, and at the airport I'd happened to mention my interest in Neil Young to my publicist. A publicist is a touring author's de facto wet nurse, and without a word of complaint, she'd chauffeured my needy, helpless ass to Young's old neighborhood.

Winnipeg, I'd been told, was a little rundown. Companies that once made their headquarters there had moved to Calgary or Vancouver. It was April, not quite spring, and the city was cast in a leached, alabaster light. Storefronts, even entire neighborhoods, were blanketed in dust. Having come from the smug, wet, hippie part of the country, I felt as though I was watching *The French Connection* on VHS: the colors had faded; everything was a little outdated and depressed. My publicist helpfully informed me that Winnipeg had received a large influx of Asian immigrants "only recently—right after the war." We stopped at 1123 Grosvenor, an address that I remembered from John Einarson's book. Driving through River Heights, the city's posh neighborhood, I couldn't help noticing just how grimy everything looked, how the trees that lined the streets were still bare.

This time around, it was cool and overcast when we arrived in Winnipeg. The first things I noticed were the bright green lawns and the gardens fat with color. According to Winnipeggers, we were in the middle of the worst summer in recent memory. People here were accustomed to steamy summers spent fending off mosquitoes and absorbing as much heat as they could to carry them through the first snowfall in, oh, October and the rest of the nutsicle-making winter season. Instead, they'd been treated to the kind of soggy summer we used to get in Vancouver—before global warming edited nature.

The four of us were adopted during our visit by Dave's uncle and aunt, Ian and Donna Stevenson. Donna, John Yellowlees' older sister, had retired after thirty years with the Canadian National Railway Company. Originally from Winnipeg, she missed out by a few years on the Squires. In the 1960s, she lived in Vancouver, where she "was wild, but not too wild," and then with Ian in Scotland, where their oldest child, Sarah, was born. Ian is a silver-haired man originally from England. Having lived in Winnipeg for nearly forty years, he lost his accent somewhere west of the Canadian Shield, and he speaks in a matter-of-fact baritone that reminds me of Johnny Cash.

On our first night in town, we went with the Stevensons to a sweet sixteen birthday party for their granddaughter, Victoria. My fingers were crossed, hoping for a community club dance, but what we got was a family gathering, with both sides of Victoria's close-knit family there—plus me, Geoff, and Mark.

While Victoria received her presents, we stood around in the kitchen talking to her mother, Sarah, who, as a teenaged Ozzy Osbourne fan, would baby-sit Dave when she visited Vancouver in the summers. We milled around until Brian, Sarah's husband, arrived with a case of beer. Full of good cheer, Brian reminded me a little of my own father—a piss-taker.

"Here," he said, handing us each a beer, "have a can of personality."

There was also Sarah's sister-in-law, a woman about my age who'd just given birth to her seventh child. She was in a T-shirt and overalls, her hair in a ponytail.

"She has seven kids," Dave said, leaning over to me, "because she always wanted a big family."

My brow fused momentarily. "But why does she want a big family?"

"I think she said seven is enough for her," Dave said. "She's going to go back to school."

She was a very nice woman and her kids were delightful. Her husband, a top Winnipeg mechanic, was wearing a T-shirt decorated with the painted handprints of their brood.

"So, you're the writer," someone asked me in the kitchen. I forget who it was.

"Yeah."

"You're writing about Neil Young."

"In a roundabout way."

"I heard that. I'm not sure I completely understand the concept of your book."

I shrugged. "That's okay. I don't either. I really, *really* have no idea. I'm open to suggestions. Can you please help me?"

"Why don't you interview Neil?" this person asked me.

"That won't happen."

"Have you tried?"

"Why bother?"

"You should at least try."

"Uhhhhh, too much trouble."

"But don't you want him to read it?" someone else asked me. "In an ideal world, wouldn't you want him to read it and call you and tell you he thinks it's a good book?"

"Not really. It'd be too embarrassing, like if he picked up the binder that fell off my desk in homeroom and saw that I'd written 'Mrs. Neil Young' all over it. I'd just die. Even worse, he might sue me."

"Why would he sue you?"

I ducked reflexively. I was so paranoid of getting sued by Neil Young that I didn't even like the word "sue." "Because he's an eccentric control-freak genius. He could sue me just for yuks. I mean, he even sued his own authorized biographer, Jimmy McDonough. Or was it McDonough who sued Neil? Maybe it was both. I forget."

I asked Sarah if she knew anyone who used to know Neil. She didn't, but she offered to take us to the bar where Burton Cummings played VLTs. In my imagination, Cummings played video lotto with sweat dripping from his dark moustache, a medallion hanging in his open shirt. Oh man, that would have been great, but anything less would have been disappointing to me. As with Neil Young, I didn't want to wreck my glorious illusion, so I had to decline.

ON FEBRUARY 5, 1964, with Beatlemania spreading from the U.K., the Squires became the first rock 'n' roll band to play at the Fourth Dimension. Part of a chain of coffeehouses—there were Fourth Dimensions in Regina and Fort William—the Winnipeg 4-D had, until then, booked only folk acts like Pete Seeger and José Feliciano and comedians like Shari Lewis (with Lamb Chop) and George Carlin. The Squires filled the club, and their set, made up of Beatles covers, went over well.

"With its drab tarpapers and snow fence décor, checkered table cloths, candles, and espresso coffee and cinnamon tea," John Einarson wrote, "the 4-D was the stereotypical bohemian coffeehouse." When you entered the 4-D, you were given a card stamped with the time; upon departure, you would present your card at the door and pay twenty-five cents an hour, plus food and drinks. Fran Gebhard worked at the 4-D when she was fifteen. "I used to drink Chinese gunpowder tea," she had told me. "I used to think I was so sophisticated."

Unlike many rock 'n' rollers, Young had been a fan of Bob Dylan since grade nine. He loved the Ian and Sylvia hit "Four Strong Winds," a tune he'd record for his 1978 album *Comes a Time*. In late 1964, at the 4-D, Young would meet a fledgling singer named Joan Anderson, later to become famous as Joni Mitchell.

John Yellowlees was the one who suggested I speak with the former co-owner of the 4-D, David Ingram. "He's that guy who advertises in the parking lot of Park Royal Shopping Mall," John had told me. "He keeps a car there covered with signs." A large, bearded man with a low conversational voice, Ingram is now an immigration tax specialist in North Vancouver. When I'd visited his office earlier that summer, I'd expected somebody older than this robust-looking man who kept pictures of his young children amidst the heaps of books and paper cluttering his workspace. Ingram, who had worked in broadcasting for forty-one years, also hosts a weekly radio show, a program he describes as an "infomercial" on tax issues.

Ingram was a one-third owner and "one-hundred-percent manager" of the Winnipeg 4-D, and had a ten-percent stake in its Regina counterpart. The Winnipeg coffeehouse opened at three in the afternoon for high-school kids. "In 1963," Ingram told me, "we had a great big massive sundae we called a 'Suffering Bastard.' It was four-fifty. You got to think how much money that was. We used to sell a lot of them." Ingram had one of the three espresso machines in all of Winnipeg, serving cups for three-fifty a shot.

He was also in charge of booking acts like Sonny Terry and Brownie McGhee, Ronnie Hawkins, and George Carlin, "when he was flat broke staying at my basement, doing hippie-dippie weatherman kind of stuff."

"What was José Feliciano like?"

"Interesting. Everybody was interesting. They were marvelous people. Bill Cosby was at the Fourth Dimension in Regina one time in summer 1963—"

I was momentarily stuck on José Feliciano, whose Christmas album my father still played during the holidays. "Did he need an escort to get around?"

"No, nope—"

"Did he have a cane?"

"I had a Cadillac limousine, an Imperial limousine; I had a Cadillac hearse, a Packard hearse; I had a TR-4—about fourteen cars. There was always somebody around who wanted to drive somebody. It worked out okay. Right now, I have five or six cars."

I brought out a picture of Neil Young with Mort, and for a moment, Ingram confused Young's hearse for one he'd owned. "What's the attraction of a hearse?" I asked him.

"People are dying to get in them."

I laughed. "Ka-boom-boom."

Another of Ingram's cars in Winnipeg inspired his most imaginative business promotion. "Somebody wrapped a '51 Pontiac around a telephone pole just around the street. I bought it, paid maybe fifty bucks for it, had it hauled over and wrapped around the pole in front of the coffeehouse. I had a '49 Cadillac ambulance that I backed up to it with the red light going around very slowly. We had a spotlight on the accident scene, some dummies—one dressed up in a police uniform and another in a white ambulance-type thing. It looked like a real accident. And I had a sign: 'If you drive, drink coffee!' "

Ingram sat back in his chair and laughed, still pleased with his ingenuity so many decades later.

"Well," I said. "It was good of you to promote responsible drinking."

He shook his head. "There were sixteen or seventeen accidents the first day and a half. It was a traffic hazard."

"You must have been pretty young."

"I was twenty-one or twenty-two back then."

"Do you remember the first time you saw Neil Young?"

"It would be the summer of '61 or something."

"What's your first memory of him?"

"He was a kid with a dream. My real memory of Neil was when his father phoned me. It was November or December, 1963. He wanted to know about his son going to Los Angeles. I encouraged Dad to let Neil go; I thought it was a great idea." Just like Fran Gebhard, Ingram seemed to know—a realization perhaps burnished by hindsight—that Young was something special. Or maybe he was that bad a student. "But he didn't really head there for another two and a half years." (Young would leave Toronto for California in March, 1966.) I asked Ingram if he was a Neil Young fan. He said he is, though he prefers talk radio to music.

David Ingram was inspired to go into his current business when one of his American acts at the 4-D was stopped by Canada Customs at the Pembina, North Dakota, border. "They held her up because the paperwork wasn't proper and the bus had left without her. I headed down in the middle of the winter and had to fill out all this paperwork. I have been, almost since that day, in the U.S.-Canadian tax and immigration business."

"When did the 4-D close down, or when did your association with it end?"

"Well, you're always associated with something," Ingram said. The 4-D was torn down to make way for a bridge, Ingram believed, in 1973.

Before the club was destroyed, a friend retrieved the 4-D's front door and brought it to Vancouver. It was displayed at the Media Club, a local pub for news types, and from there it disappeared. "I would give anything to have that back."

When our interview concluded, Ingram went through his computer database, looking up old friends.

"It's David Ingram," he would bark into the phone. "How are you? Listen, I've been talking to a fellow named Ken Chong—"

"Kevin."

"He says he's doing a book on the 4-D."

"Actually, Neil Young."

"Yeah, yeah—and Neil Young," he said. "Is it all right if he speaks with you?"

He threw the phone back onto the hook. "All right. He says he's willing to talk."

"Uh, thanks."

He spoke to several people. Between phone calls, he entered my name and contact information into his computer, typing in "Neil Young, 4-D" as my keywords. He also recommended a good mechanic for the hearse I was still planning to drive. "Tell them David Ingram sent you," he told me.

\\\|/

CHAPTER

EIGHT

THE FOUR OF US were housed comfortably in Winnipeg, in a trailer in Ian and Donna Stevenson's driveway. There were three beds, a TV and VCR, a kitchen, and a magically self-replenishing beer fridge. It was like a slumber party, but with beer. We put in some microwave popcorn and watched the Robert Redford movie *Sneakers,* which was sort of like an *A-Team* for middlebrows, and tried to watch *Attack of the Clones,* but only got halfway through that two-hour toy commercial. One night I attempted one of Dave's space cakes. Minutes after complaining that I wasn't feeling anything, I couldn't stand. I was told, only after puking behind the garage, that I had taken one of the super-sized pieces.

In the mornings we'd stumble into the house hungover, and there'd be bacon and eggs waiting for us at the dining-room table. Sarah had told us how, when Ian and Donna used to host visiting rugby teams, they would not only feed the entire team but fill their keg for them.

"I love Winnipeg hospitality," Geoff said. Mark and I nodded along vigorously as we shoveled breakfast down our throats.

"When I was a kid I used to love when Ian and Donna came to visit," Dave was saying. "Ian would make bacon and sausages for me every day."

"Oh, right," I said. "Your parents don't eat red meat."

Dave shook his head. "I had to beg my parents for steak. My mom would make it once a week, every Friday. She'd hold the steak away from her when she brought it to the table. It was like she was feeding a dog."

Geoff took his guitar to busk at the public market in the Forks, the downtown area where the Red and Assiniboine Rivers meet. Dave and Mark went off to another area called the Exchange.

I drove alone to the Crescentwood neighborhood to meet with Winnipeg novelist Miriam Toews. I'd met her at a reading a few months earlier, and before leaving Vancouver I e-mailed her. Miriam wasn't an expert on Neil Young, but she did live only a few blocks from Kelvin High School. Her latest novel, *A Complicated Kindness,* had been on the bestseller list since it first appeared that spring, winning rapturous reviews not only in Canada but in the U.S. and the U.K.

"Coffee or beer?" Miriam asked me.

I'd just had coffee, but was it already beer o'clock? I mulled it over: "I'll have a can of personality."

Miriam is disarmingly warm, funny and self-deprecating. As we sat outside in her enclosed back porch, each drinking a tall can of Czech pilsner, she peeked into the kitchen to make sure her oldest child, Owen, wasn't within earshot before telling me about secretly listening to his CDs.

"I only listen when he's out of the house." Miriam, by the way, is freakishly young to have birthed two children who are now teenagers. Owen, who was soon entering university on a basketball scholarship, had a copy of *Greendale,* she said. "For some reason, he just loves that CD."

"It's like a song cycle, a rock opera—"

"Yeah, a concept album. With grandpa sitting on his rocking chair on the porch. And it's an environmental record." Among her son's other CDs, she liked Kanye West and the Streets. "I'd never have thought he'd like that."

According to Miriam, Winnipeg is good for writers because of the low rents and the weather. "It's a very cold place in the winter. You can't really go outside without risking your life for months at a time. In that way it's conducive to staying inside and planting yourself in front of a computer and getting down to work."

I suggested we walk to Young's childhood home on Grosvenor, then to Kelvin, the school her daughter Georgia would be attending in the fall.

"When you write your book," Miriam told me on the street, "feel free to have me saying any brilliant or pithy thoughts you can think up afterward."

"Deal."

"And if for any reason, say, that I don't end up in your book," Miriam said, "that's also fine by me."

I threw my hands in the air and laughed. "Why does everyone keep telling me that?"

We walked along Grosvenor until we arrived at a three-story brick and stone house set back from the street behind gnarly old oak trees. The house, which you enter from the side, has been divided into three apartment suites. Young lived here with his mother, and later his grandfather, Bill Ragland, throughout his Kelvin years. According to Einarson, he was often left on his own by Rassy, who appeared regularly on a local television quiz show and had an active social life that included curling and golf. Young would subsist on canned spaghetti and macaroni and cheese, which he'd cook up for the Squires before their shows. The police would appear periodically in response to noise complaints. Rassy so thoroughly charmed one policeman that he actually sat in with Neil on the drums.

Miriam grew up outside of Winnipeg in a liberal Mennonite family. "When I was fifteen, sixteen, seventeen," Miriam said, "it seemed that every boy I went out with—not that I went out with a lot of them—was always learning Neil Young songs and playing them in their basement bedrooms. That was going to be the thing that impressed me, that would make me love them forever: when they mastered 'Cortez the Killer' or 'Cinnamon Girl.'"

"Songs you never need to listen to ever again," I said. I laughed, but I also cringed, thinking of the times I'd played Neil Young songs to girls. Or, even worse, pretended I was playing them to imaginary girls.

"I've got his triple album, best-of—"

"*Decade.*"

"Yeah, yeah for sure. It's kind of cool to listen to that stuff. 'Like a Hurricane.' Although *Rust Never Sleeps* is probably the best."

According to Miriam, Crescentwood is "more of a working-class neighborhood" than River Heights, which it borders and which "is an old, wealthy neighborhood. A lot of old houses, old money." As we passed into River Heights, the houses got noticeably bigger and somehow WASPier. It is that part of town where people go to imagine the house they'll buy when they strike it rich. Every city has one.

We came to Kelvin High School, formerly known as Kelvin Technical High, whose notable graduates include Scott Young and philosopher Marshall McLuhan. Neil, as his mother once pointed out, is "Kelvin's most famous dropout." The building where Young attended classes was constructed in 1964. Miriam and I approached the office and asked if there was anything related to Neil Young at the school.

Juve Furtado, the school's vice-principal, took us to the library and helped us look for Neil in old yearbooks. I didn't have my notes with me and couldn't remember which grades he'd failed or what year he dropped out, so we leafed through the yearbooks from the first half of the 1960s. At some point, Mr. Furtado mentioned that he'd played in bands later in the decade, a few years after the Squires had finished.

"We'd perform at pep rallies and other school events," he told us.

"What was the name of your band?"

"Halo Syndicate," he recalled with a laugh. "I mean, I've been in other bands and done local stuff. But it was a side thing, you know? I went into education."

"Did you do originals or covers?"

"We did a lot of covers. I still love to pick up a guitar. It's been a hobby most of my life, though I dropped the band thing years ago."

"What are the kids at Kelvin like?"

"There are a lot of talented kids." There are about 1,300 students enrolled in the school. Mr. Furtado mentioned band and choir, sports programs, and the new art rooms in a recently built wing. Two staff members, he said proudly, had put out CDs.

While at Kelvin, Young was sent to the principal's office after doing his Roy Orbison impression at the back of the classroom. Kelvin's principal, when told by Neil that he wanted to drop out, supported Neil's decision. (Was there one person in Winnipeg who thought Young should stay in school? Jeez.) "Go and give it a try," the principal said, according to John Einarson. He was confident Neil would return once he realized how difficult becoming a professional musician would be. I asked Mr. Furtado if he would ever give his students this advice.

"Obviously not. I think, today, students are more fortunate. We've got staff who recognize the talent in the students. We want the student to succeed academically, obviously, because you never know where the music will take you." He mentioned one teacher who organized a coffeehouse night and arranged for a producer to meet with the kids. Funding was provided for a songwriting workshop and studio time for a demo CD made by a couple of students. "In school, you'll always see a kid dragging his guitar around."

Young's song "Don't Be Denied" reads like the valedictorian's speech Young never made. It follows the template of the standard high-school graduation speech—chase your dreams, don't give up, think differently—but shows how pursuing your dreams can be onerous, and how it means uncertainty, leaving people behind. And possibly pissing off your parents. As Young would later say: "I received my different diplomas in back alleys and dressing rooms and motels."

On the way back, Miriam told me her daughter was looking forward to Kelvin. "I think she feels this is a new start and she's going to get back to achieving academically, which she's totally capable of doing if she puts her mind to it." I asked Miriam, theoretically, what she'd do if her daughter wanted to drop out, whether she'd encourage her to do it the same way Rassy did for Neil.

"Oh man, I'd be so of two minds," she told me. "On the one hand I'd be saying, 'Right on, go for it. Do what you have to do.' On the other hand I'd certainly suggest she finish high school."

"How much determination do you need to be a writer?" I asked.

She laughed. "You could ask yourself that question."

"I'll edit this out."

"Well, I don't know what it is. I'm not a particularly motivated person. I'm not a high achiever. I don't need the accolades or the back-patting. But there's something that compels me to write. Maybe it's my attitude problem"—she laughed—"my problem with outside authority."

"I'm *so* like that," I said, nodding like a chimp. "I *so* hate outside authority."

"I wouldn't be able to do anything for anyone else. I guess you need, as you know, a ton of self-discipline to get the job done." She joked: "I sound like an Olympic athlete. *Just came up short today, wasn't what I planned.* It's so hokey, but I really do need to write to stay relatively sane."

We said our goodbyes, and I headed for my car. I'd been planning to go straight back to the Stevensons' trailer for a pre-dinner nap, but I wanted a photo of the house on Grosvenor. I parked the car and approached the house's side entrance. There were three buzzers. I could hear the notes of a piano tinkling from one suite. Should I ring and ask to look inside? I didn't want to intrude. I pushed one doorbell, and when I got no reply, I was relieved. I decided not to press on.

In the Stevensons' back yard, Ian was grilling hamburgers for dinner. I checked my e-mail and scanned the Rustie listserv in Ian and Donna's office. From the desk chair I could hear Donna on the phone, talking about what "the boys" were doing.

"David and Mark headed to the Exchange. Kevin met with Miriam Toews, a Winnipeg writer. Kevin says she doesn't know Neil Young, but she lives near Kelvin and River Heights. Tomorrow he'll be speaking to John Einarson, the music writer—"

Later on, there was a knock on the door frame. I turned to see Donna holding a plate of cookies.

"I just happened to be baking," she said. "Do you want some?"

"Sure." I'm not the kind of guy who turns down baked goods.

Dave and Mark came home, having wandered around downtown Winnipeg and met a pretty local girl who took them to her favorite pub. It often seemed to me that Dave and Mark lived in a parallel universe where pretty female strangers, when asked for directions, offered their services as tour guides. On certain levels, I hate them.

"Where's Geoff?" Dave asked.

"Dunno," I said, with a shrug. "I'm not his mommy."

We waited, then ate dinner without him. Dave decided we'd better go find him.

"You'd think he'd be back in time for dinner," he said, as we drove down Portage, Winnipeg's main street. All of Winnipeg seemed to be at home having dinner. "If you're staying as a guest and say you'll be back for dinner, you should be back on time."

"Maybe he got lost," Mark suggested.

"He lost track of time," Dave told him.

We spent forty-five minutes looking for Geoff. When we returned, he was at the dining-room table eating a cold hamburger.

"Where were you?" Dave asked, sounding both relieved and exasperated.

"I took the wrong bus and ended up at the other end of town. I walked back for an hour."

"You should have called," Dave said.

Geoff wiped the corners of his mouth with a napkin before speaking. "Sorry, Mommy."

My cell phone rang. It was Lyn, looking for Dave. I passed him my phone and he took the call outside in the driveway.

Geoff had made enough money busking for a cup of coffee and a couple of used records. He showed me what he bought. "What's up with Dave?" he asked me.

I shrugged. Shrugging is for me what hand-gesturing is for Mediterranean people. "He loves a little too hard."

CHAPTER

NINE

SINCE 1972, Winnipeg's official motto has been "Unum Cum Virtute Multorum," Latin for "one with the strength of many." The city is also known as "Winterpeg," "the Peg," and, because of its geographic position as a middle point between eastern and western Canada, "the Gateway City." Which reminds me of the term "gateway drug" and makes me think of Winnipeg as the place you go before visiting Heroin Falls and Cracktown.

At some point Winnipeg's slogan, at least on the highway signs as one enters town, became "One Great City." "One Great City" also happens to be the title of an intriguing song by a Winnipeg band, the Weakerthans. While the song is memorable for its refrain, "I hate Winnipeg," there's an attention to detail—"a darker gray is breaking through a lighter one," another stalled car "in the turning lane"—that complicates this offhand loathing.

Miriam Toews suggested I get in touch with Weakerthans singer and lyricist John K. Samson. Although the acerbic lyricism of Samson's songs seems more reminiscent of Tom Waits or Elvis Costello than of Young, and the band's music has a post-punk snap with nary a thirteen-minute guitar solo, Samson was kind enough to meet with me at Fort Rouge coffeehouse to talk about Neil Young. There was some overlap in the experiences of Young and Samson, a Kelvin grad, but also some differences. Young left Winnipeg, Samson stayed. Young came from an era of rock stars; Samson grew up with punk, a genre and approach that is openly suspicious, if not disdainful, of rock-star excess.

Samson's lyrics have a literary quality that extends beyond his word choice and precise, marbled imagery. Songs with titles like "Pamphleteer" and "Uncorrected Proofs" allude to Samson's role as an editor at Arbeiter Ring, a Winnipeg publishing collective. Arbeiter Ring, named after a Jewish fraternal organization that took part in the 1919 Winnipeg General Strike and set up anarchist Emma Goldman's visits to the city, publishes books on "contemporary politics, culture, and social issues" from a left-wing perspective. "We always barely break even," Samson told me. "It's kind of strange. I play in a rock band, and the rock band supports my day job in an office. It's kind of the opposite of everyone else." Other songs feature epigraphs from Martin Amis or mention French theorists Michel Foucault and Jacques Derrida. And if you go to their website (theweakerthans.org), you'll find the Weakerthans' lyrics set not in verse, but in paragraphs. They read like something between inner monologue and prose poetry: "Memory will rust and erode into lists of all that you gave me: some matches, a blanket, this pain in my chest, the best parts of Lonely, duct-tape and soldered wires, new words for old desires, and every birthday card I threw away."

I mentioned a recent article in the *Globe and Mail* by Carl Wilson, in which Wilson suggested that "fiction and rock are ever-more-specialized interests, whose overlapping audiences at this late date might as well bunk down together." I asked Samson, who'd grown up with a punk do-it-yourself aesthetic, whether there were any upsides to occupying the fringe.

"There's definitely value in it. I read a lot of poetry. I think there's a lot of democratic power in forms that are marginalized. And I think of Winnipeg as a great metaphor for that. The place itself is so marginalized. I think that's one of the reasons the arts community is so vibrant. People always talk about the winters and people having to stay indoors— uh, yeah, maybe. But I think it has more to do with the actual physical isolation of the place, which spurs people to create things. It's got all the greatness and lousiness of both big cities and small towns, which makes it a conflicted place. It's a place that's constantly unsure of itself. It lives off reflected light. Everything is always elsewhere—"

"Life Is Elsewhere," I suggested, name-dropping a Milan Kundera novel.

"Even when it comes to things like Neil Young. It's all reflected. He's only been here three times since he left, but people claim him. It seems strange, the ferocity with which they claim him, and other people who've left. You don't always pay attention to what actually happens here. It's all nostalgia, it's all in the past."

"Have you ever thought about leaving?"

"Yeah, I think about leaving all the time, but I'm always drawn back here. I think of Winnipeg as my subject, the thing I write about, that I'm always writing about, that I'm always trying to get right. I think writers, for the most part, are saying the same thing over and over again, trying to get it right."

"Variations on a theme."

"Yeah, and I guess I'm comfortable with the fact that this is what I'm writing about. This is what I'm going to try and get right. Even if I leave, I'll always be writing about this place."

"I think of writers like James Joyce, who wrote about Dublin from a distance. You don't find it hard to write about Winnipeg being in Winnipeg?"

"I do. I feel very closed in sometimes. I totally understand why people leave. You have to leave. But I spend four months a year away from this place. I get a nice perspective on the community and the buildings"—here, I'm reminded of the beginning to the Weakerthans' "Left and Leaving": "My city's still breathing (but barely it's true) through buildings gone missing like teeth"—"and on what Winnipeg means. I'm still trying to work out what I feel about this place."

Samson enjoyed his time at Kelvin, he told me. He first started playing music while there, in a band with the guitarist he still plays with, Stephen Carroll, as part of the punk scene in bars downtown. "Draft night at the Albert was Thursday night, and everyone played in a band, and everyone played on draft night. They got fifty bucks and a case of beer.

That's the community I came out of: anyone can play if they want to play, and should if they want to."

"Do you think music is more manufactured than it was before?" I asked.

"That's what people always say. It's a cop-out that people use. I think music's becoming more creative, more democratic. Especially with the means of production—I hate to sound like a Marxist, I probably am—which are so much more available to everyone now. Recording on computers, peer-to-peer sharing. There's an expanse of indie labels that seem to do well. There's always the crap that people are going to sell at Wal-Mart. It just seems to me that it's easier for musicians to do something these days."

"Some would say rock music is balkanized, that it's another niche among niches. That there aren't any more *Exile on Main Street*s, or Neil Young—"

"There's a very real sense that history is speeding up. It's very difficult to get a grasp on anything for more than five minutes—to think about it, and write about it, and communicate it. Maybe you're right. There's something to it."

"I was just arguing, you know, what other people—"

"Right. But I think there are more *Exile on Main Street*s being produced today than there ever have been, albums that have that same spirit and integrity. I don't think they're as noticed." Samson mentioned a Broken Social Scene record that was playing in the coffeehouse: "It's not on the top of the charts, but it still has a profound effect. Maybe the market is diluted. But I think it's a good thing."

Samson's early memories of Neil Young were family trips spent listening to *Harvest* over and over again on his Walkman. "I loved his voice because it was so unaffected. It was so simple, he used what he had, and instead of that being limiting, it was exactly the opposite. He never had the fake English accent. You got to love him for that, when everyone tried to affect it. The same thing happened with punk."

Samson was a bassist before moving on to acoustic guitar. "I was in a punk-rock group called Propagandhi when I saw the movie *Dead Man*. The next day I bought my first electric guitar. I was so overwhelmed by the way that movie sounded and what Young did with sound." He went into a local music store. "I said, 'I want to sound like Neil Young.' And, of course, everyone in there sighed. People probably came in there saying that all the time. I immediately realized that that was way too much guitar for me, so I got a cheap Ibanez Talman." Samson expressed admiration for Young's guitar solos, a spontaneity that he wished he could better tap into. "He makes something profound with, like, four notes."

"Guitar solos are so out of fashion. No one plays them anymore."

"I certainly don't. But you've got to admire his twenty-minute guitar solos."

"Is there anything in Neil Young's music that reminds you of Winnipeg?"

"Yes, it's something intangible. It's working with the materials at hand and trying to make something worthwhile. I think that's the spirit of arts in Winnipeg: using what you have, not being limited by that, being empowered by that. In other ways it doesn't remind me of Winnipeg at all."

"The California rock—"

"Oh, yeah. There's something incredibly American to a lot of it, of everything post-*Harvest*. And what I think of as those dark years—"

"His pro-Reagan albums?"

"Yeah, they have to be taken in context, but they do have to be looked at in a serious way. I think they're really disappointing. They seem very American, in the worst sense of the word. Artists should be held accountable for their politics. That's one of the problems I have with Neil Young. Sometimes there's a reactionary vein in his songs. Then again, he has written some of the greatest protest songs I know. The form itself is so powerful, it's so immediate—that's political, too. It redeems any reservations I have about him."

"He's an environmentalist, too."

"Oh, yeah."

"He's definitely not ideological."

"Exactly, whereas I am a very ideological person. But I can't think of a better protest song than 'Rockin' in the Free World.'"

"It's also a meathead frat-boy album."

"I know, it's true."

Throughout our conversation, I returned to my whiny, it's-all-been-done jag several times, only to have Samson pull me from the brink of despair. "Do you think of rock 'n' roll as more of a tradition, like folk music?" I asked.

"I guess people have been saying that since—forever," he told me. "I'm all for being derivative, in a way. Pop songs are ready-made tools. Neil Young does this especially well. You can use these forms, because people understand them. And you can do something different with them—lyrically. Melody is a mysterious thing.

"Sometimes you don't want to mess with the delicate machines that songs are," Samson told me. "Sometimes messing with them, analyzing, screws them up. The songs are the questions." I left my conversation with John K. Samson thinking rock 'n' roll is in good hands.

I'D ARRANGED to meet John Einarson at Earl Grey Junior High, on the very steps where Young and his friend Ken Koblun would sit dreaming about being stars. John is a high-school teacher, though at a nearby private school. In addition to teaching, he's somehow managed to write, at a prodigious pace, several books on Young, Buffalo Springfield, and the Winnipeg music scene. Earlier that day he'd been working on a television documentary about Buffy Sainte-Marie. *Don't Be Denied*—which expands on *Aurora,* Einarson's booklet on the Squires that was published by the NYAS—covers Young's musical beginnings in Canada. Since its 1992 publication, it has been a resource tool for every major Young biographer. Einarson's book on Buffalo Springfield, *For What It's Worth,* has been recently updated and reissued.

John is trim. The day we met, he wore wire-rimmed glasses and a red polo shirt. To look at him and to look at me, with my hipster glasses and ratty cardigan, was to see two generations of rock nerds, men—and it's almost always men who are rock nerds—whose eyewear and studious fascination with the minutiae of rock 'n' roll belie the hedonism and abandon that the music supposedly represents. In his demeanor, and to a certain extent in his elegant, unpretentious prose, John demonstrates the qualities of someone born to teach: a deep well of patience for the recitation of dusty facts and an enthusiasm sparked when approached by a curious mind. Since I'd contacted him earlier that summer, John had become my most valuable resource, always ready with the phone numbers I'd asked for and other helpful suggestions.

Young came to Earl Grey in 1960 for grade nine, and it was here that he'd been the "new kid." Though he soon made friends, the move was not without its rough patches. The second verse of "Don't Be Denied" recalls his initial reception: "When we got to Winnipeg / I checked in to school / I wore white bucks on my feet / When I learned the golden rule / The punches came fast and hard / Lying on my back in the school yard."

The first thing I wanted to know from John Einarson was what exactly "white bucks" were.

This was an easy one for him: "White bucks are white slip-on shoes."

"They were a little after my time."

John laughed. "Pat Boone used to wear white bucks with a white sports coat and a pink carnation. And they were popular in the late fifties." As Young told Jimmy McDonough in *Shakey:* "There was nothin' *new* about white bucks by the time I started wearin' white bucks. They were like, *out. No one* was wearing them. That's when I got mine. They were enough of a statement to piss people off. They set me apart."

"And this got Neil Young beaten up?" I asked John.

"The thing is, when you come from another community and you're the new kid in school, you sometimes have to prove yourself. I guess the tough guys picked on Neil and he had to show he was tough and hit them with dictionaries—"

I'd read this story before, but I wanted to hear him tell it. "Can you tell me about the dictionary?"

"Apparently, somebody was giving him a hard time in English class, so he went up to the front of the classroom, picked up a great big dictionary— very calm, very nonchalant—then walked back, whacked the guy on the back of the head with it, and returned the dictionary to the front desk."

In *Shakey,* Young claimed the incident occurred a year before, in Toronto, when he came to the defense of a boy named Gary Renzetti. The outcome was no different. "Of course he was ejected and sent to the principal's office," John continued. "Very often his white bucks were seen parked outside the principal's office."

"What were the Squires like?"

"It's interesting. Looking back, myth becomes greater than reality. I've heard the Squires described as the top band in Winnipeg. I wouldn't even put the Squires in the top ten—maybe number ten, if you were generous. They were largely a South End band. The thing that set the Squires apart from the other three hundred or so bands around the city at the time was the volume of original material they were doing, all penned by Neil—few other bands, with the exception of Chad Allan and the Reflections, were doing as much original material. And when Neil started singing, that made them unique, too, because he had such a strange singing voice. People gave him a hard time about his singing voice, but it was something he wanted to do and he stuck with it. The thing is, he had a distinctive voice."

The first live show John saw was Burton Cummings and the Deverons at a community club. Although he grew up three blocks from Young, he missed the Squires by a few months. "They played Grant Park High School several times, because Allan Bates and Kenny Smyth went there, but I was in grade seven. They were in grade eleven or twelve. My brother saw the Squires because he was about the same age, and he knew Kenny Smyth. They were like neighborhood heroes. And Neil was a 'hard rock.' He had the Cuban-heel boots, which would later become Beatle boots, and the leather jacket. There was the perception that he was a tough guy, when, in fact, he wasn't. There are stories of him organizing a student revolt at Kelvin, stories about him jumping out of the classroom window from the second floor. Did he skip out of class? Absolutely. Did he lip off teachers? Sure. Did he fail? Yep, twice. He was focused on music. That's all he wanted to do."

Around this time, we were interrupted by an Earl Grey teacher who wanted to know why two grown men were sitting on the steps of a junior high school. We explained the Neil Young connection.

"Is there a shrine to Neil inside?" John asked.

Laughing at the rock nerds, the teacher shook her head and left.

I mentioned to John my surprise that Young, whom I'd have assumed to be a nerd in high school, was actually popular with both boys and girls. Maybe I was projecting, or maybe Neil was both nerd and stud, the way any teenager can shift between possible selves—geek and rocker, loner and popular guy. In some ways, Young has continued to juggle those identities through the decades.

"He was in a band," John told me. "Therefore, he was cool. Girls wanted to know him. Guys who played guitars or were in a band wanted to know him. He definitely had cool credibility. The jocks weren't interested in him at all. There was always the dichotomy between the jock guys and the growing rock scene."

"Are the divisions the same these days at your high school?"

"Oh yeah, for sure. If you're on the hockey team in our school, you're the big man on campus." For the past fourteen years, Einarson has been part of a school program called "The Rock Show" involving 120 kids. Students spend a year learning songs and perform at a concert. "One of the first shows we did was called 'Young and the Restless: A Tribute to Neil Young.' We opened with 'Don't Be Denied,' then we did 'The Sultan' and went through his career, ending with 'Rockin' in the Free World.' It was a lot of fun for them."

"So your students know about Neil Young?"

"Absolutely, and not just because of me. I teach Canadian Studies, a compulsory course in this province. And part of that is Canadian culture and the arts. We talk about Canadian music, the CRTC"—the government organization that regulates broadcasting, which began to enforce quotas of Canadian content in the 1970s—"and the evolution of the Canadian music industry. They learn about Neil Young. But I don't have to educate anybody about him. There are sixty-year-olds who know Neil Young and there are fourteen-year-olds who know Neil Young. It's simply astounding that he has endured."

Einarson recalled seeing Young play on TV in 1967 with his big orange Gretsch and in a Confederate Army uniform; already John knew about Neil's connection to his neighborhood. His favorite Buffalo Springfield song was "Nowadays Clancy Can't Even Sing." "When I was writing *Don't*

Be Denied, in the fall of 1991," he said, "in my classroom I had a student named Adam Smith. His father was Clancy Smith, who inspired the song."

Clancy was a Kelvin student whose multiple sclerosis kept him isolated from other students. "He was a kind of persecuted member of the community," Young told Einarson. "He used to do something, sing or something, and then he wasn't able to do it anymore...[A]ll the other problems that were seemingly important didn't mean anything anymore because he couldn't do what he wanted to do."

Young wrote this song in 1965, during one of his most despondent periods as a fledgling musician. "The song really moved me," Einarson told me. "If I had to rank my top ten favorite songs by anybody, it would certainly be in my top five. Maybe not number one, but possibly number three. The first Buffalo Springfield album appeared in Canada in December 1966, and it was heavily hyped in Winnipeg. Neil's mother came on the radio. She came on CKRC; the deejay pulled the needle off the record because Mrs. Young was there. They began playing cut after cut. The only news that filtered into the entertainment newspaper was kind of bizarre. I remember a short little blurb that said: 'Winnipegger Neil Young is now in California writing songs for Sonny and Cher.' "

I asked John how he was able to interview Young for *Don't Be Denied.* He'd been writing a series of two-page articles for the *Winnipeg Sun* entitled "Rockrospect," he said. ("Terrible title. I didn't make that up.") Each article focused on a different Winnipeg band, including the Shondels, the Deverons, and the Orfans. One of the bands was the Squires. From those articles, he was approached to write a book about the Winnipeg music scene, which would be published as *Shakin' All Over.*

"It was the summer of 1985. It was the last time Neil's mom came up to Winnipeg. She used to drive up on her own every summer from Florida because she had a lot of family and friends living here. I heard she was in town, got her number, called her up, and did an article about her. She was helping to raise money for cerebral palsy. She was a celebrity here in the 1960s, long before Neil Young was Neil Young. She used to be on *Twenty Questions* every week. I told her about my book and she said, 'You've got to talk to Neil.' She gave me his number. A few days later I worked up the courage to call. The funny thing was, someone had sent him the articles. 'I have them right here,' he said."

An interview was set up. "It was amazing the recollection he had all about Winnipeg," Einarson said. "Here's a guy who's played Woodstock and Farm Aid and Live Aid, and he could remember what he was wearing the night he played Glenwood Community Club in the spring of 1964."

In 1987, to coincide with the publication of his book, John organized a concert celebrating Winnipeg's 1960s music scene, also called Shakin' All Over. The concert date was tied to the weekend of Kelvin High's seventy-fifth anniversary reunion. Young attended both. "That's when he jammed with Randy Bachman, the first time they ever played together, even though they already knew each other." Young also reunited the Squires at a local club, the Blue Note Café.

"A few years later when I wanted to do *Don't Be Denied* I called Neil up and told him what I wanted to do," John continued. He was invited down to Young's ranch. "If I'd gone through his management, it wouldn't have happened. They exist to keep distractions like me away from Neil. But this was something that was important to him. His Winnipeg roots are very important to him; he thinks of himself as a Winnipegger."

Young's biographers have noted that while Neil has become infamous for his disdain of nostalgia and for never looking back, he is also meticulous in his efforts to document every period of his career. When Einarson visited Broken Arrow, Young's ranch in northern California, in 1991, he was taken to the building on the ranch where Young's long-awaited Archives were being organized. (Over a decade later, rumors still circulate about their imminent release.) There were already eighty tracks, along with a booklet that had a page devoted to every song.

For the Shakin' All Over show, John played onstage not only with Young, but with Randy Bachman and Burton Cummings. "I was beside myself playing with them."

"What did you guys play?"

"Neil came out, and we did 'Just Like Tom Thumb's Blues' in the key of A. And we did 'Down by the River,' 'American Woman'—with me telling Neil the chords—then 'Taking Care of Business.' That was just a thrill."

"Were you in bands as a teenager?" I asked John.

"I played in bands throughout the sixties and seventies."

"What were they called?"

He laughed with embarrassment. "I was in Red Ryder, though it was a different band than the one that played with Tom Cochrane. And a band called Euphoria. Actually, we opened for Led Zeppelin—"

I shat myself. "YOU OPENED FOR LED ZEPPELIN?"

John smiled. "We were the sound-check band, I think. That was on August 29, 1970. It was called the Man-Pop Festival, and it was outside. We were an opening act, along with Chilliwack, the Youngbloods, Iron Butterfly, Ides of March. But a couple acts after us, it rained. They were going to move the concert indoors. They created a makeshift PA out of a bunch of Garnet amps that all the local bands had, moved everyone from the football field into the arena, threw together a stage from a bunch of risers. The Youngbloods played, the Ides of March played, Iron Butterfly played. Except Zeppelin had a contract that said if it rained they didn't have to play; they still got their fifty grand. This was around the time of *Led Zeppelin II,* so they were only making fifty grand, which was a lot of money back then." *Back then?*

"They were staying at the International Inn, a hotel by the airport, partying it up. A local singer named Diane Heatherington—bless her, she's dead now—went to the International Inn, knocked on their door. She *chewed their ears out.* She'd never met Led Zeppelin in her life; they didn't know who she was. All of a sudden there's this"—John paused, reaching deep into his word-cupboard for the appropriate term—"*chick* standing at the door, saying, 'You've got an obligation, thirteen thousand there, they sat out in the rain, you go play.' And they did. They came and played at two in the morning. It's in Led Zeppelin lore as The Concert They Never Had to Give. And it was here in Winnipeg. I opened the show."

Through his writing, Einarson stays in touch with his rock 'n' roll days. "I guess I'm reliving much of my own youth, the music that I loved, the artists I admired. I get a chance to write about them and meet them." John finds it easier to work now that his own children are adults and no longer need to be chauffeured around, and he uses his summers off to conduct research. "It's my obsession, it's what I love." He was now working on a book profiling sixty prominent Winnipeg musicians, *Made In Manitoba: A Musical Legacy,* to be published in time for the 2005 Junos.

In his office at school, John told me, he has Neil Young posters and photos. Recently, he splurged and bought a Gretsch White Falcon, the kind of guitar Bachman played and Young used exclusively with Buffalo Springfield.

"How much was that?" I asked. "Three grand?"

"Five grand."

"Ho*ly.*"

"My mid-life crisis."

I laughed. "I'm a latent guitar player. When I buy a Gretsch White Falcon, then I'll know—"

"I told my wife, 'It's cheaper than a sports car and safer than a girlfriend.'"

John had brought for me to keep some rare photos of Young with Buffalo Springfield and, on a CD-R, a couple of Squires songs that he made me promise not to bootleg. I offered him my profuse thanks as we parted. I was a block or two from Earl Grey when a car came whipping around the corner. John burst out like an undercover cop, with one more interview lead that had come to mind.

"If you go to Fort Rouge Travel, a few blocks from here," he told me, "you'll find someone who once kicked Neil Young out of his band."

Carmine LaRosa was behind a desk in his travel agency when I surprised him with my MiniDisc recorder. "I didn't fire Neil Young from the band," he said, his voice tinged with an Italian accent. "He quit."

LaRosa was reluctant to be interviewed but intrigued by my recorder. "I've been looking for something to record my own songs, when I'm at home with my guitar. How does it sound? Does it play cassettes?" I showed him how the MiniDisc slid into the player and played some tape I'd recorded as he tilted an ear to the speaker. Only after this demonstration did he agree to speak.

"How long have you been working as a travel agent?" I asked him.

"I've been here since 1979."

"But you didn't fire Neil Young from your band."

"No, I did not fire Neil Young from the band," he said with a laugh. "He did play with me for a while—as a guitar player, not as a singer."

"What was the name of your band?"

"We were called the Thunderstorms." Carmine was the lead singer of the Thunderstorms, and he still played music of the "late fifties and early sixties" at a local restaurant.

"Why did Neil leave the band?" I asked.

"Well, he left the band because we did a few gigs at the community clubs and he was ready to move on to Toronto—and, as you know, to better things."

"What do you remember about him from that time?" I asked him.

"Well, not very much at that age. He was quite withdrawn as a teenager. As far as his singing was concerned, he was not the best. We used him mainly as a rhythm guitar player." He laughed again, amazed not so much by how far Neil Young has come, but by what a lousy singer he used to be—and sort of still is.

1 *Neil Young with Nardwuar the Human Serviette and Bev Davies, who got aced out of a seat in Mort Two. Nardwuar and Bev wanted to know what became of the sleeping bag she'd lent Neil in 1966. The sleeping bag, it turned out, had its own tangled history. (Photo courtesy of Nardwuar the Human Serviette.)*

2 *Geoff Thompson needed to piss at every railroad track he saw. He's a strange dude. (Photo courtesy of Dave Yellowlees.)*

3 *Geoff also belongs to a long, noble tradition of rockers in knee pants: Angus Young of AC/DC, Geoff, and ... I can't think of anyone else.*

4 *Brilliant novelist and super-cool Winnipeg resident Miriam Toews.*

5 *Music biographer and high-school teacher John Einarson, on the same steps of Earl Grey Junior High where Neil Young sat dreaming of being a star.*

1

3

2

5

4

CHAPTER

ELEVEN

WINNIPEG HAD BEEN too kind to us. We didn't deserve the hospitality, and what we wanted was to sink back to our level, out on the highway in search of more meat sticks and roadkill. We intended to reach Thunder Bay by nightfall. It had warmed in the last couple of days, and ninety minutes outside of Winnipeg we decided to stop at Whiteshell Provincial Park to see Falcon Lake. We parked near a pebbly public beach and took off our shoes. Although there were a few hardy kids in the lake, the water was chilly, and after getting our feet wet we were content to sit by the concession stand and have a beer. Or, in my case, a lime margarita.

At the annual benefit concert for the Bridge School, set up by Neil and Pegi Young to aid severely disabled children, Young would introduce "Four Strong Winds" with a story about his time at Falcon Lake: "I used to listen to this song when I was sixteen or seventeen. I had my little band and we went up to a lake near Winnipeg, Manitoba, and got a gig up there. Paid twenty-five dollars a week, for the three of us. We did pretty well, we had a lot of money left over for partying. Anyway, I used to go down to this place and put a little money in the jukebox, stand in front of this thing, and listen to this vinyl record play this thing, over and over again. I miss that."

A resort area popular with Winnipeggers, Falcon Lake was where Neil Young met his most serious high-school girlfriend, Pam Smith, in 1963. A year later, Young returned for another camping trip and convinced a hotel manager to let the Squires play. Ken Koblun agreed to go; the rest of the band had other plans and declined. Young, upset at his bandmates' unwillingness to place music above all else, disbanded the Squires.

Young's time with Pam and the weeks he spent camping with friends were memorable enough to inspire a 1967 song called "Falcon Lake (Ash on the Floor)," an instrumental only recently released on the 2001 Buffalo Springfield boxed set. The melody of "Falcon Lake" would reappear in "Here We Are in the Years," a wistful ode to country life from Young's first album. "Here We Are in the Years" hints at the environmentalism and wariness of city life that would show up in his later work: "Go to the country, take the dog / Look at the sky without the smog / See the world, laugh at the farmers feeding hogs / Eat hot dogs."

On our way out of the park, we set off the car alarm yet again, annoying some party boys who had towed a motorboat to the lake behind their pick-up truck. They shook their heads and snickered at us. Screw you guys, I thought, we're almost in Ontario. We were only minutes away.

Upon crossing the provincial border, the first things we noticed were that the roads were better (presumably because Ontario is a richer province) and that, on either side, the forests were thinned out by clearcuts— like a hopeless combover, barely covering the surrounding hillside. We were driving along the Canadian Shield, a plateau of ancient rock, mostly granite, that covers half the country and extends to the Arctic tundra. Traffic, too, was thin: this is the part of the Trans-Canada truckers go through the States to avoid. For long stretches, the road tapered to two lanes. Cell-phone reception vanished. It was just the car, the road, and the flint-colored sky. I began to wonder why the explorers and fur traders had even bothered. If I'd been a trapper, I'd have traded a thousand pelts just to buy an SUV and turn back for the Old World.

Geoff was driving. With his long hair and the muzzle he'd grown, which was the color of dark chocolate, he looked like a cross between a *White Album*–era George Harrison and a cartoon bulldog. He sat close up to the steering wheel, almost hugging it. Dave was riding shotgun, playing with his digital video camera. He recorded us in black and white, then in a sepia hue, then solarized like the cover of *After the Gold Rush*. Every few minutes or so, he'd show us a new setting, or he'd rewind and show us footage of us ten seconds earlier. The metabolism of the day had been accelerated. We were getting back into the groove of traveling, that inward, shelled-off state where travel is measured not in kilometers or hours but in tanks of gas and album lengths. Having been fed a big breakfast in Winnipeg and sent off with cookies, we skipped lunch. We were in a trance, our bodies glued to the car upholstery, the narrow road pulling us along like a leash. Between long silent spells, having passed the map book around, someone would speak.

We were listening to a CD of Neil Diamond's greatest hits. "Kentucky Woman" was playing.

"Women love Neil Diamond," I pointed out. I was speaking to break out of my fog, to hear the sound of a voice. "It's a strange phenomenon."

"Oh yeah," Geoff said. "I've noticed that."

"If you're at a party and you want women to start dancing with each other, you put on 'Sweet Caroline' and they all start dancing. It just happens," I informed him.

Geoff laughed. "You're full of fun facts."

"My friend's wife saw him in concert and when he did 'Girl, You'll Be A Woman Soon' he pulled a woman from the audience and sang it to her. When he finished the song, he returned the woman to her seat and said to her boyfriend, '*She's ready for you now.*'"

"I think you're obsessed with the wrong Neil."

As we approached Thunder Bay, which was known as Fort William and Port Arthur before the amalgamation of the two cities in 1970, we listened to the other Neil. On the CD that John Einarson had given me were the Squires songs "Mustang" and "I Wonder," both recorded on April 2, 1964, again at CKRC with Harry Taylor. "Mustang" is a Shadows-influenced instrumental along the lines of "Aurora," though with more of an up-tempo groove, some sudden stops, and busy drumming. One of Young's earliest vocals, "I Wonder" shows the influence the British Invasion had had on Young, his vocals as Merseybeaten as they'd ever get. His voice is almost unrecognizable. "One can hardly tell," Einarson wrote in *Don't Be Denied,* "that this is the same voice that, years later, would be parodied as the voice only cats could love." Even so, Young's vocal charms were distinctive enough for Harry Taylor to advise him, "You're a good guitar player, kid—but you'll never make it as a singer." At least Taylor was right about Young's guitar-playing. After the first verse, the song breaks off into the kind of guitar solo that George Harrison could have proudly claimed: intricately constructed, elegantly phrased, with a little whang-bar flourish that delivers the song back to the verse.

Young would reuse the melody of "I Wonder" for "Don't Pity Me Babe," a Dylanesque acoustic song that exists only as a widely bootlegged demo, appearing in finished form as "Don't Cry No Tears," a mid-tempo song that blends California rock with fuzz guitar on his 1975 album *Zuma.* "Well, I wonder who's with her tonight / And I wonder who's holding her tight," he sings in both "I Wonder" and "Don't Cry No Tears," "But there's nothing I can say / To make him go away."

In *Shakey,* Young admitted that "I Wonder" might possibly be about his relationship with Pam Smith. Young broke up with her at the end of 1963, after they'd dated nearly five months. "I think he was afraid of a commitment," Smith told Einarson. "Even the thought of commitments scared him." Young was a gentlemanly boyfriend, but he always chose the guitar over the girl. Pam Smith also had to help move band equipment. A few months after they'd broken up, while they were at a Dairy Queen, Young told her he still loved her and wanted to go steady again. "You love me," she blurted at Young, too flustered to react more thoughtfully. "I love ice cream." Decades later, when asked by Jimmy McDonough whether he remembered this put-down, Young responded with palpable understatement: "Yeah. I'm sure I thought about that for a couple of weeks."

In the 1964 prototype of the song, the verse ends: "Well, I never cared too much anyway / Well, I guess that I'll forget her someday." Eleven years later, on *Zuma,* these last two lines were replaced: "Old true love ain't too hard to see / Don't cry no tears around me." The younger Young's unconvincing display of male bravado in "I Wonder" has evolved into a lament for a true love that has become plainly visible only in retrospect.

The title of the 1975 song "Don't Cry No Tears" may also confirm Young's inability to deal with personal confrontation, especially from emotional women. He would tell McDonough: "[My] mom's biggest tool to get me to do things would be to cry... So now, to this day, if a woman starts crying I can't—I can't—I can't handle it." Then again, Young may have just changed the lyrics because the new lines sounded better. Listening to the song, I stared out into the highway. We were still a long way from where we needed to be.

BY 1963, the Squires had begun hitting the road. Their first out-of-town gig was at a high-school dance in Portage la Prairie, an hour west of Winnipeg, in November. Another show later that month in Dauphin, Manitoba, for which they traveled by bus four hundred kilometers north, netted them $125. Not quite Led Zeppelin money, but the Squires' biggest payout yet.

Soon after breaking up the Squires in the summer of 1964, Young would look to reform the group with new members. That fall, he recruited Bill Edmondson, a buddy from high school, and Jeff Wuckert, the only piano player the Squires would ever have. The revamped group adopted a bluesier direction. Young, influenced by the harmonica playing of Jimmy Reed and John Lennon on "I Should Have Known Better," began to play the harp. They also took on a new name, Neil Young and the Squires. Young had already started to think strategically, hoping to build himself a reputation.

The band also needed a new ride. Up until then, the Squires had arrived to shows around the city in Rassy's car, with its unreliable heater, or in Ken Smyth's father's Chrysler. Neil bought a 1948 Buick Roadmaster hearse that he named Mortimer Hearseburg, or Mort. The hearse was old and falling apart, but it was roomy enough to fit the band members and their equipment, with black curtains to conceal the group's gear, and it had a side door and a tray that opened onto the sidewalk. The latest version of the Squires often performed at the 4-D, playing for meals in lieu of cash. A photograph of the band appeared in the *Winnipeg Free Press,* showing them in ascots and black vests made by Wuckert's mother. The clothes would outlast Wuckert's brief stint with the group.

When Neil Young and the Squires left for Fort William, Ontario, to look for a gig on October 12, 1964, they went without Wuckert, whose father had forbidden him from going so far from home. There had been philosophical differences as well. Wuckert told Einarson: "I wanted to play in a band but I never liked the lifestyle, the grubby clothes and casual habits. Neil did."

Young, Koblun, and Edmondson landed a week-long engagement at the Flamingo Club-Tavern, or, as it was known, the Flame, where the three of them were paid $325, plus accommodation and meals. "They'd played some clubs in Winnipeg," Einarson told me. "The Twilight Zone, but that was a teen club. But when they went to play the Flamingo in Fort William, it was an older crowd."

The Squires were finally a professional touring band. In a letter to his father, Young reveled in his newfound independence: "I'm not particularly worried about where we go right now, as long as we get paid and improve ourselves." The Squires capitalized on the allure of being an out-of-town band. "Because being the unknown," Neil told McDonough, "being from out of town, makes the mind open wider. People look at you, they have no preconceptions."

The shows at the Flamingo went over well enough that the Squires were offered a two-week stint at $350 a week. Young's group returned to Winnipeg for a Halloween dance at the River Heights Community Club and to get union cards, then headed straight back. With Young's time as a Winnipeg musician now history, Fort William would prove to be the next crucial phase in his apprenticeship.

For the band's second engagement at the Flamingo, posters were made up with the group's publicity photo and a caption below it that read: " 'Rock 'n Rolling' Neil Young and the Squires: Enjoy the swinging music of Neil Young and the Squires, just recently returned from an Eastern Tour. Recording stars under the 'Vee' Label." The Squires were doing fewer instrumentals as Young honed the group's vocal harmonies. This bluesier version of the group played originals like "Hello Lonely Woman" ("Well, hello lonely woman / Won't you take a walk with me?") and "Find Another Shoulder." Young would revive "Hello Lonely Woman" in live shows on his tour with the Bluenotes, the R&B group he put together after the 1987 Squires reunion.

They'd also cover "Farmer John," a 1950s hit by Don and Dewey, an R&B duo from Los Angeles. It was with this song that Young first experienced musical transcendence on the guitar. "Things just got to another place, it was gone," he said in *Don't Be Denied*. "And the people would say, 'What the Hell was that?'... People knew they had been watching a normal band playing these cool songs, then all of a sudden we went berserk and they didn't know what was happening." Curt Vigg, a musician I would meet later in our trip in Ohio, described these moments in Young's guitar-playing as Young's "peace-of-mind zone."

Young does a freewheeling rendition of "Farmer John" on his 1990 album *Ragged Glory:* "Farmer John, I'm in love with your daughter / Yeah, the one with champagne eyes." By recording this song in his midforties, replete with baying background vocals from Crazy Horse, Young might have come off as a lunatic cradle-robber, but instead gives the impression of someone playfully acknowledging and toying with the idea that rock 'n' roll is only for the biologically youthful. Whenever I hear this song I'm reminded of why novelist John Irving has called Young "one of my heroes—along with Bob Dylan." According to Irving, "they're not afraid to embarrass themselves—and you've got to be able to do that."

The second Flamingo engagement would also be memorable for Young because it would be his first birthday—his nineteenth—away from home and his mother's smothering affection. Stuck in his room at the Victoria Hotel on November 12, 1964, Neil would pour his anxieties into one of his most candid and most popular songs, "Sugar Mountain": "Now you say you're leaving home / Cause you want to be alone / Ain't it funny how you feel / When you're finding out it's real."

On Sugar Mountain, the singer is reunited with both parents, but not everything here is as innocent as balloons and "candy floss" (one of the rare Canadianisms to pop up among the Americanized usages in Young's songwriting). Young's early nostalgia for waning childhood clashes with his excitement for first experiences. What gives the song its edge is the "girl down the aisle" who's written a "hidden note," or the "first cigarette" you have while "you're underneath the stairs." Vladimir Nabokov famously described art as the sum of "beauty plus pity." Even at nineteen, Young was aware of how beauty is given dimension, a tragic shadow, by its impermanence.

"'I Wonder' and 'Mustang' were written in April 1964," Einarson had told me in Winnipeg. "In November 1964, Neil wrote 'Sugar Mountain.' It's like day and night—the maturity. Then again, they represent the dichotomy of his sound and style. He was a rocker, he was listening to the Kinks and the Dave Clark Five, and 'I Wonder' represents that. But he was also listening to folk music: Bob Dylan, Joan Baez, Buffy Sainte-Marie." Whenever I hear the song, I'm reminded of the canoeing trip I took in high school with a guide who claimed his age was "nineteen and twelve-thirds," thus allowing him to sneak into Sugar Mountain.

That November, Young and the Squires played a few gigs at the Fourth Dimension in Fort William, where Young mingled with the local folkies. The band also befriended CJLX deejay Ray Dee (short for Delatinsky), who would become the Squires' first impresario, booking them gigs and bringing them down to the station to make tapes. There, Young recorded another version of "I Wonder" and a newer song, "I'll Love You Forever," which Dee mixed in with a tape of ocean sounds. These were the first occasions that Young felt his music's essence was captured on tape. Dee sent the demo to Capitol Records, who nonetheless rejected the band.

Back in Winnipeg, Neil Young and the Squires imploded once again. Young fired Edmondson because he was too in love with his girlfriend to tour. Firing band members—friends—was no easy task, but it was a responsibility Young didn't shirk. Music was his top priority, and the ice was already forming in his veins. The Squires' drum stool was briefly occupied by half a dozen players before the band found fifteen-year-old Randy Peterson, who was then dropped on account of his still being in grade nine. Bob Clark, a drummer who could read music, was eventually found. A talented rhythm guitarist, Doug Campbell, was added until his parents forbade him from going to Churchill, Manitoba, to play at the Hudson Hotel—where, during one show, the bar started rumbling after a polar bear burrowed underneath the building and tried to stand up—and he, too, got the sack.

In April 1965, the band took Mort back to Fort William. To save on gas, Young would coast down hills with his foot on the clutch and pull the car out of gear. The damage inflicted on the transmission would come to haunt him. The Squires worked out an agreement with the Fort William 4-D management, where they played afternoon shows and opened for headliners in exchange for a room at the Sea-Vue Motel and free food. In his sets, Young began to fuse his folk and rock influences: old folk staples like "She'll Be Coming 'round the Mountain" and "Oh Susanna" were given rocked-out arrangements; a song like "Tom Dooley" was played in a minor key. His experiments seemed to anticipate the success of the Byrds, whose jangling, electrified rendition of Bob Dylan's "Mr. Tambourine Man" had not yet been released.

On April 18, 1965, a young musician named Stephen Stills, who was touring as a singer-guitarist with the folk group the Company, caught one of Young's sets. In *Don't Be Denied,* Einarson likened their meeting to "the day John Lennon first encountered Paul McCartney at a Liverpool church-sponsored street party or the day Mick Jagger ran into Keith Richards, an arm full of blues albums at his side, on an East London train," though some might say their legendary encounter would come later, in California. A multi-instrumentalist who could play electric guitar, bass, and drums, Stills had grown up in Dallas, New Orleans, and Latin America and was educated at a military school. Like Young, he had played in rock bands as a teenager, then dabbled in the folk scene of Greenwich Village, where he'd been in the Au Go-Go Singers with Richie Furay, another future Buffalo Springfield member.

Stills was impressed with Young's guitar-playing skills and vision; Young was impressed with Stills's soul-inflected, made-for-radio voice. With both of them staying at the Sea-Vue, they had, in Stills's words, "a great time running around in Neil's hearse and drinking good strong Canadian beer and being young and having a good time." The two of them shared their songs and spoke of collaborating in the future. Stills gave Young his New York City address so they might reconvene after an entry visa for Neil could be worked out and the Company's tour was finished.

In a matter of weeks, Neil Young and the Squires established themselves in the Fort William scene, jamming with local musicians onstage and after hours. Ray Dee landed them shows at the Polish Legion Hall, Westgate High School, a dance in Port Arthur, and an opening slot for big-time crooners Jay and the Americans. Even so, the Squires rarely made over forty-five dollars a show and relied on handouts from their parents. For a set of weekend shows at Smitty's Pancake House, the Squires played under the name the High Flying Birds, after a song Stills had played with the Company. Obviously, Stills had stuck in Young's mind.

In June 1965, after a show at Smitty's, Terry Erickson, a good friend of the band who'd occasionally sit in with them on guitar, asked Young for a favor. He had a gig in Sudbury, about 650 kilometers of desolate highway to the east, and needed a ride. Young, who had another engagement at Smitty's the next weekend, agreed, for a lark. Erickson, wearing a Nazi-era helmet, piled his equipment and Honda motorcycle into Mort, and along with Squires drummer Bob Clark and two other musicians, he and Neil headed out on an adventure. Young borrowed thirty bucks from Dee and told the deejay that he planned to visit Toronto to ask his father for some money to get to Los Angeles, though not before returning to Fort William.

And the rest is rock 'n' roll history. A knocking sound that was detected in Sault Ste. Marie went undiagnosed by a local mechanic. The knocking got louder and louder until Mort came to a stop near Iron Bridge. The transmission dropped from the hearse, falling out on the highway. With Mort dead on the road, Young started laughing hysterically. He was in shock.

Mort was taken to a junkyard in Blind River while a local garage looked around for a new transmission. The other guys in the car hitch-hiked back to Fort William to play their gigs, but Neil refused to abandon his hearse. He remained in Blind River with Erickson. After a couple of days in a motel, they decided to take the motorcycle to North Bay, so that Erickson could convince his dad to cash some bonds and finance a trip for the two of them to England. When this proved unsuccessful, they left for Toronto to hit up Young's father for money.

For weeks afterward, Young kept tabs on Mort in Blind River. He would even return from Toronto to check on Mort before finally giving up. And yet he'd left Fort William, and his friends and bandmates, without a word.

Some, like Ray Dee, would not hear from Young for almost thirty years. When Young learned through Einarson that Dee had Squires recordings from 1965, he invited Dee to his ranch for a reunion. According to *Shakey,* Neil offered him an apology, and when asked why he'd never called, told Dee: "Look, when the hearse broke down, I didn't have the money to fix it. It died. The hearse was my identity. That machine was my soul. That was *me.* I couldn't come back and face anybody there."

(In his tribute to Mort, "Long May You Run," Young sings: "Well, it was back in Blind River in 1962 / When I last saw you alive / But we missed that shift on the long decline / Long may you run." As in many of his autobiographical songs, Young fudges the facts. Here, he changes 1965 to 1962, possibly because "five" and "alive" is a more predictable, if better-fitting, rhyme than "alive" and "decline.")

When Young returned to Thunder Bay in 1992 to receive an honorary doctorate at Lakehead University, it was his first visit in nearly thirty years. About Fort William, he said in his convocation speech: "A lot of things happened to me here that were really important in the rest of my life. The first and most important thing that happened to me here was meeting my friend Ray Dee." Young offered the same explanation for his sudden departure that he'd given his old friend: "I almost became that hearse myself I was so attached to it. It was part of my personality and it was kind of like a walking stick I had... One day I took a trip out of town in the hearse and the darn thing broke down—it wouldn't go anywhere—so I couldn't come back here without that thing."

A FOG BEGAN slathering the highway about forty-five minutes outside Thunder Bay. We hit town after a full day on the road and drove along the edge of Lake Superior, the grain elevators and port facilities draped in shadow. Looking for the Flamingo, we found a storefront at the address—

a furniture rental business, I think, though it was dark—and then continued past a giant casino and uphill until we found the Sea-Vue Motel. When I checked in I told the man at the desk that I was staying there because of Neil Young.

"Oh yeah," he said, nodding. "He mentioned this place the last time he was in town."

"He gave a convocation speech at Lakehead University," I told him, as I filled out the registration form.

Taking my credit card, the man at the desk shrugged, as if to show he wouldn't disagree even if he wanted to. "And I saw him on TV. He does a lot of work with disabled kids. Good for him."

There was a woman sitting in a chair behind the desk. "Yeah, I saw that, too."

"Do you know which room he was in?" I asked.

"Uh, I think the manager lives in that one." He looked over to the woman. She nodded. "Yeah, that's where they stayed."

"It's really foggy here. Does that have anything to do with Lake Superior?"

He hesitated. "Yeah, sure."

"And is it always so foggy?" I asked.

His jaw expanded as though he were turning a toothpick in his mouth. "Okay, yeah."

I was handed a key to the kind of soiled motel room that Willy Loman from *Death of a Salesman* might have killed himself in. It was brown and pea-soup colored, run-down in a skanky way. There were two beds, a sticky bathroom door, and a closet nook in which two disconsolate wire hangers dangled.

"This isn't the worst place we've stayed at." Trying to be upbeat, I reminded Geoff and Dave of a motel in Reno. "You know, the one with the huge blood stain on the wall?" I remember thinking that the diamond-shaped stain looked like the Shroud of Turin.

"But I slept really well there," Dave said. "This is definitely the worst."

Geoff had brought out his guitar and was working on his own "Sugar Mountain," a song provisionally entitled "Pudding Loaf." He was in agreement with Dave that this place might be our worst. "The beds here are kind of funky."

I looked at the beds. "A lot of marmalade on those bedspreads."

To divert our attention from the room, I brought out my tape recorder. "Geoff, what do you know about Thunder Bay?"

"I know it used to be two towns, and now it's one town. I know that Paul Shaffer"—from the David Letterman show—"is from Thunder Bay. The End."

Mark joined us. He had been smoking outside. "There were two hookers in the parking lot who started making out."

"Were they putting on a show for you?" Dave asked.

"Not much of a show."

We ordered pizza and lay in bed watching TV. George W. Bush was waving to the Republican National Convention as confetti fell across the screen. This place was way too depressing.

\\ l /

CHAPTER

TWELVE

THERE WAS STILL A FOG over town the next morning when
we went for Finnish pancakes. My attempts to speak with anyone Neil-
related in Thunder Bay that morning had failed. The number I had for
Terry Erickson no longer worked, and when I finally reached Ray Dee—
whose wife had answered every time I'd tried his number in the previous
month—he answered gruffly, saying he was back only for the day and
was too busy to speak. Ironically, he'd been at the Finnish pancake place
an hour earlier. Before hanging up, Dee did mention that he still ran
three radio stations and that he hoped to make some money when Young
released his Archives boxed set, which would include some of the recordings Dee had made. I asked him about the release date; like everyone else,
he had no idea.

Mark was behind the wheel when we returned to the Trans-Canada.
We drove along the edge of Lake Superior, surrounded by rock and trees.
With half a tank of gas remaining we filled up in Wawa, because we'd
been told there wouldn't be another gas station for three and a half hours.
At Old Woman Bay, we pulled off the highway into the lot and began
walking along the pebbly beach. The water reflected the light of cool sun.
Mark had bought some taco chips and he passed the bag around. Across
the water was a steep rock face that was supposed to look like a stern

old woman. We were nowhere, far, far away from home with weeks to go. We were in transit. It was perfect.

The bay would be our last stop for what seemed like years. We drove and drove and drove as the Trans-Canada curved around Lake Superior. The sun seemed to be setting earlier than usual. We sat there numb and listless. We grew impatient as we turned, again and again, to the map book. Blind River was only three fingertips away—why was it taking so long? It was nightfall when we reached Sault Ste. Marie and bought hot dogs for the hibachi and beer. In the parking lot of the supermarket, I somehow lost the keys. We started looking around the car. There were no keys in the ignition.

"I had them going into the Beer Store," I said, molesting myself and my pockets.

"Maybe you dropped them there," Mark suggested.

I smacked the heel of my palm against my head. "I don't even smoke dope and I'm this absentminded."

We returned to the Beer Store and looked around. Neither of the two cashiers could help.

"Did I give one of you guys the keys?" I asked them on the way back to the car.

"No."

"Are you sure?"

"Yeah."

"They might be in the back," Dave suggested, pointing through the suv's rear window. We'd already filled the back with our cases of beer. "The doors are still unlocked."

"But the car alarm will go off as soon as we open them," I said. "If the keys aren't back there, the car will be honking for at least twenty minutes, until CAA arrives."

"It's the only place they could be," Geoff said.

"Okay, then. On three—"

"One. Two. Three."

As we opened the back door, the car started throwing its tantrum. We started pulling out bags and beer. Underneath Geoff's Red Stripe and on top of Dave's Carling were the keys. I pressed the button on the keychain to silence the alarm. We returned to the highway. With my blood returning from its boil, I sat in the back seat and took sips from an oversized can of Foster's.

We stopped long enough in Blind River, population 3,600, to take a photo of the town's sign, then continued on through the night until we found a campsite on Manitoulin Island, between Lake Huron and Georgian Bay. We set up the tent in the glare of our headlights before roasting some hot dogs and chicken skewers.

"Once again," Dave said at the grill, "the hibachi saves the Dave."

"You really love that thing," I said to him.

"I really miss it," Dave said, turning over a chicken skewer and handing a hot dog to Mark, who was wearing a headband with a flashlight on it. "We used to eat really good when Mark and I were living together. When Mark moved out, it was like a divorce, and I lost custody of the kids."

Mark nodded. "Dave was really broken up about the hibachi."

"Lyn was upset when Mark moved out, too, because she used to borrow his razor blades. Now she has to buy them herself."

Mark laughed, his flashlight bright in our eyes. "That's why those blades went so fast."

"Why don't you buy a new hibachi?" I asked Dave. "How much would one cost—fifty bucks?"

Dave shook his head. "I don't know."

I tilted my head and gave a smarmy nod, like a sitcom dad imparting wisdom to his bed-wetting son. "Maybe it's not the hibachi you miss, Dave. Maybe the hibachi symbolizes something else, something deeper. Maybe it's Mark's love and companionship that you actually cherish and long for."

Dave handed me a hot dog. "Screw you."

THE NEXT DAY we caught the ferry across the cloudy Georgian Bay. On the other side, we stopped at a national park to look for some caves Mark had gotten high in years before. Following a forest path lined with day-trippers, we wound down a rocky ledge to a pebbly white beach where families were swimming in the misty lake. Farther out in the bay, scuba divers edged off a boat. On either side were steep limestone cliffs. I let

Dave and Mark go to their caves while I walked, slowly and carefully in my leather ankle boots, along the top of the escarpment. I startled some kids who were smoking up while listening to "Baba O'Riley" by the Who.

Back on the highway, I used my cell phone to call Brian Moniz and arrange to meet him in Owen Sound. When I first wrote to John Einarson about my intention to retrace Neil Young's journey to California, he told me to contact Brian, who had extensively researched the hearse trip, to which he had an intimate connection. Brian, it turns out, was conceived during that hearse trip and later given up for adoption. Only when he was an adult did he learn the identity of his mother, Tannis Neiman.

I had spoken with Brian a couple of times on the phone. Each time I found him eager and excited to speak about his mother and her adventures, and about his love of rock 'n' roll, only to reach a point in our conversation where he'd catch himself and realize that he was talking to not only a stranger but a writer. He wasn't so much looking out for himself, as he was concerned that his mother—a woman he'd never met—might be mischaracterized, or that I might try to overstate his connection to Neil Young.

A month before leaving Vancouver, I sent Brian a copy of my first novel, which is about a teenaged boy whose parents had been folksingers in the 1960s. It had been inspired partly by the section in John Einarson's book about Neil Young's time on the Yorkville coffeehouse circuit and partly by a remaindered copy of Margaret Trudeau's autobiography, *Beyond Reason*. I found the title on a diner jukebox, a B-side to a one-hit wonder. I just liked the sound of the name, but in interviews and in reply to essay-writing high-school kids who e-mailed me, I'd suggested my novel was about people on the B-side of their lives.

To be honest, I was a little anxious about Brian's reaction. My book's narrator was a boy whose mother was a beautiful half-Native folksinger who died before he ever met her. Tannis Neiman, Brian's mother, happened to be a beautiful part-Native folksinger who died before he could meet her. I'd made up my story; he'd lived his. I was relieved when Brian called to say he liked it.

A few days later, I got an e-mail from him: "Here's the song I wrote about my mom. I don't play this for a lot of people. But after reading your book, why not." Attached to the e-mail was an MP3 entitled "Tannis." The ballad began with a twelve-string guitar, then, over it, a mournful slide. Brian sang with a rock balladeer's rasp: "She wore rose-colored glasses to hide her big brown eyes / She played for tips in coffeehouses back in 1965." A chill crept across the back of my neck as I listened. Here were two life stories in three minutes and forty-eight seconds; he'd gotten it right. "I keep playing my song until it reaches you," he sang. "From the son you couldn't keep to the mother I never knew."

Owen Sound is a town of about twenty thousand people. The Sydenham River, full of water the color of chocolate milk, runs through a downtown area lined with brick buildings. Brian and I had agreed to meet at a Tim Hortons, but since there is approximately one Tim Hortons for every six people in Ontario, we ended up at the wrong one. After asking for directions, we eventually found the right donut shop. I bought coffees and a box of donut holes. This would be my first interview in the company of my friends, and I wanted to make sure they were prepared.

"Brian's a cool guy," I told them. "But he doesn't know me and I don't want to scare him."

"No problem, boss," Geoff said.

"And he's got kids—so, please please please, you can't smoke up in front of them."

"Of course," Dave said. "You know, I've got friends with kids. Do you think I'm that irresponsible?"

"Uhhhhh, no."

It was midway through the Labor Day long weekend, and Brian, who had been at his in-laws' property out of town, arrived in shorts. He had the traces of a goatee and wore a baseball cap. Like me, he'd brought a couple of his friends. We introduced ourselves, a little awkwardly, and then our respective entourages from opposite sides of the country. It felt a little like two rival gangs meeting to negotiate a peace treaty and divide turf.

"Let's go back to my house," Brian said. "I want to show you some of my mother's stuff." We grabbed our coffees and followed Brian's car to a small brick house with a huge back yard. He led us inside to a wood-paneled den, his personal shrine to rock 'n' roll. On the walls and shelves were guitars; a framed issue of *Crawdaddy* with John Lennon on the cover and a *Rolling Stone* starring Bob Dylan; photos of Jimi Hendrix;

publicity photos of Brian with his old bands; a plastic figurine of Michael Anthony—the bassist from Van Halen—whom Brian had seen in concert early that summer, and backstage passes to a couple of shows.

In a poster for the Mariposa Folk Festival from the early 1970s, a tall, striking woman with high cheekbones and long, dark hair strums a guitar. "That's my mom," Brian said proudly. He led us to another photo of Tannis Neiman that was taken years later. Tannis stares into the camera while Neil Young, in a blazer with a lapel pin shaped like a treble clef and a white headband, watches her. With his familiar lopsided smile, he gazes at her reverently, as if to make sure she doesn't disappear. The photo was taken in 1987, shortly before Neiman died of cancer. "They say Neil never looked happier," Brian told us.

After the tour of Brian's den, we sat in his kitchen and sipped our coffee. "My mother went on a trip with Neil a really long time ago, when he first made it with Buffalo Springfield," Brian explained to my friends, the way you explain things to people who already know your story.

When Neil Young met Tannis Neiman in Yorkville, she was a folksinger originally from St. Boniface, Manitoba, who shared with Young the dream of making a life out of music. In those days, Neiman lived with Bev Davies and their friend Jeanine Hollingshead.

"Tannis was a folkie in the sixties and she came to Yorkville like all the others did," Hollingshead would tell me later. "She played Monday night hoots at the Riverboat. She went down to Florida with Buffy Sainte-Marie, played in Buffalo with John Kay and the Sparrow." According to her friend Hollingshead, Tannis was brash, outspoken, and funny.

"I didn't start looking until after my adoptive parents passed away," Brian said in his kitchen, "maybe five years ago. My wife wanted to know my medical history for our kids, because I had none." Brian learned from the Children's Aid Society that his mother was a folksinger named Neiman and that he was conceived in Albuquerque, New Mexico, in 1966. His wife Karen's research on the Canadian music scene in the 1960s brought him to Tannis and her front-row seat in rock 'n' roll history.

"I should tell you now: Neil Young is not my father," he said. "That's what everyone wants to know when they hear my story." Brian grew up on bands like Led Zeppelin and Van Halen, and he owned a copy of *Rust Never Sleeps* on vinyl when he was eight. After meeting his mother's friends like Hollingshead and Neil's brother, Bob Young, Brian was pointed in the direction of a man who worked with Tannis at the Igloo, an Albuquerque coffeehouse. Brian and his family have since met his biological father, who now lives in San Diego.

I asked him if I could bring out my tape recorder.

"Maybe later." He still wasn't too thrilled to be speaking on the record, and I didn't want to push it. "Why don't we just hang out?" I was like that fifteen-year-old in *Almost Famous*, without the redemption of being the alter ego of Cameron Crowe. I was the enemy.

We finished our coffee and headed over to Brian's in-laws', where he and his family were spending the weekend. After picking up beer and more hot dogs, we drove behind a house into a large yard. Brian's family—his wife Karen and their kids Amber, Stacy, and Lennon—were gathered around a fire with some friends. We parked behind the fire in a wooded area, next to what was probably the world's nicest, best-smelling outhouse. Geoff and I struggled to set up the tent while Dave and Mark sat at the campfire and quickly made friends.

"How do they do it?" I asked Geoff. At some point, we realized we'd put the tent poles in the wrong sleeves and were now correcting ourselves. "What's their secret?" I need to concoct a *book* to meet new people.

Geoff laughed. "They're extra tall. They're easygoing."

"They know how to set up a tent." We realized we'd put the tent poles into the correct sleeves the first time around. This was the last time I'd try to put up the tent. One of Brian's friends eventually came to our aid.

To the side of the campfire was a small trailer lined with bunk beds where Brian's family slept when they visited. Brian took me inside and showed me his mother's Martin twelve-string guitar and the strap that had once belonged to Stephen Stills. In her will, Tannis had left her guitar to Buffalo Springfield bassist Bruce Palmer, who passed it on to Brian.

"When I met Bruce," Brian told me, "I asked him if I could take a picture with it. He wasn't sure if he wanted to do that, and I left it at that. Then he phoned me and said he wanted to give me the guitar. I told him

I didn't want it, I just wanted a picture with it. It went back and forth for a little while, and then finally I came to my senses. It's one of my prized possessions." After picking up the guitar, he opened the case to find a card that read: "To Brian, from Tannis."

This was the guitar I'd heard on the recording Brian sent me. He had restrung the Martin upside-down to play left-handed. His mother, who was also a leftie, had taught herself to play right-handed. "Since I've had it, I've written more songs with this guitar than in my entire life."

Geoff unpacked his guitar and his little amplifier from the car, and everyone sat around the fire and swapped songs. Geoff played a couple of his own songs. Brian—who, like Geoff, drove a delivery truck as a day job—played an original he'd written about Yorkville and one for his new friend Rosie Rowbotham, a convicted marijuana trafficker who was now working as a CBC Radio broadcaster. At separate trials on unrelated drug charges, Neil Young and Norman Mailer had testified in Rowbotham's defense. "I like writing songs about history," Brian said.

Then the campfire sing-along commenced. Brian and Geoff played "Helpless." When Brian sang, his eyes would rise toward his forehead like a church steeple. Geoff played "You Can't Always Get What You Want" by the Rolling Stones. Brian played "Wonderwall" by Oasis, one of his favorite contemporary acts, along with Kid Rock. Brian's friend played "She Talks to Angels" by the Black Crowes, whom Brian hated because they'd once made fun of Oasis onstage.

Brian's three-year-old approached me. "I'm Lennon," he said.

I shook the boy's hand.

"Tell the story," I said to Brian, "about how your mother hung up on John Lennon."

Bev Davies had told me this story. Brian laughed. "You tell it. You know it better than me."

"I think, when the Beatles played Toronto in 1965," I said, "Tannis and Bev sent John Lennon a telegram inviting him for tea. I guess he got a kick out of it and called them. Tannis answered the phone and, thinking it was a joke, hung up on him. When he called again, she realized it wasn't a joke. Lennon thanked them for the invite, but told them that he couldn't get out of the hotel—you know, Beatlemania. Your mom was a cool lady."

I cannot imagine how it would feel if some stranger arrived at my house and started telling me stories about what a mother I never knew did forty years ago. I could only speak for myself—I was having fun. This was what I'd wanted from the trip all along. To meet new people, to get to know them, to step outside my routines and habits. All the initial awkwardness had disappeared. Of course, by now I was fairly hammered. Brian offered me a cigarette.

"Listen, maybe tomorrow we can talk," I said to him. "I won't ask you anything rude or invasive. And you don't have to answer anything you don't want to answer."

Brian laughed and took a drag. "I feel like Billy Crudup in *Almost Famous*. And you're that teenaged virgin—"

"Oh, really?" I said, feigning confusion. "I don't think I saw that movie."

He shrugged. "Let's do the interview now."

I grabbed my microphone and fumbled in the dark with the tape recorder. As I said before, I was hammered.

"When you found out about your mother," I asked Brian for the record, "did things make sense to you?"

"I found out where I'm coming from," he said. "I've always been a writer, I've always been a strummer."

("He's his own self," Hollingshead would later tell me, "just like she was her own self. They're both like rebels, like outlaws. There's so much similarity for me. He has the same eyes; he has the same smile.")

"What kind of musician was she?"

"She played Mariposa. She played a few gigs with Kris Kristofferson, she played with John Kay from Steppenwolf." Earlier that summer, Brian and Karen had attended a Steppenwolf concert and met Kay backstage. "I'm sure she and Neil played a few times together. Her music, the little I've heard of it, was very folk. She stuck to her folk roots. It also sounded a little bit country."

A few years earlier, at a benefit for Young's Bridge School held at Toronto's Hard Rock Cafe, Brian had earned a standing ovation for his song about Tannis. And yet he had still not met Neil Young. Although Brian met Bruce Palmer for the first time backstage at one of Young's shows, he had been unable to break through Young's notoriously protective throng of handlers, even with Palmer there to introduce him. "If you met Neil Young," I asked him, "what would you say to him?"

"I'd say hello. I'd tell him who I was, then I'd ask him to tell me a story about my mother. I want to know who she was."

THE NEXT MORNING, after stumbling out of our tent, we accompanied Brian to a brunch-time open mike. We went to Ted's Range Road Diner out on an otherwise empty country road, an intimate, funky place with an arching roof. From outside it was noisy with the weekend crowd and the sound of music. When we entered, the host of the open mike, a long-haired man in white cut-off jeans, was playing "Thrasher," from *Rust Never Sleeps*. A couple who looked around retirement age played some hootenanny-era folk on an acoustic guitar and a Celtic drum called a bodhran. "It rhymes with 'moron,'" the woman playing it told me.

Brian played his song about Rosie, then Geoff took the stage with his guitar and practice amplifier. As he ran through a couple of his own songs and "Dead Flowers" by the Rolling Stones, against the slurping chatter and chair scrapes of the brunchers, I shook my head in respect. I've always admired Geoff's fearlessness, his willingness to try anything. This was a guy who once streaked a Little League baseball team on a dare—I wonder where that videotape went?

Outside, some of the musicians who'd just played gathered around talking about local gigs. "It's always the same," one of them griped. "If you're from Toronto, you get twice as much here as someone from Owen Sound."

Brian insisted that I speak with Beaker Granger, the guy in the white cut-offs, who'd had a run-in with Neil. "It was three or four years ago, when Neil was being inducted into Canada's Walk of Fame. We went down to the ceremony. After it was over, they left the side gate open to the Royal Alex Theatre. We got into the ballroom and we saw Neil with some people. We ended up following them and I yelled, 'Hey, Neil.' I scared them. They all turned around and I asked Neil to sign the album I'd brought with me. The manager was completely in my face, wouldn't budge. He was doing his job. There are so many lunatics out there. I'm a good crazy, not a bad crazy. Anyway, this has all turned into a song for me, entitled 'Standing in the Hallway with a Startled Neil Young.' "

Brian plays twice a week at local bars. "There's a lot of good music in Owen Sound, a lot of talented musicians," he told me. "Just because they don't sell a million copies doesn't mean what they're doing is worthless. It's worth it to me even when just one person comes up after my set and tells me they liked my stuff."

It was not yet noon, and we decided to leave for Toronto before the brunt of the holiday traffic flooded back on Monday. Dave approached me, his sunglasses hooked into the collar of his striped polo shirt, holding the map book in front of him. I was expecting him to suggest a route we could take into the city.

"We've decided we need a name," he told me.

"A name?"

"For the four of us. You know, like the A-Team."

"What do you have in mind?"

"How about Team Crazy Horse? You know, because of Neil Young."

"Right, I got that."

"*If you have a problem, if no one else can help, and if you can find them, maybe you can hire* Team Crazy Horse."

Across the parking lot, Brian was still chatting with his musician buddies. I told him we were leaving, and that I'd be in touch.

"Part of me wishes I could come along," he said.

"You know, the car seats five."

"Karen and I were thinking about driving all the way down there, taking Route 66, the parts left of it, down to Albuquerque, then L.A."

"The whole family?"

"No way. Are you kidding me?" Brian asked. *"Are we there yet? How much longer?"*

"Oh yeah." I pointed to Dave, Geoff, and Mark, who were huddled by the car. They piled their hands on top of one another and then threw them in the air: *"Go, Team Crazy Horse!"* I shook my head very, very ruefully. "I know, I know."

1

2

3

4

1   *Mark Latham, yours truly, and Dave Yellowlees
    stayed in style in the trailer of Ian and Donna
    Stevenson in Winnipeg. Later that night, I barfed
    up one of Dave's space cakes. (Photo courtesy of
    Donna Stevenson.)*

2   *Here I am outside Neil Young's former Winnipeg
    address.*

3   *The best thing about Mark is that he's always
    willing to share his taco chips. He's also good at
    setting up tents.*

4   *Geoff at Falcon Lake, outside of Winnipeg. He had
    shaved about twelve minutes before this photo
    was taken, I shit you not.*

\\|/

CHAPTER

THIRTEEN

IN A GLOBE AND MAIL COLUMN on June 15, 1965, entitled "The Hearse Dealer," Scott Young wrote about receiving a call from a "member of the younger generation." "I am dirty and hungry," a thinly veiled version of his son Neil told him. In the column, Neil arrives by train from North Bay—though most accounts have him hitchhiking (and being picked up by some meatheads who tossed him into a ditch while jeering "Hippie!"), traveling from Sudbury with Terry Erickson on his motorcycle, or a combination of both.

While this detail remains in dispute, there's no reason to doubt Scott's physical description of his younger son: "He's six feet tall and weighs less than 140—long legs in tight tan pants, a very dirty shirt under a good sweater, long hair hanging down at the back and brushed low on his forehead at the front, a big smile." Scott would provide the food and bed that his son had gone without on his travels. From his father's house, Young visited the Yorkville area and was impressed by its music scene. The Neil Young who arrived in Toronto was "full of beans, hope, and the assurance of being nineteen with all life ahead."

Soon the rest of the Squires—Ken Koblun, who was living off an advance for a show the band never played in Fort William, and Bob Clark—met up with Neil and Terry at Scott's house in the upscale Rosedale neighborhood. They were polite young men who observed a Neil-imposed one AM curfew and devoured anything edible placed in front of them. To get Neil started in Toronto, Scott arranged and cosigned a four hundred dollar bank loan that Neil was supposed to repay in monthly installments of twenty-five dollars. (Neil eventually defaulted; Scott would cover the payments.) Neil and the band found an apartment on Huron Street and, through Scott, a rehearsal space in the lobby of the Poor Alex Theatre.

In Toronto, the music scene was divided into camps. Rock 'n' roll was played in Yonge Street bars like the Bohemian Embassy and Le Coq d'Or, where Ronnie Hawkins performed with the Hawks (later to become Bob Dylan's back-up band and famous in their own right as the Band). The folkies strummed their acoustic guitars in the coffeehouses of the Yorkville district. Unlike in Fort William, you had to choose one scene or the other. Young tried to avoid this partisanship, following folk acts like the Allan Ward Trio and Lonnie Johnson while keeping his eye on rock bands like the Sparrow, an earlier incarnation of Steppenwolf that included a young bass player named Bruce Palmer.

Soon after his arrival, Young made contact with Martin Onrot, who managed the Allan Ward Trio and had run a folk club called the Fifth Peg. Onrot was the one who suggested the Squires change their name: Hawkins's backing band had recently released a single under the name the Canadian Squires. Neil's band adopted Onrot's suggestion, Four to Go, though they never played a gig under that moniker. Onrot was unable to find them shows or attract record label interest from promoters and producers, who saw something too unfamiliar in Young's music. Clark and Erickson left the band for Winnipeg and Liverpool respectively, replaced by Jim Ackroyd and Geordie McDonald. But by the end of the summer, Four to Go had come and gone. Young was writing at a super-humanly torrid pace—that is, his normal rate of output—but he would never play any of his songs with a band in Toronto. "I think the problem was that people were telling us what to do, what to sound like," Neil told Einarson, "rather than the cool thing we had happening in Fort William. Toronto was all locked up."

By the end of the summer, Young had gone for a four-dollar haircut at a place called Mister Ivan's and was working at a Coles bookstore to pay off his loan. He'd last five weeks before he was fired. Without a band, Young would decide to make his mark in Toronto as a solo folksinger, an endeavor that wouldn't be much of a success, either. He was living at a boarding house at 88 Isabella, an address he'd eulogize in his song "Ambulance Blues." For many critics, including Johnny Rogan, the song is Young's finest achievement. "Oh, Isabella, proud Isabella," he wails, "They tore you down and plowed you under." In this cryptic song, Young seems to have toked up on a decade's discontent, as allusions to then-topical figures—Patty Hearst, Richard Nixon—merge with his long-buried resentment and frustration about his time in Toronto. "Well, I'm up in T.O. keepin' jive alive," he sings, "And out on the corner it's half past five / But the subways are empty / And so are the cafés / Except for the Farmer's Market / And I still can hear him say / You're all just pissin' in the wind / You don't know it but you are."

WE WERE LISTENING to Geoff's Yoko Ono CD as we left Owen Sound, moving across the soft curves of the countryside and through placid bedroom communities. It was a mixed CD: there was a little Yoko squealing, a little Yoko whispering, and some Yoko screaming to funk guitar. So far we'd been tolerant of our musical differences. But now Dave and Mark were open in their loathing.

"She sounds like Sullivan banging on a toy drum," said Dave. "This music is driving me crazy."

Mark, who was normally the most affable person in the car, was buoyed by Dave's vociferousness. "I could listen to something else."

"It's self-indulgent," Dave was saying. "It's self-indulgent shit."

Geoff looked at me, painting over his displeasure with a smirk. "This guy is a Zappa fan," he spat out. He had a point there. We'd spent three hours en route to Manitoulin Island listening to Frank Zappa singing about "poop chutes."

I didn't mind Yoko so much, maybe because my expectations were very low, and I was just happy my ears weren't spitting blood. We found ourselves engulfed by the Greater Toronto sprawl, passing outlets and strip malls in the outlying suburbs before getting onto the 401. The double-digit-laned highway was full, and traffic moved at a slow-medium speed. Between swatches of prefab townhouses, we saw giant billboards advertising city news teams and the airtimes of U.S. television shows broadcast on local stations. After seeing one particular billboard ad over and over again for two hours, I was almost hypnotically compelled to pull us over and go back-to-school shopping for my hypothetical pre-teen son or daughter. This was definitely a change from the sleepy Trans-Canada. I'd misread the map book and, having long passed the right exit, we entered Toronto from Don Mills.

Toronto is Canada's largest urban center, a place I like more for its neighborhoods and brick rowhouses than for its skyline composed of buildings with the same dull sheen as nonstick frying pans. After dropping us off downtown, Mark took the car to visit an old friend in London, where he'd gone to high school. He'd meet up with us later that week.

The hostel we'd been planning to stay at had no more empty beds. We were directed to a hotel, the newly crowned winner of our search for the worst motel/hotel ever, a flophouse with high ceilings and linoleum floors. As we were about to enter our room, a woman and a man who seemed to want to be a woman appeared at the doorway. "Do you mind if we use your room for a couple of minutes?" asked the woman who was a woman. It was as though we were in a Charles Bukowski novel. We turned her down and resigned ourselves to a restless night.

I hid my valuables under a small hillock of dirty underwear before suggesting we get something to eat. We picked a pho noodle place on Spadina, just outside the city's thrumming Chinatown. We were starving. We sat in a covered patio area on a side street, the broth vapor only briefly overwhelming the smell of exhaust.

"While we're here," Geoff was saying, "I should starting looking at flights back from Las Vegas."

"You need to be home," I asked, shoveling thin-sliced beef and rice noodles into my mouth, "when, again?"

"I work Tuesday. I should fly back on Monday."

"Are you sure," Dave asked, "that you just can't take another week off?"

"It's probably not a good idea." Although Geoff was generally in good spirits, there would be lulls when we'd catch him sitting on some steps nursing a cup of coffee, or taking an extra glance at a child Sullivan's age, and we'd realize how homesick he was. "I'm going to drive down to Auburn for Farm Aid. Sarah and I were talking about making a trip out of it."

"Oh, okay," Dave said, not sounding convinced. "Do you want to borrow my credit card?"

Geoff doesn't own a credit card; he likes paying as he goes. "Uh, well, I was thinking I could get a standby ticket."

"That could be risky. And expensive."

"I don't think it'll be a problem."

"Like I told you before, you should just quit your job," Dave insisted. "Take out a student loan and go back to school and get a trade."

Geoff half-smiled, swallowing the words in his mouth with a gulp of broth. Dave was not suggesting Geoff abandon music. What he said made sense. There were plenty of times, especially recently, when I'd daydreamed about becoming a plumber. And yet if Geoff were to take a trade, if he were to get a decent job and earn decent money, music might easily turn into a side interest, a hobby. I didn't like Dave's advice either. I had my own interest in Geoff playing music. He was doing what I had given up and what others weren't around to do.

It would be wrong to write about Neil Young, my garage-band hero, without also talking about my friend John Zivanovic, someone who was a big part of my garage-band years. John and I were in the same grade at Catholic school, and he picked up the drums around the same time I decided to play guitar. We started playing with Geoff the summer I turned sixteen. Throughout high school and into my first year at university, the three of us played in bands together. I chose band practice over my prom.

I remember envying John for getting out of gym class because of his heart condition. He was a good friend. He was half-Croatian and half-Filipino and had curly hair. He was a drummer. I'd been with John the first time I saw Neil Young and Crazy Horse. The first time I ever smelled pudenda was when John came up to me in my basement, fresh from getting to third base with his girlfriend, and brought his fingers to my nose. He was the funniest person I've ever known, and yet only among his friends, because he was shy. He died at twenty-two. It wasn't a car wreck or drugs, but a heart attack. It was cruel.

Geoff had a show the night of John's death. It was in July, a month before I left for grad school in New York. I was leaving home for the first time, something I'd long wanted to do, and now that I was getting what I'd wanted, I was scared shitless. I called John's house. We were no longer playing together, but we kept in touch and, with Geoff, drank espresso until three in the morning at an all-night Italian coffeehouse called the Pofi Bar. John's brother Peter answered the phone: "John died today." He'd come home and found his younger brother on his bedroom floor. Peter's voice was flat and slow. He was still in shock.

I'd called John to see if he wanted to come with me to watch Geoff perform that night. Peter was also in a band. He knew how stressful it was to perform live, and he made me promise not to tell Geoff about John until after he finished playing. I remember sitting through Geoff's set, swallowing another double scotch, just waiting to ruin his night.

Peter had always been a thoughtful, intelligent man, but he was uncommonly generous—heroic—in the moments and days after John's death and his funeral. At the Zivanovics' house, after the wake, he found the time to take us into John's room and tell us how much we'd meant to his brother, how his brother would want us to know that. On the floor of John's bedroom was a pair of underwear that the paramedics had snipped off before taking him away.

I left home, grew older, and moved back. Through the years, sporadically, I've tried to keep my friend in my memory. The last time I went to John's grave was in 2002, around the fifth anniversary of his death. I remember that day distinctly because it was a particularly mopey period of my life. I'd asked Geoff to come with me. It was summer, and he came riding up the street on his bike, without a shirt on, sporting a thick, dark moustache. If you wanted to be nice, you'd say he looked like Frank Zappa; if you wanted to be unkind, that guy from Hall and Oates, but without a shirt on.

Geoff had grown the moustache in part because he could, but also, I suspected, because he was in a rut. This is how men express themselves: not by talking, but through goofy facial hair. I was in a rut, too. I'd been dumped, and when I'm depressed, I have a terrible habit of seeking out misery. We went to John's grave not only because I wanted to mourn my friend, but also, I'm embarrassed to say, because I wanted to exult in my own sadness.

It was the first time we'd been to the cemetery since John's burial, and we roamed among the gravestones until we found his marker. On one side of his name was his high-school grad photo; on the other was an engraving of a set of drums, his love.

I was afraid of forgetting—not about forgetting him, but about forgetting that he was gone. There were times I half felt he was just another person I'd lost touch with, someone whose career or schooling had taken him to another city, someone who was too busy with his wife and his kids to call. There were times, in my dreams, when I'd felt I could just reach for a phone and speak to him. In the years that have passed since that visit to John's grave, I've grown to think of old friendships as phone calls from the police station: once you hang up, you don't get another call.

Afterward, Geoff and I had gone for fried chicken and then for drinks, sulking in tandem. The next day, Geoff called and asked if I wanted to go on a trip. I agreed without hesitation, but neither of us had the time to go away for as long as we'd have liked. Instead, Chong and Oates settled on going to Vancouver Island to visit Dave, who was more effusive and fun-loving than either of us. We needed him to make us better. We drank beer and played cards at Dave's kitchen table. We went to the lake and ate pepperoni sticks and jack cheese. I don't think we solved any of our vexing issues, but we still had one another.

The next time I saw Geoff, a couple of months later, he told me he was going to be a father. That sad, sad moustache had been shaved off.

A car passed us, turning onto Spadina, blaring Bon Jovi's "Livin' on a Prayer." Geoff looked at me: "I wrote that song for you."

\ | /

CHAPTER

FOURTEEN

NICHOLAS JENNINGS suggested we meet on Yorkville Avenue at the modern-day equivalent to the freewheeling bohemian coffeehouse, a jaunty little speakeasy they called Starbucks. Jennings, a music writer for a national magazine, was in the process of completing a television adaptation of his entertaining and illuminating history of the Yorkville music scene, *Before the Gold Rush.*

According to Jennings, the Yorkville coffeehouse circuit was a result of the drinking age being twenty-one. "There really was no place," he explained, "for young people in Toronto to go hear live music legally. If you could get fake ID or fool the guy at the door, you could get into a club on Yonge Street like Le Coq d'Or. A number of entrepreneurs opened a string of coffeehouses in the ground floors of what were turn-of-the-century Victorian rowhouses. Typically, what the owners did would be to open up the main floor of the house and put in tables with red and white checkered tablecloths and Chianti wine bottles with candles stuck in them. This would be the seating area. And there would be some kind of makeshift stage for performers."

In the early sixties, Yorkville was a haven for folksingers. Singer Ian Tyson, for instance, arrived from Vancouver in 1960 and debuted at the Village Corner on Avenue Road, which Jennings described as "Hipster's

Heaven: a smoky room with dark blue walls and a large mural of black slaves being unshackled." Tyson's future singing partner and wife, Sylvia Fricker, played at the Bohemian Embassy, south of Yorkville. She sang traditional English and Appalachian songs between readings by poets like Margaret Atwood and Earle Birney. Bob Dylan would show up at the Bohemian Embassy in 1962, but he wouldn't be allowed to play because the guy who ran the poetry nights didn't recognize him.

After the Beatles had taken off and Dylan had gone electric, these coffeehouses began hosting rock 'n' roll, much like what happened at the 4-D in Winnipeg. When Young arrived in Toronto, the Byrds' "Mr. Tambourine Man" was number one. "The red and white checkered tablecloths," said Jennings, "gave way to dance floors. At the peak of Yorkville's cultural hippie heyday in the mid-sixties, there were about forty or more clubs and coffeehouses offering live music every day of the week. Many of them were side by side. Chez Monique, Café El Patio, the Riverboat, the Flick, the New Gate of Cleve, the Half Beat. Boris' Red Gas Room was a big R & B hangout around the corner from Yorkville along Avenue Road." The Devil's Den, El Patio, and the Purple Onion were just starting to alternate between rock and folk acts.

Across the street from where we were sitting was the building that once housed the Riverboat. "Back in the old folky days," Young sang in "Ambulance Blues," "The air was magic when we played / The Riverboat was rockin' in the rain." Like proud Isabella, it was soon to be torn down to build a high-end hotel.

"The Riverboat was the pre-eminent coffeehouse," said Jennings. "It was run by a German immigrant named Bernie Fiedler, who was a coffee salesman originally. Fiedler designed it to look like the inside of a riverboat, so there were pine-paneled walls with brass portholes." The Riverboat was a long narrow basement room that sat about 120 people. The seats were booths, and no seat was farther than fifty feet from the stage. It was an intimate space, especially for big-name acts like Sonny Terry and Brownie McGhee, Phil Ochs, Gordon Lightfoot, and Joni Mitchell. "There was always a lineup. On the biggest nights, Fiedler would turn over the crowd several times. There'd be a seven o'clock show and an eight-thirty show and a ten o'clock show. Visiting celebrities had to go to the Riverboat. Bernie Fiedler booked them all. He turned it into the showcase venue in Yorkville. And it was a launching pad for a lot of up-and-coming singer-songwriters."

"But Neil Young couldn't get a gig there?"

"Bernie Fiedler was a talent-spotter, but for whatever reason he didn't see the talent in Neil Young. Neil tried very hard to get a main-stage showcase night at the Riverboat. But the only time he ever got to play there was a Hoot Night, when he managed to get onstage with a couple other local folksingers, including Vicky Taylor." Vicky Taylor, I knew from my reading, was a Yorkville fixture whose encouragement buoyed Young during these struggling times. She was the first—of many, it would turn out—to compare him to Dylan, and she let him crash at her apartment on Avenue Road. "They performed as the Public Utilities"—in Rogan's book, it's the Public Futilities—"and did a folk satire number: a bit of theater, some humor, and some serious folk music." (According to Taylor, Fiedler teased Neil: "Why don't you just pack up your guitar and go home. You're never going anywhere with that voice." Young replied: "Someday you're going to come and beg me to play in your club and I won't come!") "That was the only time Neil got to perform at the Riverboat until he came back to Toronto as a major star in February 1969. Bernie Fiedler saw the error of his ways and booked him for a full week."

"But he did play at the Cellar, right?"

After Four to Go came and went, Neil tried remaking himself as a folksinger. "He had his twelve-string and people would often see this tall, skinny figure walking along Yorkville Avenue. He played mostly at open mike nights at different coffeehouses like the Half Beat, the New Gate of Cleve, and the Cellar." Young would cover songs by Bob Dylan and Phil Ochs and do originals like "Sugar Mountain."

During Young's solo Yorkville period, he composed more introspective songs like "The Rent Is Always Due" and "Don't Pity Me Babe," whose ponderous wordplay was plainly indebted to Dylan. His most successful composition from this period was "Nowadays Clancy Can't Even Sing." "Who's that stomping all over my face?" Richie Furay sings in the Buffalo

Springfield recording. "Where's that silhouette I'm trying to trace? / Who's putting sponge in the bells I once rung?" Eventually, the song moves from paranoid impotence to self-accusation: "And who's all hung-up on that happiness thing? / Who's trying to tune all the bells that he rings?" As John Einarson told me: " 'Clancy' is a song about frustration, about alienation, about feeling there's nothing happening in your life and career, but still having hope and courage to carry on." In the final verse, Young seems to assert his resiliency in the face of almost certain doom: "Who should be sleeping, but is writing this song / Wishing and a-hoping he weren't so damned wrong."

In October 1965, Young, Koblun, and Geordie McDonald traveled to Vermont to play at a ski resort called the Wobbly Barn. Afterward, Young and Koblun made a trip to New York so that Neil could look up Stephen Stills. Arriving at the address he'd been given, Young instead came upon Stills's former bandmate Richie Furay, who told him that Stills had left for California to be at folk rock's epicenter. Furay was impressed enough by Young's originals that he made him record "Clancy" into a tape recorder and write out the lyrics so that Furay could learn it. Furay himself would soon be lured to California by a bongload of hot smoke from Stills about his great (i.e., nonexistent, still hypothetical) new band.

Neil returned to New York that November for a demo recording session at Elektra Records. He was led to a tape vault and made to sing into a creaky tape recorder that an engineer had placed on a metal chair. "Just turn it on and let it run," he was told. He recorded seven songs, including "Nowadays Clancy Can't Even Sing" and "Sugar Mountain." On the widely circulated bootleg of this session, you can hear Young trying to wedge himself into the circumscribed folk mold. The tone of his voice is earnest, his phrasing is stiff, and the songs are not leavened by his trippy imagination or his lacerating sense of humor.

In January 1966, Young's luck changed. While carrying an amplifier along Yorkville Avenue, he met bassist Bruce Palmer, who was a year younger than Neil but already married at the time. Palmer's father was an orchestra leader who played violin and occasionally sang through a megaphone; his mother was a painter. At seventeen, Palmer had played around Yorkville as a member of the Swinging Doors, an R & B group featuring saxophones, mohair suits, and Rick James on vocals and guitar. Palmer moved on to join Jack London and the Sparrows, a band that took advantage of London's English accent in the midst of the British Invasion. (One of the Sparrows, Dennis McCrohan, known as Dennis Edmonton at the time, would go on to write Steppenwolf's "Born to Be Wild" under yet another stage name, Mars Bonfire.)

As Palmer later recounted to John Einarson, the entire band had to go around Toronto speaking in fake British accents, even among old friends. During one performance, London (real name: Dave Marden), who'd emigrated to Canada as a child, accidentally spoke in a Canadian accent. The crowd reacted by throwing things onstage. Palmer eventually got so fed up with the phoniness that he arranged to switch bands with Nick St. Nicholas, the bassist of the Mynah Birds. "It was like a hockey trade with the Mynah Birds," he told Einarson.

I finished my pumpkin scone, and Jennings and I set off to stroll by the upscale boutiques and restaurants that now occupy Yorkville's rowhouses. Nicholas had given Yorkville walking tours in the past, he said, and was always pleasantly surprised by the turnout. He pointed out the old addresses of places like the Upper Crust and the Cosmic Visitor before stopping on the corner of Hazelton at the site of the old Mynah Bird, which was owned by Colin Kerr. "Kerr actually owned a mynah bird named Raja, and he was convinced that this talking bird would make him a millionaire. He would tell anyone who'd listen that Raja would get on *The Ed Sullivan Show* and *The Tonight Show,* and he was a bird imbued with incredible good luck. Kerr did everything possible to promote this bird, to such an extent that he opened a club called the Mynah Bird." Kerr began by actually selling mynah birds. He then drastically switched gears and turned the Mynah Bird into a body-painting club. Customers could paint sections of a naked woman whose body parts had been numbered and priced.

The next logical—relatively logical—step for Kerr was to form a band. Fronting the Mynah Birds was Palmer's old bandmate, Ricky James Matthews, who then fancied himself a black Mick Jagger. The Mynah Birds recorded one single for Columbia Records: "The Mynah Bird Hop," a calypso number that featured Raja's squawking, and its B-side, "The Mynah Bird Song." Raja would accompany the band to their shows, which consisted largely of Stones covers. "To resemble Raja, the band was dressed in black turtlenecks, black pants, and yellow shoes," Jennings said. "Bruce Palmer once told me that that was the last straw. They all rebelled. They left Colin Kerr at that point." Neil Young was in the Mynah Birds for three months in 1966.

The Mynah Birds soon found a new backer in John Craig Eaton, heir to the Eaton's department store fortune. "John Craig Eaton was dabbling in the rock scene," said Jennings, "and thought there was money to be made and invested in the group. He bought Neil, Palmer, Ricky Matthews, and the rest of the band"—John Yachimak on rhythm guitar and Ritchie Grand on drums—"all their equipment." They rehearsed at Eaton's house, used his limousine to get to shows, and were given spending money. For Eaton, the band was as much a hobby as it was an investment. "He'd come into our dressing room in his trench coat and stride up and down like Knute Rockne," Palmer told Scott Young, "telling us to go out there and knock 'em dead."

Having traded in his orange electric Gretsch, Young played his leads in the Mynah Birds on a twelve-string acoustic guitar until Eaton bought him a Rickenbacker electric and an amplifier. For the only time in his career, he was content to play a supporting role behind the charismatic and domineering James. The two future musical superstars collaborated on a couple of songs that have never been released, "I'll Wait Forever" and "It's My Time." James would also introduce Young to amphetamines. "I remember at one high-school gig," Young said in *Don't Be Denied,* "I was so high that I jumped off the stage and pulled my guitar jack out in the middle of a song."

Young had played only a handful of shows with the group before they signed a long-term record deal with Motown, arranged by their manager, Morley Shulman. James notwithstanding, they were the first "white" act signed to the label. The band was sent to Detroit in March 1966, and while they recorded for five or six nights with Smokey Robinson, they were given deluxe treatment. "[I]f we needed something, or if they thought we weren't strong enough," Young later told Cameron Crowe, "a couple of Motown singers would just walk right in. And they'd Motown us!"

The dream ended abruptly when James was arrested for being AWOL from the U.S. Navy. He would serve jail time, not for the last time in his life, before resurfacing a decade later as a funk star. Motown ended the session and canceled the Mynah Birds' contract. When the remaining members of the band returned to Toronto, they also discovered that their manager, Shulman, had used their $25,000 advance to overdose on heroin. (It's amazing to think that all this happened to Young in under two months, approximately half the time it takes for me to change the water filter in my refrigerator.) Young was back to zero.

Nicholas Jennings worked at the Riverboat in the seventies, but by then, he said, "Yorkville had already been subjected to the makeover we see today." By the eighties, the coffeehouses were priced out by high rents and pushed to redundancy by a lowered drinking age. Jennings played in the clubs and coffeehouses of Vancouver in the mid-seventies before realizing he'd have more success writing about music. "I was a very good Neil Young and Murray McLauchlan cover artist, but I never came up with my own sound." He told me about the dozens of CDs by unknown bands that now end up on his desk every week. There are usually at least one or two he finds exceptional.

"Do you think Canadian musicians have it easier today?" I asked him.

"I think Canadian musicians today have it much easier. People like Joni Mitchell and Neil Young flew south because there was no music industry here: no management, no record companies, no quality recording studios. If you took your 45 into a Canadian radio station, it would often wind up in the wastepaper basket. There was a stigma against our own. Today, we have a record industry, and thanks to Canadian content regulations, radio stations have—*had*—to play Canadian music. Which meant the record industry had to grow up. There's a wealth of Canadian music that can compete on the world stage."

"What do you think of Neil Young's recent output?"

"I think Neil still has moments of pure genius. Like Bob Dylan or Leonard Cohen, Neil never releases an album that doesn't have some moment of brilliance or charm. My feeling is that he's not as consistent as he used to be, but I always find something to enjoy."

After strolling down Yorkville, we turned onto Avenue Road, where Jennings pointed out the rowhouse where Vicky Taylor lived. Before we parted, I asked Nicholas how his appreciation of rock 'n' roll has changed as he's gotten older.

"There's no question that rock 'n' roll was once a young person's music," he told me, "but like the blues and like jazz I think it's grown up. There's the knock about some rock 'n' rollers being geriatric, going out on tour and trying to recapture their youth. But if you look at blues and jazz artists they don't get the same knock. If you can still perform passionately, there's no age limit."

"Even the Rolling Stones?"

He smiled genially. "Well, I still think Mick Jagger can entertain—"

\\ | /

CHAPTER

FIFTEEN

SO FAR AS Neil Young fans go, I'd say I'm slightly *above* above-average. Before embarking on my trip, I owned most of Neil's thirty-something official albums, having made a wide berth around much of his critically lambasted 1980s material (I do have *Trans* and *Landing on Water* on vinyl, but not a functioning record player), and I had read a couple of his biographies. On a Neil fandom scale of one to ten, I would say I'm a seven-point-five or a seven-point-five-one. I'm not a completist.

In the course of researching this book, I'd already met a lot of people who claimed to be or to know *Neil Young's biggest fan.* Usually this person turned out to be somebody who owned a copy of *Decade* and had taped "Harvest Moon" off the radio. None of them, I think, compares to the Rusties who make up the online community of Neil Young fans. Unlike everyone else in the world, Rusties didn't need me to explain why I wanted to take a hearse to Blind River or L.A. These people understood.

Earlier in the summer, I'd found the e-mail address of one Toronto Rustie, Sharry Wilson, and introduced myself with a long, semi-coherent e-mail. We'd met on a soggy day in June, when I was in Toronto for an artist's residency. We'd also gotten together with Harry Oesterreicher, a Rustie visiting from Seattle, and gone to a number of Neil Young landmarks, like Neil's star on Canada's Walk of Fame, his old address at 88 Isabella, and the former location of the Coles bookstore where Neil held his one and only day job.

Through Sharry I gained my first foothold in the realm of Rustiedom. There are at least four thousand members of the Rust List. There are also about four hundred members of a splinter chat group, Human Highway, who go off-topic to discuss politics and are known as "Zumans." A lot of fans belong to both listservs. There are separate Neil Young lists for German, Dutch, and Brazilian fans. Rusties post articles on Neil and reviews of his shows. They circulate hundreds of bootleg CDs and VCDs (a format that is being phased out as more traders buy DVD-burners). There are live shows from four decades available, performances and appearances on TV talk shows, copies of Neil's hard-to-find first movie, *Journey Through the Past*. There is even a VCD of Young's appearance on a televised celebrity golf tournament. Some fans offer trades or freebies; others looking for a particular show post a "grovel" or a "B & P," blanks and postage. The strict rule about these bootlegs is that no one makes a profit.

When I think of Neil Young fans, all types of people come to mind. Young, old, middle-aged. Turtleneck-swaddled types and guys whose relationship with trucker hats shrieks with authenticity. Punk rockers and hippies. Yuppies and farmers. The mindlessly ironic and the cringingly earnest. Though the median Rustie is probably somewhere in his forties, Sharry believes that Rusties range "anywhere from fourteen to sixty-four in age."

One Rustie who contacted me, Bill Neuschulz, recalled how Young brought him closer to his dying father. Neuschulz had recently lost his job, he wrote. "I was very lucky to take that unexpected free time and spend a great deal of it with my father before he died last Christmas morning. I remember how he would love to listen to his favourites: Tony Bennett, the Rat Pack, Benny Goodman, Artie Shaw. He surprised me one afternoon, while I was preparing dinner, when he asked me to put on some music."

His father had heard Neuschulz playing a Neil Young solo tour compilation at his sister's house and wanted to hear more. Bill made him a copy of the solo comp. "He told me, 'that guy is really good, has he done anything else?' I just smiled. I was with him over four months of the year and I was pleasantly surprised to go over many times and find him listening to that '99 comp. I haven't told many about this, but Neil was a comfort to him and I am so very grateful for that."

"The music of Neil Young, more than those of the others artists, vibrates my atoms which enter an infinite dance and then lose the control of their trajectory," French Rustie Denis Stephan told me, by e-mail, writing in his peculiar, lyrical, and beguilingly off-kilter English. "His songs pile up with a lot of emotional excitation. It is happiness in a pure state. His melodies match very well with his voice: they are simple, effective, and very beautiful. Neil is perhaps not a virtuoso of the guitar, but an alchemist who, in his laboratory, explores the heart of the sounds with his instrument, the guitar, in order to transcribe life."

Rustie Joost Groen has come to North America from the Netherlands to see Young on four visits, and has seen him play twenty-three times in total. "I don't really prefer either acoustic or electric Neil," he told me on the phone. "Both have their advantages. When you're at an acoustic Neil concert, you hardly ever know what's going to happen. Like what happened in Chicago in 1999: I was very privileged to be in the audience when Neil played 'On the Beach' for the first time in twenty-four years. You can imagine, I was really *through-the-roof*. And if Neil is going electric, mainly through Crazy Horse, the amount of energy transferred by him is so immense."

Some Rusties have met Neil. Some have autographs or guitar picks. The best piece of Young memorabilia might belong to Stephen Cross, from Wichita, Kansas, who has a chunk of Neil's hair. "It was on March 17, 1991, at the Myriad in Oklahoma City," Cross wrote me. He went to the show early and happened to see Neil's bus outside. "I didn't see any security at that moment so I walked past the barricades like I knew what I was doing."

Cross approached Neil's bus looking for an autograph but couldn't find him. "Just then a roadie came up to me and told me that Neil had just had his hair cut." The roadie pointed to a chair. "There was a fairly decent pile of hair next to the chair, so, feeling a bit embarrassed, I reached down and put a small handful in my coat pocket. When Neil walked out on stage for the show he was sporting a 'new' shorter haircut, like the one pictured on the *Weld* poster."

When I mentioned Cross's memento to Joost Groen in conversation, he immediately informed me: "That was the time Kim Gordon from Sonic Youth cut his hair on the Smell the Horse tour." How and why does Joost know this? you might ask. Let's just say that the "Dutch boy" haircut was a seminal moment in Young's career.

Rusties post descriptions of their Neil dreams; there are a lot of them. They compose Neil haikus, post top-ten lists of his most romantic songs, or attempt to sum him up in three words. (My favorite three-word summary is Sharry's: "Wannabe Chicken Farmer," alluding to Neil's childhood business selling eggs in Pickering, Ontario, and to a grade-school report, reproduced in *Neil and Me,* in which young Young announced his plans to attend the Ontario Agricultural College). Like other online sub-sects, the Rusties have developed their own set of acronyms, such as "NNC" for posts with "no Neil content" and "HOGTT," or "Heart of Gold Toe-Tapper," a phrase coined by Rustie and novelist Robert Clark Young (no relation) to describe casual Neil fans.

Before and after concerts, Rusties usually hold gatherings known as "Rust Fests." At the concerts themselves, Rusties often sit in specially arranged "Rust Rows" that guarantee them tickets, usually sold before general release. "I've met dozens, both here and in the States," British Rustie Jules Gray told me. "I went to the States specifically to meet Rusties. People I'd never met before. People here thought I was crazy, but it was one of the best times in my life and I'm so glad I did it."

"The Rustie community is the most friendly, most convivial that ever was!" Denis Stephan added in his e-mail. "It is a fact! Everywhere on the Net or at the time of festivals, or in shows, the Rusties are formidable. Of course, there are some grumpy persons, I don't deny it. But love which is given there can only pulverize their bad mood like snows under the sun."

There's definitely a level of obsessiveness among Rusties, a need to collect and perfect sets that is reminiscent of their famously intense object of attention. Yet this urge to completism is often independent of Young and carries over to other interests: one Rustie I met is a big fan of science fiction; a lot of Rusties like Bob Dylan and the Grateful Dead, or newer acts like Wilco and Gillian Welch. Neuschulz, for instance, has been to 450 Grateful Dead shows. (He's seen Neil play only 150 times.) These are fans who stick with artists during fallow periods, long after an artist's been labeled a has-been by critics; fans who make music a part of their lives.

A singer like Neil Young is both rewarding and challenging for super-fans. His staggering productivity keeps collectors scrambling. "I have about 450 live bootlegs," Joost Groen told me over the phone. "I'm not a completist."

But it's mostly what Young doesn't put out that bothers Rusties. According to his biographers, Young has at least a dozen albums' worth of material, including the now legendary *Homegrown* album, that have been shelved at the last moment. The multi-disc Archives has been promised for over a decade, delayed because of Young's perfectionism and his ongoing anguish over the digital recording process. "Did you ever go into a shower and turn it on and have it come out tiny little ice cubes?" Young asked McDonough. "[CD technology is] like gettin' hit with somethin' rather than havin' it flow over ya. It's almost taking music and making a weapon out of it—do physical damage to people without touching them." Young's hesitation has prompted the release of a five-disc bootleg compilation named *Archives Be Damned 2000* (or ABD2K) and the formation of a half-joking online support group.

Over the decades, many critics have argued that Young's output is erratic. As Young himself put it in an interview: "One week I'm a jerk, the next I'm a genius." The contenders for the worst Neil Young album would probably be *Everybody's Rockin'*, Young's lackluster attempt at rockabilly, and *Life* and *Landing On Water,* two eighties synth-rock albums. (Over the years, some critically bitch-smacked albums have been reclaimed by fans. Young's electronica album, *Trans,* is an endearingly weird curio in many a music lover's collection. And if the clunky production on *Re*Ac*Tor* can be ignored, its goofy brand of proto-grunge rocks.)

Rusties usually have a kind word to say about even Young's most derided albums, singling out a choice cut or a particularly nice vocal. These fans have come to the same conclusion as critic Xan Brooks, who wrote: "For years I've figured that the trick to being a Neil Young fan was to turn an indulgent blind eye (and deaf ear) to the man's shabbier moments. It was, I thought, entirely possible to revere Young as one of the key players of popular music, while conveniently ignoring the myriad of rubbish he's recorded. These days I'm not so sure. Increasingly, it's dawning on me that if you love Young, you have to accept the whole package... Good Neil, bad Neil: you can't have one without the other." It's not slavish devotion that elicits such boosterism (well, not completely) but the realization that Young's lesser works are inextricable from—and redeemed by—his masterpieces. Regardless of its appeal, what links all of his work is his conviction and the relentless pursuit of his specific vision.

On the Toronto leg of my road journey, Sharry Wilson and I decided to make a trip to the site of Young's childhood, the town of Omemee. Mark had returned the night before with my car and was spending the day hanging around the city with Dave, while Geoff got ready for another solo show that night. I picked Sharry up at her house on the northern edge of the city. Sharry is originally from Toronto, and her first Neil Young show was the late show at Massey Hall on January 19, 1971, as part of Young's Journey Through the Past solo tour. "I was a bit too young to attend performances in the coffeehouses and clubs in Yorkville's heyday," she told me, "but I do remember the scene and going down there to shop at the boutiques and stare at the hippies."

Sharry had been Rustie of the Month for July 2004, a distinction given only to truly exceptional Neil Young fans and community members. "It's something that you have to earn by being a list presence in some special way," she told me as we moved along the 401, "or else by doing something selfless for the list, such as putting together a tour comp, or doing something special for the Bridge School, or being a really good trader."

We turned off the 401 onto a smaller highway, heading toward Peterborough. After one wrong turn and a couple of stops to ask for directions, we found Omemee, the "town in north Ontario" mentioned in the song "Helpless." (Actually, Omemee is in south-central Ontario.) We parked by the Pigeon River, where Young used to go fishing with his big brother. I was reminded of the song "Mellow My Mind," a relatively upbeat cut from

Tonight's the Night in which Young sings about being "a schoolboy on good time / Jugglin' nickels and dimes / Satisfied with the fish on the line." A few old bridges cross the river, and farther back is an old mill. Omemee is a town of 1,100 with a main drag spanning a few blocks that included a diner, a Legion Hall that might have been around during Young's time, and some storefronts.

Approaching our car was a stout older man with a head of thick white hair who'd come from his house on the edge of the tiny river.

"Are you lost?" he asked us.

"No," I said. "This is our destination."

"We're looking for Neil Young's house," said Sharry. "Kevin's writing a book on Neil Young fans—"

"Well, uh, actually, that's only one element of my story," I started to say. "I mean, it's also part biography, part travel memoir about my own journey of self-discovery—"

"It's up King Street," the man said, pointing down the road. He also gave us directions to Scott Young Public School and to Scott Young's farm. The elder Young wouldn't be there now, he said, only a caretaker.

"And Neil used to go fishing here?" Sharry asked.

"Yes, that's true. My grandfather used to pull fishing hooks from his and Bob's fingers."

"Do you know him?" I asked.

"Of course I do," he said. The man's name, we would learn on our visit to Scott Young School, was Jay Hayes. Hayes appears in *Shakey* and is referred to as a "good friend" by Scott Young in his autobiography, *A Writer's Life*. While it was a nice coincidence to be greeted by a family friend of the Youngs, it also gave Sharry and me an idea of how closely people are linked to one another, over decades, in this small, peaceful place. "Life was real basic and simple in that town," Young said in *Shakey*. "Walk to school, walk back. Everybody knew who you were. Everybody knew everybody." Here, it seemed, was the kind of rural idyll Young would return to both in his life and in his music.

"Could I interview you?" I asked Jay Hayes.

He smiled, shook his head, then returned to his porch.

The Young family moved to Omemee in August 1948, when the Neiler was not yet three, and remained there until 1952. "Omemee life was great for kids," Scott Young wrote. "Neil had a sandbox always full of turtles, which kept escaping. Bigger kids pulled him in their wagons, once so fast that he crashed and lost half of one of his permanent teeth. We went tobogganing." Neil attended Lady Eaton Elementary School (named after the grandmother of the businessman who'd sponsor the Mynah Birds), where he was a mischievous student. He had a dog named Skippy who followed him around.

In "Helpless," Omemee appears as a refuge in Young's recollection: "There is a town in north Ontario / With dream comfort memory to spare / And in my mind I still need a place to go / All my changes were there." William Wordsworth, who also devoted a few words to childhood, suggested that poetry originates from "emotion recollected in tranquillity." The song's piano part creates a space for tranquillity, three chords played in a solemn, slipper-footed march as Young summons old emotions, calling attention to the distance between now and then, between childhood and adult reality, ungrammatical childhood ardor merging with adult language in the jumbled word-cluster "dream comfort memory," before recapturing, in the second verse, memories through the imagery and perspective of an adolescent: "Blue, blue windows behind the stars / Yellow moon on the rise / Big birds flying across the sky / Throwing shadows on our eyes."

Sharry and I had lunch before our next stop, Scott Young Public School, the middle school named in honor of Scott Young, the novelist, sportswriter, and member of the Hockey Hall of Fame, who passed away in June 2005. After reading *Neil and Me,* Sharry wrote Scott, care of his publisher, to tell him how much she enjoyed the book and to ask for contact information for the NYAS. "He wrote me a very nice letter," she told me, "and I thought it was exceptionally nice of him. He also sent along his own personal copy of *Broken Arrow* and told me to return it to him when I was finished looking at it."

By the school's front office was a display case full of Scott's books, including *100 Years of Dropping the Puck: A History of the OHA;* one of his murder mysteries, *The Shaman's Knife; A Writer's Life,* and, of course,

Neil and Me. There was also a photo of the dapper author at the school's dedication ceremony in 1993. We told the school's secretary why we were there and, like a pair of superannuated juvenile delinquents, waited in the office for the vice-principal.

The vice-principal escorted us to a teacher named Bill Damery, who's been at the school since its opening and met Neil and Scott when they appeared at its dedication and its ten-year anniversary ceremony in 2003. Yet another guitar-playing teacher, Damery has posters of Stratocasters and Les Pauls on the walls of his classroom. It was Damery who identified Jay Hayes for us. He also told us that when Neil played in Toronto he stayed at his father's farm, which Scott sold when he moved to Ireland in 1989 and Neil bought back in 1994 when Scott decided to return. Young made local headlines for purchasing a guitar in Peterborough; the owner of the music store, who didn't normally accept cheques, must have thought Young was good for the money.

Damery suggested we visit Young's childhood home. The owners of the house, the Bococks, were friendly people, he said, and would let us look inside. We thanked Mr. Damery and turned back onto King Street.

The Youngs' old house, which is only a few blocks from the school, is a red brick home with an enclosed front porch and apple trees in the yard. As a former lieutenant in the Canadian Navy, Scott bought the house through the Veterans' Land Act, a settlement plan for ex-soldiers. Like tourists at Stonehenge, Sharry and I took pictures of each other in front of the house. We knocked on the front porch door and were just about to leave when a frail, slender woman came slowly to the entrance.

"Hi, we're Neil Young fans."

"We don't mean to bother you. This was the house Neil Young grew up in—"

"Do you mind if we take a look inside? I mean, only if it's no trouble for you."

If Mrs. Bocock was a little surprised by our request, she was too gracious to show it. "You can come in, but I'm afraid the house is a mess."

The house was not at all a mess. We walked through the kitchen and into the front drawing room, its walls filled with old photos and reminders of a family's lifetime. Mrs. Bocock was in the kitchen, on the phone. "Can I call you back?" we could hear her saying. "There are two fans of Neil Young, the singer, here to look at the house."

Mrs. Bocock explained that she'd bought the house in 1955 from the Youngs, who'd rented out the place after leaving in 1952. There were three bedrooms and a bathroom on the second floor; this had been the first home in which Neil had a room of his own. Mrs. Bocock waited at the bottom of the stairs as we took a look.

Young's time in Omemee coincided with the polio epidemic, and Neil would contract the life-threatening disease in the summer of 1951. One evening Scott discovered Neil groaning in his bedroom, complaining that his back hurt. The next day, Neil had a temperature of one hundred degrees Fahrenheit, and the Youngs' family doctor advised them to take him to the Hospital for Sick Children in Toronto. For the entire drive there, Neil lay on the back seat of the car clutching his new toy train.

"Writing this now, I keep asking myself," Scott Young wrote, "what were you thinking? I don't know what I was thinking. One of the bad things about having polio in the family is the sound of the term. There is so much dread and fear and hopelessness in the word that if a man wants to do things he has to do, the things I was doing, he has to keep it from his mind."

A test confirmed that Neil had the disease. A masked nurse wheeled the five-year-old into an isolation ward. "So we waited. The waiting began immediately." The family spent a week in quarantine, calling the hospital every day for updates on Neil. After six days, the hospital phoned to tell them Neil had recovered. Neil had spent the week sitting in the hospital bed "half upright, holding the sides to keep himself there because it hurt his back so much to lie down." He'd fall asleep and loosen his grip, only to wake up crying in pain. When the family arrived at the hospital to take him home, the first thing he said to them was, "I didn't die, did I?"

On the third floor of the house was an attic room filled with boxes and a desk for sewing. Above the desk was a window that looked out onto a barn that had been converted to a garage. According to *Shakey,* trains used to travel behind the house, and Young would put pennies on the tracks.

"I bet Scott Young wrote here," Sharry said, as we looked around. "You can tell this is a perfect writer's room."

"Maybe," I said. In my experience, it depended on the writer. Just as there are some writers who keep messy desks and others who need orderly surfaces, there are writers who prefer to work in the center of a house, or at least in a comfortable office. They aren't content to place their life's work in a spare room. Everyone else in the house has to adjust to their single-mindedness; they won't be the ones to bend.

Novelist Margaret Atwood has suggested that the unifying theme of Canadian literature is survival. Her metaphor has been the source of much debate and discussion, especially among younger writers looking for apple carts and orthodoxies to overturn. Insofar as making money is concerned, one might argue with less disagreement that survival is the unifying theme for *writers* of Canadian literature. Scott Young cobbled together a living selling short stories, which Rassy typed, to magazines like *The Saturday Evening Post* and *Collier's.* "For most of Neil's childhood," Young wrote, "we lived the boom-or-bust life of trying to make it from my fiction." Neil has credited his father for his own independence, a tip of the hat that Scott graciously shared with Rassy, "who never once said, or even hinted, that the uncertain life of a freelance writer bothered her."

Scott Young would have to return to salaried work when the market for short fiction withered in the freshly omnipresent glare of television. In *A Writer's Life,* he described his brief tenure working as a public relations man for an aviation company in the 1950s. After complimenting him on his work, Young's boss predicted that he wouldn't last long.

"What makes you think I'm not permanent here?" Scott asked.

"You strike me as basically a loner, not really comfortable in a team work situation, which ours has to be."

Both Sharry and I know what it means to avoid teamwork situations. Sharry is a freelance proofreader, primarily for Harlequin Books, working out of her house. Neither of us can handle nine-to-five slogging. We like waking up when we do and working at our own pace, even if the pay isn't as good.

In *Neil and Me,* Scott wrote about dealing with the rejection that came from sending out his stories: "The only way I could keep on doing that was to believe that any editor who didn't like a story of mine had to be a mental case." This works, I know firsthand, but sometimes it isn't enough. You can't live off indignation. There was another passage in *Neil and Me* that felt more relevant to my troubles. When talking to his son about writing, Scott said: "I tried to represent myself as always trying to do my best work, whether it pleased others or not." Neil later told his father he learned from him "that the most vivid way to get an idea across was to lay oneself bare in the knowledge that others would identify with the bareness, the sometimes painful truth."

Sharry and I repeated our apologies to Mrs. Bocock, then left to find Scott's farm, about fifteen minutes outside of Omemee. It was late in the afternoon, and I had tentative dinner plans in Toronto, but I didn't want to disappoint Sharry. The official Rustie protocol was *not* to stalk and harass Neil at his house, but we'd been assured by Mr. Damery that none of the Youngs would be at the farm. Damery and Jay Hayes had given us approximate directions, a couple of street names and a rough description of the home. Sharry got more vague directions from a store owner who was protective of the Youngs. Those instructions led us to one gravelly dirt road, then another.

The roads dipped and crested along the countryside. I'd drive down one hill slowly but have to accelerate to get up the next one.

"It's a little bumpy, isn't it?" I asked.

"Yes."

"What time did you have to be home?"

"I shouldn't be too late."

We passed one property. "Does that look like Scott's house?"

"I think Mr. Damery said it was a chalet-style home."

The car had skidded once by the time we found one of the streets we were looking for. We continued slowly along the dirt road for another five minutes.

"Do you think we're going the wrong way?" I asked Sharry as we climbed to the top of another hill.

"Possibly," Sharry said. "Anyway, it's getting late. Maybe we should call it a day."

I eased the car down slowly, but it skidded a second time, and this time we slid ten feet before stopping in a dirt haze. A newspaper headline flashed before my eyes:

TWO IDIOT FANS DIE IN CAR CRASH OUTSIDE
NEIL YOUNG'S DAD'S FARM
Frustrated minor Canadian novelist
working on a biography (sort of)

Okay, I admit it would have to be a slow news day. Sharry and I decided to call off our quest and turned back for Toronto.

1   *I remember you well at the Sea-Vue Motel. In this*
    Thunder Bay motel, where Neil Young stayed with
    the Squires in 1965, there was a lot of marmalade
    on the bedspreads.

2   *Here I am on the outskirts of Blind River, Ontario.*
    I was very excited about the Home & Sports Show
    in Blind River, but my friends reminded me to focus
    on this book—crap.

3   *Brian Moniz, raspy rock balladeer, playing the twelve-*
    string guitar of his mother, folksinger Tannis Neiman.

4   *Geoff and Dave enjoying the ferry ride across*
    Georgian Bay. I'm pretty sure they're already drunk.
    Deadbeats.

CHAPTER

SIXTEEN

I GOT BACK from Omemee about forty-five minutes before Geoff's second Toronto show. His first gig had been before an open mike at a pub across the lane from the Poor Alex Theatre where Neil rehearsed with Four to Go. Over the evening, the pub had grown half full, not bad for a Monday, even if almost everyone there was a musician. I was surprised by how talented the performers were, how frequently they surged beyond competency, even the tall guy who sang like Tiny Tim and the dolorous young woman in the blue-tinted glasses who should probably be kept from sharp objects.

"Another due paid," Geoff had said after the first show, offering his oversized grin. He'd made a check-mark motion with his hand, then slung his guitar over his shoulder. That was the full extent of his complaining about the often inglorious trials of being a musician. Geoff isn't a whiner. I offered to carry his practice amp. Geoff and Dave had driven fifteen hours with me so I could read in front of that one woman at the bookstore in northern California. I'd be his roadie any day.

Tonight, Geoff was going to be playing a bar in Kensington Market, a tasting menu of ethnicities in downtown Toronto. Since our first night, we'd been sleeping in bunk beds at a hostel in the neighborhood, and every evening when I returned from my interviews I'd find my friends on the hostel's back-alley patio drinking beer with their newfound friends. Dave and Mark would be playing dominoes with a Japanese woman or a Russian card game with two Germans. Geoff would be at his guitar, in the middle of a twelve-bar blues jam with Sagi, an Israeli man looking for a job in Canada.

Geoff was already at the bar when I arrived back to unload my recording gear. At the hostel, I told Dave and Mark about my near-death experience on the dirt roads outside Omemee.

"Why didn't you use the four-wheel drive?" Dave asked, clutching a can of Carling.

"I don't know how to use it."

"You just turn it on."

"It's not so hard," Mark said.

"Don't you first have to put it in neutral," I asked, "and turn some lever above the rearview mirror?"

"Why didn't you do that?" Dave asked, snickering at my effete helplessness.

"Well, I'm here, I'm alive, and the car is still running."

Before Geoff's show, I had barely enough time to meet my friend Sara and her husband Alan for a quick dinner near Kensington Market. Sara and I know each other from graduate writing school. She's an American, a former hippie girl from New Jersey who went to the same high school as Jack Kerouac; Alan's a British physicist. The two of them had moved from Sheffield, England, to Toronto, where Alan is working on a post-doc. Sara had just returned from yet another wedding: a friend of ours from grad school had gotten married in Vermont to the father of her newborn child.

"Our policy regarding whether to travel for a wedding is simple," she told me. "If you came to our wedding, we'll go to yours."

"My wedding-travel policy is *no more*," I told her.

That year alone, Sara and Alan had crisscrossed the English-speaking world to attend weddings in Kamloops, British Columbia, the U.K.—"it was a kilts and saris wedding: the groom was Scottish and the bride was Indian"—and New England. They had one more wedding left in the fall in the U.K. I was going to break my wedding-travel policy to witness the nuptials of another mutual friend in New Jersey. This same friend had RSVP'd to Sara's wedding and failed to appear. He hadn't even canceled, and Sara was still steaming about it.

"I'm hoping Darren invites me to his wedding, just so I can say no to him," she was saying, with foamy indignation. "At least I'll have the decency to let him know I'm not going."

After our meal, Sara and I went on to the bar to see Geoff perform. Mark and Dave arrived shortly after us with about a dozen people from the hostel. Among them were Ryan and Pippa, two Australians who had decided to move to Canada after sitting through a traffic jam in Sydney, and Kelsey, a snowboarder, also from Australia, who was hoping to wind up in Banff by the end of the year.

After my first drink, I switched from beer to Irish whiskey: a dozen or so nights of consecutive drinking had been rough on the body, and we were only halfway there. The small, narrow bar had huge front windows that opened onto the street. At one point, Geoff's set was disrupted by the sound of a garbage truck making the rounds. Between originals, he played a couple of Neil Young covers, "When You Dance, I Can Really Love" and "Everybody's Alone," and premiered a new song entitled "Canadian Freeloaders Society"—the song he'd written after "Pudding Loaf," his ode to Thunder Bay, failed to come together.

"Is that also a Neil Young song?" Sara asked me.

"Uh-uh."

"Your friend's *good*."

Between sets, Sara and I went out to smoke; I bummed a cigarette. She was planning a bowling night for her thirtieth birthday party.

"I had to ask for ten-pin bowling," she told me.

I laughed. "Yeah, we have five-pin bowling in Canada. I don't know why. I used to belong to a league when I was eight or nine, but I stopped going because I wanted to watch a Saturday-morning cartoon starring Rubik the Cube—"

"I'm turning thirty," she said.

"I know."

"You don't understand. *I'm turning thirty.*"

"Sorry."

"It's okay. You're only twenty-nine."

Sara and I have anxiety issues in common; perhaps this was why we've remained friends. "Do you have that thing," I asked her, "where you drink too much coffee and wake up full of death anxiety?"

"Yeah. That's when I know I've had too much coffee."

"I have a friend on Paxil," I said. "It helps him."

"I have a friend on something from the same family of drugs."

"Paxil's second cousin by marriage?"

Sara laughed. "I saw a *New Yorker* cartoon that reminded me of you. I was thinking to myself, 'This is just like Kevin's sense of humor.' I forget how it goes. Oh, I remember it now—"

She described the cartoon and recited the caption. I hate *New Yorker* cartoons. Across the street was a head shop and café called Roach-O-Rama. Dave had spent some time there in the past couple of days. I interrupted Sara.

"Hey, I've been meaning to ask you this. Do you want one of Dave's space cakes? You can take one home with you."

"Okay." She paused. "You're not going to write about me taking a space cake, are you?"

"Of course not," I told her. "I mean, what does that have to do with Neil Young?"

"You're a writer. I know you," she said, her eyes glinting with foreknowledge. "You'll find a way."

CHAPTER

SEVENTEEN

JEANINE HOLLINGSHEAD AND I had arranged to meet at a pub near her house. We'd spoken on the phone about a month before. I dialed the number I had and asked for her.

"And who's calling?" a woman asked. There was a dry snap to her voice, and you could tell she wouldn't go for any bullshit.

"My name's Kevin Chong. Bev Davies gave me your number—"

"Oh, *really*." She laughed. We talked for an hour, even though Jeanine told me she had very little to say, and she said to call her again when I was in Toronto.

Jeanine's name had come up several times back in Vancouver when I spoke with Bev Davies. Bev herself is mentioned in a couple of Young biographies, including *Shakey* and the Rogan biography, which describes her as "an art-school kid from Bellevue [*sic;* actually it's Belleville], Ontario, who had come to Yorkville in the spring of 1965 in search of beatnik heaven."

"Do you remember the first time you saw Neil Young?" I'd asked Bev, when we spoke.

"I was walking down Avenue Road going south with Tannis Neiman and this guy was walking toward us, really tall, and he had one of those red mack lumberjack shirts on, carrying a guitar. Tannis said, 'Hi, Neil.'

And he walked by. And I said, 'Who. Is. *He?*' That was the first time I'd seen him. He'd been in town about six months."

"So you got a crush on him?"

"A really really really big crush."

"What was it about him?"

"We ran a coffeehouse for a while"—the Cellar—"and he used to show up late at night after the Mynah Birds gigs. We'd just lock the doors and he'd sit up on stage and write music." Bev remembered the two of them discussing the work of M.C. Escher and "boxes that turn inside out...I used to like it in words. I think he used some of that wordplay in his songs. Like 'Looking through a keyhole in an open door,'" from Buffalo Springfield's "Out of My Mind."

Neil would often talk about California, and according to Hollingshead Bev was the one who "practically engineered" the trip.

"Do you remember Neil's hearse?" I asked her.

"Yeah. I only saw it, I never I rode in it anywhere. I was at his house when he went out and bought it. He bought it somewhere east of Toronto, toward Hamilton or something."

Our conversation in Vancouver had taken place the day after Rick James's death was announced. In the Rogan bio, Bev talked about having nightmares about Rick James the day before the hearse left Toronto. "Can you tell me about those nightmares?" I asked her.

"I went back further with Rick James than Neil. I knew him when I went to art school and he played in a band called the Sailors. They wore sailor suits. We didn't know Ricky was actually an escaped sailor. I never got along with him, particularly, and with his connection to Neil, I figured that if there was anybody who was going to sabotage me in this world and make sure that I didn't get to do what I wanted to do, it was Ricky James Matthews. So I was surprised to find out that it was Tannis who had stopped me from going to California in the hearse, because I always assumed that it had something to do with Ricky James."

"What did you do instead?"

"Bruce Palmer took me to his sister's place that night because they were all leaving early the next morning and I refused to go back to my apartment. And Bruce had a dollar, and he said, 'Here's a dollar, it's all the money that I got.' And I hitchhiked down to New York and it cost ten cents to cross the border, because you had to say you were going to see the American side of Niagara Falls and put ten cents in a turnstile."

Bev told me she still listens to Neil on the radio. "I always stop doing what I do, unless I'm driving. I enjoy his music, but I don't buy his CDs. He has enough money." She prefers his earlier stuff. "I like the Neil Young from before they figured out how to record his voice really well, and once they did that they took some kind of the edge off him that I really liked in the Buffalo Springfield and the early Neil Young, that scratchy voice. Now they've got that equipment, so he goes in and he sounds like everyone else."

"He was more nervous back then," I suggested. "With Buffalo Spring-field and his first album."

"Maybe," she said, not at all swayed.

"They made Neil tell me," Bev Davies said. "I remember sitting at one of the windows at the Cellar, a little archway, when he told me I couldn't go. And I was *crying and crying and crying.* I'd already taken all my belongings to my parents' in Belleville, because I was going to California."

Bev moved to Vancouver in the seventies. She had almost been reunited with Neil one time when she befriended Dennis Hopper, a friend of Young's who'd come to Vancouver to film the movie *Out of the Blue.*

"How did you know Dennis Hopper?"

"Didn't. Just phoned him. I met him after the Grey Cup game"—I hadn't realized Hopper was a Canadian Football League fan—"and so he looked in rough shape. Francis Ford Coppola was there, too. We were at Hopper's hotel, and he said, 'Have you seen *Apocalypse Now?*' And I said, 'No, I haven't.' 'Well, I'd like you to meet Francis Ford Coppola.' I said to Coppola, 'I heard that's a good movie.' Then when I saw it, I was dumb-struck. If I'd seen the movie before I met him, I would have fallen over."

"Not to mention *The Godfather.*"

"Well, yeah. That's not a girl movie the same way *Apocalypse Now* is, but anyway—"

Too-shay.

"Neil was going to score *Out of the Blue*," she continued. "Dennis was going to phone me when Neil arrived. I'd explained that I knew him and hadn't seen him in years and years. Dennis gave me a call as Neil left. He'd only stayed here one day, saw the movie, said, 'You can use the song "Out of the Blue" but I'm not going to score the movie.'" So a couple more decades would pass before Bev met Neil again.

"Do you regret not going on the trip?" I asked her.

"I guess that's one of the reasons I like to see Neil when he's in town. I just feel that my life could have gone a different way. It went the way that it did; I have no regrets—my life is fine. I really enjoy where I am and what I've done in my life. I just like to see somebody that I knew so long ago and go, *'You did real good, kid.'*"

JEANINE HAD PICKED an upscale English pub to meet at. The place was in the middle of its dinner rush when she arrived wearing a T-shirt from a folk festival. She had dark eyes and her hair was short and dark. From our earlier conversations, I knew that Jeanine has worked with musicians all her life. In high school, she promoted dances. Since her Yorkville days, she's worked at folk festivals across the country and is now the office manager of a small record company. "We're not a major label," she told me. "We make folk and blues. I'm the person who does everything but recording and singing and playing." She plays mandolin, but as a strictly non-professional pursuit.

A waiter seated us at a table on a pleasant back patio. It turned out that I was about the twentieth writer to approach Jeanine asking about three weeks in her life nearly four decades before. "Every two or three years for the last thirty years someone has called about something. In one case, it was Jimmy McDonough, who called over and over for years. Apparently he didn't get his book cleared right away, so he kept coming back looking for more quotes. Johnny Rogan, Dave Bidini, our friend Nicholas Jennings. I kind of liked talking to Neil's dad. I thought *Neil and Me* was a pretty good example of what could be said about how serendipitous that whole trip was."

"It's a very loving book," I said. "It's a sweet tribute, coming from a father who admitted he wasn't a perfect parent to a son whose music he seems to genuinely appreciate."

"I thought so. He captured the feeling between him and his son. Scott was a fairly significant writer and Young was something of an upstart. Scott was very proud of Neil."

"Some fathers would consider it competition. Like Loudon Wainwright III and Rufus."

"The fact that Scott wanted to do a rewrite of the book"—for the updated 1997 edition—"and get the facts a little straighter spoke to what a writer he is. Anyway, there's always someone who wants to know about that trip. I get to answer the same questions every two or three years. Neil gets to answer them every two or three weeks for his whole life. It's part of rock 'n' roll history," she said, with a little resignation in her voice. "I just happened to be there."

I could see Jeanine wasn't exactly thrilled to be going through this again. I decided to get her drunk. We had beers with dinner, and then a couple more.

Jeanine entered the Neil Young story around the time of the Mynah Birds' inglorious demise. The band had had a tantalizing brush with success in Motown. With Rick James in jail, Young was back in Toronto, without a band or a hope of success. Bev Davies recalled being with him at an all-night diner called Websters. Young was playing "California Dreamin'" on the jukebox and talking about leaving. Later, while playing chess at the Cellar, Young and Bruce Palmer (who was drinking coffee laced with acid) hatched their plan.

"By 1966, I knew I had to leave Canada," Young told John Einarson, "and the sounds I liked were coming from California." Young also knew that Stephen Stills was already there. "I knew that if I went down there I could take a shot at making it."

To raise money for a car and expenses, Young sold everything he owned, and then some. "I didn't realize until later that he pawned a bunch of equipment to get the money," Bev Davies had told me, "but I was with him earlier that day, and he was trying to pawn his Rickenbacker guitar"—the guitar that John Craig Eaton had bought him. "He came out of one pawnshop, out of the saloon doors where you met with someone private. He came out just doubled over, laughing, and he said, 'They offered me twenty-five dollars for my Rickenbacker guitar.' I guess they thought it was hot."

Young also sold a Traynor guitar amp and a bass amp that Eaton had bought for him. When he returned to Toronto as a rock star in 1971, Eaton took him to court. Young's concert earnings were garnisheed to pay the businessman back. Neil would fork over the money—and then some—without a fight. "I had to shit on a lot of people...to get where I am now, especially in the beginning," he explained years later to Einarson. "There was no other way. I had almost no conscience for what I had to do. If I could justify it in terms of furthering my goal, I would do it."

Looking over the classifieds, Young found a 1953 Pontiac hearse. He saw it as an omen, and after buying the car, he named it Mort Two. On March 22, 1966, the hearse left from the Cellar carrying Young, Palmer, Tannis Neiman, a Yorkville regular named Judy Mack, a guy named Mike Gallagher who had some money for the trip and has never been heard from since, and Jeanine Hollingshead.

Jeanine was a close friend and occasional roommate of both Bev and Tannis. She had attended hairdressing school and held waitressing jobs at Yorkville haunts like the Purple Onion, the Penny Farthing, and the Red Lantern. She worked the door at the Riverboat for a period in the 1970s. Of her friends, Jeanine was the sensible one. "As Bev said, I was the don't-give-up-your-day-job girl," she told me. "Someone had to have cash."

I nodded. Maybe it doesn't mean a lot to be the most sensible teenaged hippie in a hearse, but in some way I felt Jeanine was a kindred spirit. Because I know what it's like to be a sensible person drawn to others less moored by propriety. It's always been my feeling that the crazies make you better, even when you half-disapprove of them. As Johnny Rogan put it, Jeanine "revelled in the highjinks and giddier pursuits of her companions." Jeanine, Bev, and Tannis formed a folk group called Tannis & Two with the bassist from Luke and the Apostles and recorded a two-track demo. They also designed a twelve-foot banner with the slogan "Tannis

Sings Folk Blues," which they paraded in front of a sound booth to get the attention of a local deejay and record-label owner.

"Bev was talking about how she had a crush on Neil," I said to Jeanine. "But you were immune to his charms."

"He was charming. I just didn't have a crush on him. We were fighting for sleeping space in the coffeehouse. There wasn't a lot of room for romantic interest. We were all huddled together for warmth. He was just another tall skinny guy trying to ace me out of my warm spot next to the furnace." Jeanine remembered Neil having a Beatle haircut and a black rayon shirt with pink polka dots on it. "But Neil had a certain charm with the ladies"—apparently, Tannis, Judy Mack, and Vicky Taylor were all, to some degree, in love with him—"and I guess I was impervious to it because I wasn't looking at anybody that way."

I reminded Jeanine about something she had said on the phone, how she missed out on "free love" because she was afraid of getting pregnant.

"That's an individual choice," she told me. "I remember at that time doing a radio interview on free love, and me, in my own naïve way, saying, 'I don't think there's as much going on as everyone thinks there is.' But that was just me. Obviously, there was a huge amount of free love going on." Jeanine wanted to see the world instead of raising children, and she lived off and on for years in New York, and for brief periods in London and Amsterdam. She and Tannis and Bev would frequently trade apartments with one another in different cities.

"So, you were the only other driver of the hearse besides Neil?" I asked, having read that somewhere.

"I had the only other driver's license—no, I shouldn't say that. I could drive a standard. Bruce and Judy knew how to drive; Mike and Tannis couldn't drive. I could go (a) because I could drive the thing, and (b) because I had my share of the gas money. It was that simple. Bev got aced out. I always felt bad about that."

"I heard the sleeping bag was well used."

She smiled. "I can imagine it had its own history, I suppose."

"I'm sorry to be asking you this for the eighteenth time in your life, but what are your memories of that trip?"

"My memories of that trip are of being with good pals, having no idea where we were going or what we were getting into. It was just like the song said, California dreamin'. It was March in Toronto, it was miserable. In three days we were in sunshine and good weather. My whole purpose then was to see something of America. My big dream was to see Vancouver and the west coast. I'd never been to Vancouver, and even if I needed to go to California to get there, I'd go. It was simple for me."

"What's it like to drive a hearse?"

"Very slow. Especially when you're trying to get through the Sandia Mountains in New Mexico, and your gearshift is slipping and your transmission is shot. It's like a big old limousine. It was a long, heavy car. It went slow up the hills and fast down them."

"There were six people in the hearse," I said. "How did you all fit in there?"

"Three in the front, three in the back," she told me. "Or two in the front, four in the back. It depended on whether it was day or night, whether we were sleeping or driving."

"Was it hard to sleep back there?"

"Oh, you want to hear about the rollers?" She laughed, hard. "The hearse hadn't really been disengaged from its funereal *accoutrements*"—now I was the one laughing—"so the rollers would dig into the back of your sleeping bag. It was okay when we were sitting sideways and sitting up, but when you went to get your eight hours of sleep, it could have been a little more comfortable."

Jeanine was along for the ride until Albuquerque. That was where Mort Two broke down, Neil collapsed in exhaustion, Jeanine was injured in a kitchen explosion, and Tannis conceived Brian. "We needed to rest. We'd burned ourselves up going that far."

Both Jeanine and Tannis worked at a place called the Igloo. "Tannis went onstage a few times. It wasn't too hard to work in a coffeehouse. If you picked up a dish and took it to the kitchen, you were working there."

The two of them finally got to Los Angeles from Albuquerque in May 1966. They spotted the hearse on the Sunset Strip, in the parking lot of Ben Frank's, a popular diner. Young and Palmer were in Mort Two with Stephen Stills. Welcoming them to L.A., Young enthused about his new band and their exploits. But when Neil asked Jeanine and Tannis if they wanted to meet the Byrds, Tannis angrily turned him down. "Fuck off, you fucking pillhead," she told him. Jeanine wasn't sure why Tannis was so angry. She thought perhaps Tannis mistakenly believed that Neil had chosen Judy Mack over her. Eventually, Jeanine and Tannis left for Vancouver.

"How long were you in Vancouver?"

"Two or three months. We got there by the middle of May. We were back to Toronto by the end of June, early July." They needed to get home on account of Tannis's pregnancy. Traveling along the Trans-Canada, Jeanine and Tannis slept in odd places and got rides from strange people. At one point, they were picked up by a man who offered them his car. They were amazed by his generosity until they realized the car had been stolen and was out of gas.

"When was the last time you saw Neil?"

"In the seventies. He screamed at me, gave me a big hug, said I was the girl who'd driven his hearse." She shrugged. "It was true."

"Are you a Neil Young fan?"

"Only by accident. I don't dislike him. I have a couple of favorites. One is his country-revival album."

"*Old Ways*?" I asked, with some surprise.

"Love it. He always had the potential to have gone that road, but he went his own way instead. He was a pretty brave guy. He had his own thing."

To finish our evening, Jeanine and I ordered a final round and talked about our dogs. I went to use the washroom, and when I returned, Jeanine was talking to the couple at the table next to ours.

"I was just telling them," Jeanine said, pointing at my MiniDisc recorder, "why you were interviewing me."

"Jeanine's a part of rock 'n' roll history," I told them.

They nodded enthusiastically. "I'm a huge fan of his," the man at the table said to us. *"Harvest, Tonight's the Night—"*

"How do you feel about being part of rock 'n' roll history?" I asked her.

"It's okay. I'm glad I was there. There's something to be said for being in the thick of it. You don't always know that's what you're doing. Later on, it becomes clear you've been somewhere significant. I was along for the ride."

I paid the bill and we stumbled out of the pub. Jeanine lived nearby in an apartment in a house owned by folksinger Sylvia Tyson. Recently, Tyson had taken her to a rock documentary called *Festival Express,* and Jeanine was recommending I see it.

"This night wasn't nearly as bad as I thought it would be," she told me.

"Yes!" I pumped my fist in the air. "That was the best I could hope for."

Jeanine walked me to my subway station and, wishing me luck on the rest of my journey, gave me a hug. I thanked her again.

1

2

3

4

5

1 *Neil Young reunited with Tannis Neiman shortly before she died in 1987. (Photo courtesy of Brian Moniz.)*

2 *Jeanine Hollingshead, the other hearse driver in 1966. I had to get Jeanine drunk before she would talk to me. Without booze, I am very hard to take. I am the first to admit that.*

3 *Here I am in Omemee, Ontario, outside Neil Young's childhood home. Soon afterward, I would startle the frail, elderly owner of the house by asking if I could come inside.*

4 *Sharry Wilson, Rustie and fact-checker extra-ordinaire, in Omemee, Ontario.*

5 *If you're ever in Owen Sound, Ontario, check out the Sunday brunch-time open mike at Ted's Range Road Diner. (Photo courtesy of Dave Yellowlees.)*

CHAPTER

EIGHTEEN

THE CANADA-U.S. border crossing is a ritual trauma for Canadians, a violation that marks our essence. And it's always less anguish-inducing returning to Canada than it is leaving. Entering the States, you first have to get past the U.S. border guard.

On his journey south from Toronto in 1966, Neil Young chose to avoid the most popular crossing points in Windsor and Niagara Falls. Fearing that he and his hippie friends would be hassled, he followed the advice of other musicians and drove north to the border crossing at Sault Ste. Marie, a seven-hour detour. The customs official there was an old man in a rocking chair who asked them what their business was in the United States. Young had his story ready. Producing identification with his mother's address, he told them that he was visiting Rassy in Winnipeg and going through the States as a shortcut.

Long-haired potheads, then and now, tremble at the border. And for good reason: it's as though they have "Probe Me" stenciled on their foreheads. Of Team Crazy Horse, Mark, the sandal-wearing tree-planter, had had the most trouble getting into the States in the past, and he was therefore the most anxious. Before we left Toronto, he vacuumed the car. Dave gave away his remaining space cakes to people at the hostel and the staff of Roach-O-Rama.

With Mark driving, we left downtown Toronto's staccato traffic and traveled along southern Ontario's knotted westbound highways. We had decided to cross at Niagara Falls, the most logical U.S. entry point for our journey. Just before we got to the border, Dave and Geoff mailed the rest of their joints back home. After we had stopped at the duty-free to buy cigarettes and change our money, my friends decided I would drive us into the U.S. Being Asian, I was, by default, the most respectable-looking. I took this racial profiling in stride; I never had trouble crossing the border.

"I hate this," Mark said. "I'm so nervous, I think I'm going to throw up."

Dave tried to reassure him. "Kev's a pro at border crossings."

"That's because I have nothing to hide," I said, looking at them in the rearview mirror. "Except, perhaps, for any joints you might have stashed in sandwiches. Geoff and Dave, I'm looking at you."

On our way to one Neil Young concert in Washington, Dave and Geoff had wrapped joints in plastic and hidden them in peanut butter and jelly sandwiches. Of course they hadn't bothered to tell me. I had been per-fectly oblivious, like any other unwitting drug mule.

Dave laughed. "Yeah, that was pretty funny."

Anyone who's grown up in Canada has had a fear of the border guard bred into them by their parents, whether on a day trip to outlet malls in Bellingham or a week-long drive to the Grand Canyon. As children, we were made to feel that the fate of nations—or at least of our trip to Disneyland—hinged on whether or not we fidgeted in the back seat. As adults, we've come understand our parents' anxiety. Border guards are bad cops working without a good cop in sight. They try to rattle us with invasive personal questions and insinuate defects in our character and motives. They revel in our paranoia, hoping to squirm our secrets from us.

Since the attacks on September 11, 2001, these guards have grown exponentially stricter. Driver's licenses are no longer enough to get a Cana-dian citizen across the border, and the passports and birth certificates we provide instead are vetted and doubly scrutinized. Every nervous answer we give, every questionable excuse we offer, is compared to the profile of a terrorist. Mark's paranoia wasn't very far off-target.

We crossed a bridge that took us over the Niagara River and stopped at a booth occupied by a stocky gray-haired man.

"Where are you headed?" he barked at me.

"Cleveland, then Los Angeles."

"Why are you going? How long will you be away?"

Unlike some friends, whose border-guard strategy is never to offer more information than they are required to, my approach is to bore my interrogator with detail. "We'll be away three weeks; Geoff will be flying out of Las Vegas on Monday. I'm a writer. I'm doing a book on Neil Young. We're retracing the trip he took from Toronto to Los Angeles in 1966, when he formed Buffalo Springfield. Its publication date is—"

The border guard was not interested in my book. He jerked his head from the booth and looked at everyone in the car. "Where were you born?" he asked us all.

"Hong Kong."

"Jasper."

"Vancouver."

"Edmonton."

"What do you guys do for a living?"

"I'm a writer."

"I'm a welder."

"I drive a delivery truck."

"I plant trees."

"How did you all get so much time off?"

"I'm actually working on this Neil Young project—"

"No, not you." He was tired of hearing from me—my plan was working. "I mean, the other guys in the car."

"I quit my job to go on this trip."

The border guard actually laughed—a first. He was warming to us, we thought, but then the stern look returned to his face.

"I had some vacation time banked."

"I don't work during the winter."

The guard asked us how much money we were bringing in and ran our passports and Geoff's birth certificate through his computer. And then, with avuncular good cheer, he wished us a pleasant journey.

As we drove to the American side of the Falls, trying to orient ourselves to another highway system, Mark let out a sigh. "That was the easiest border crossing I've ever been through."

"Well," I told him, "you've never traveled with me."

It was a four-hour drive from the border to Cleveland. Once we'd passed the smokestacks and factories of Buffalo, we entered highway country. We were in the limbo world that exists between here and there, moving along the I-90, which curves along Lake Erie, toward Ohio. To either side of the road were fields, highway signs advertising steakhouses and top-forty deejays, motels flashing their single-room rates on blinking signs, gas stations, truck stops, and swirling overpasses.

Outside of Erie, Pennsylvania, we stopped to fill our tank and visit Taco Bell, a ritual on all trips with Geoff and Dave. In this instance, the joint Taco Bell–KFC restaurant was located in a strip mall beside a furniture warehouse. Across the street were a multiplex movie theater and a Chinese buffet.

It had taken Mark a while to recover from his hyperventilating at the border, and he was still uneasy as he tucked into his crispy chicken taco. "I can't wait to get back home," he was already saying. "Everything's different here—the laws, the people. I feel guilty of being a Canadian."

"Don't ruin Taco Bell for me," Dave told him.

"We're going to pay for this," Geoff said, "in about an hour."

Dave stuffed half a burrito in his mouth. "I don't care."

The four of us started giggling like maniacs, while the Americans in the restaurant observed us with caution. They knew we were foreigners because when I'd tried to pay for my food with exact change, the cashier had combed through my change and turned back my Canadian pennies with a patriotic sneer.

We filled up and returned to the highway, where we soon came to a toll booth. Dave had a plastic bag full of American change that Lyn had given him to pay our tolls.

Growing up in Canada, cultural identity was almost an article of faith. Our distinctiveness from the United States was something we believed in but couldn't exactly see. (I've met francophones from Quebec, though, who feel equally foreign in English Canada and the U.S., who find the two indistinguishable.) Three hours into the States, I definitely felt we were in another country. Yet it was hard to pinpoint the root of my dislocation. It was more than the non-metric highway signs and the American flags hanging from buildings and painted on car doors and the mud flaps of trucks. My sense of foreignness seemed related to highway culture itself. Many of the amenities here could be found along the Trans-Canada, but there was nothing back home of this garish magnitude or with the zealousness of these roads, reaching aggressively into the distance.

Recently, the Canadian government's refusal to join the U.S.-led invasion of Iraq and Canadians' widespread support for legislation like gay marriage and the decriminalization of marijuana suggest that we are deliberately choosing a path that leads us away from American society, a significant portion of which—if not its entirety—has remained steadfast in its political and cultural conservatism. Even Americans have noticed the growing differences, and articles in the *New Yorker* and the *Washington Post* have referred to our country as "Berkeley North." When I'd visited New York earlier that year, the same friends who'd once loudly mocked my home and native land were now joking about emigrating should the election not come out the way they wanted. This was reason enough to be smug.

Over the years, Neil Young has stubbornly remained a Canadian citizen, unwilling to shed his ties to his home country. In 1969, on his first trip back to Toronto since Buffalo Springfield, he told the *Globe and Mail*'s Ritchie Yorke: "I want to come back to live in Canada soon. I'm trying to get an artist's visa, which allows you to move around from country to country. As soon as I can get it I'll move back." In his convocation speech at Lakehead University, more than three decades later, Young spoke of Canada fondly, though from the perspective of an outsider: "I've always missed the uniqueness of the Canadian people and the beautiful natural surroundings that we have so close to places like this where you can drive five minutes and go fishing or see some beautiful clean air and clean water. I hope that Canada can continue to preserve what's left." More recently, Young told McDonough: "To me, Canada is my family, where I grew up, memories of bein' young and bein' open to ideas. And then tryin' to get outta Canada because it was limiting."

In Young's music, Canada appears mainly as an oasis of nostalgia. "Now I'm going back to Canada on a journey through the past," he sings on *Time Fades Away,* an album recorded at the depth of his disillusionment with stardom. "And I won't be back till February comes." Twenty years later, in "One of These Days" from *Harvest Moon,* an album about being in the September of one's life, he muses about writing a long letter to old friends scattered afar: "From down in L.A., all the way to Nashville / From New York City, to my Canadian prairie home."

Young has been in the United States for almost forty years, and much of the power and timeliness of his music comes from his reaction to American life. Many of his best songs—"Everybody Knows This Is Nowhere," "Human Highway," "Powderfinger," "Captain Kennedy"—play on and contribute to the idea of it, finding inspiration in the sounds of his adopted country.

A song like "Sail Away," for instance, captures the incongruities—the capaciousness—of Americana with a wistful eloquence similar to that of Willie Nelson: "I could live inside a tepee, I could die in Penthouse 35 / You could lose me on the freeway, but I would still make it back alive." Later, Young sings: "See the losers in the best bars, meet the winners in the dives / Where the people are the real stars, all the rest of their lives."

Young's love for his adopted homeland is more explicit—jingoistic, some would say—in his song "Hawks & Doves": "I ain't tongue-tied, just don't got nothin' to say," he sings, before putting *nothin'* into words: "I'm proud to be livin' in the U.S.A." In the next verse, as "U.S.A., U.S.A." is repeated in the background, he warns the foes of America in Iran: "Ready to go, willin' to stay and pay / So my sweet love can dance another free day."

Despite his unwillingness to take U.S. citizenship, Young has been unafraid to comment on American politics from an American point of view. In the 1970s, he took whacks at hippiedom's dark overlord, President Richard Nixon, in "Ohio," "Ambulance Blues," and the improvised only-in-concert "Goodbye, Dick." "Thirty-three years later, 'Ohio' remains the touchstone for American protest rock," Richard Byrne wrote recently in *The American Prospect*. "In its mere 55 words (one repeated verse book-ending a repeated chorus), it proved more articulate than any other such song from that era." Yet Young also extended his sympathy to Nixon in "Campaigner," written after his resignation and disgrace. Here, he reminds his listeners: "Even Richard Nixon has got soul."

According to the newspapers I'd been reading, Ohio was a swing state in the forthcoming election, dominated by Democrats in its northern, metropolitan areas and mostly Republican in the south. Driving toward Cleveland, however, our initial impression of the area came from a bumper sticker we saw: "I'd Travel 10,000 Miles to Kill a Camel." On the sticker was a picture of an Arab on a camel.

I was reminded of Young's "Mideast Vacation," a song about somebody going "lookin' for Khaddafi aboard Air Force One." The song ends with the narrator leaving his hotel room to confront anti-American Arabs: "I was Rambo in the disco, I was shootin' to the beat / When they burned me in effigy, my vacation was complete."

It's a subject of debate whether this song is a parody—"one of Young's most amusing and sardonic songs," notes Rogan—or an expression of a Ronald Reagan wet dream. Around the time this song was written, Young made headlines when he outed himself as a Reagan supporter. "Don't you think it's better that Russia and these other countries think that [Reagan's] a trigger-happy cowboy," he said in an interview, "than think it's Jimmy Carter, who wants to give back the Panama Canal?" Reagan also appears in a cringe-inducing couplet from *Everybody's Rockin'*: "When Ronnie and Nancy do the bop on the lawn / They're rockin' in the White House all night long."

The sun was setting, and I had to lower the visor over the steering wheel as we approached Cleveland. Riding shotgun, Geoff put on *Old Ways*, Neil Young's country album that Jeanine liked so much. Recorded with Nashville session players and featuring duets with Willie Nelson and Waylon Jennings, *Old Ways* was released in 1985—an earlier version of the album had been rejected by David Geffen in 1983—in the middle of Young's new-style-every-album era. "When I was a younger man, got lucky with a rock 'n' roll band, struck gold in Hollywood," he sings in "Get Back to the Country," "All that time I knew I would get back to the country, back where it all began." In interviews, he announced that he was giving up rock 'n' roll, a young man's music, to age gracefully as a country artist. (This was before the spangled, navel-baring Shania Twain era of country music.) Young, who'd previously adapted elements of country in his sound, went full bore in this new direction, setting his songs to two-step rhythms and garnishing them with Jew's harps and fiddles.

Young's turn to traditionalism reflected not only his disenchantment with the rock industry, but also the reactionary strain that was emerging in his political views. On *Old Ways'* title track, he echoes Ronald Reagan's message of optimistic self-reliance: "The economy was getting so bad, I had to lay myself off / Well, working was a habit I had, so I kept showin' up anyway / Then one day things turned around." In another song from that period, "Nothing Is Perfect," he reminds us: "There's women and men on the workforce / Doing forty hours plus overtime / So the hostages held at the airport / Can come home to something worthwhile." Around this period, Young also gave an interview to *Melody Maker* in which he commented about AIDS: "You go to a supermarket and you see a faggot behind the fuckin' cash register, you don't want him to handle your potatoes." (Oddly enough, in 1993, Young's piano ballad "Philadelphia" would win him an Oscar nomination for its appearance in the Tom Hanks AIDS drama of the same name.)

Music writer Dave Marsh, who'd already written a dismissive essay on Young in *The Rolling Stone Illustrated History of Rock & Roll,* reacted furiously to Young's pro-Republicanism. Marsh made the rather hyperbolically personal argument that, by supporting Reagan, Young had had a hand in the death of Marsh's father. "By supporting Ronald Reagan he killed my father… It's real simple," he told Justin Mitchell in an interview. "Neil Young said, and stuck to it, that Ronald Reagan's politics have been great for America. My father died because he couldn't get a disability pension. It's literally true that he had to continue working in a way that killed him at 57 years old. And I hold Neil Young personally responsible for what he supports."

Some of Young's fans ignore this period or offer excuses for Neil: he was grumpy because of his record company problems; he only wanted to generate publicity; he was adopting a role. But many fans continue to be let down by his pro-Reagan sentiments. There are listeners of a certain vintage who know Young only for these comments and have avoided him for that reason.

"I thought Neil was entitled to his own opinion," I would later hear from Deb Navickas, a Pittsburgh Rustie, when I asked her about Young's Reagan comments. "I didn't necessarily agree with it. Sometimes I get a little upset that he gets political in the United States, because as far as I know, he still has Canadian citizenship. I'm a bit of an isolationist as far as that goes. But then again, he lives here, he pays taxes, so he's entitled to speak up as he pleases."

Young would later say that his Reagan comments were made in an irate mood and that his support for the president was never absolute. "I don't have a view," he told an interviewer in 1989. "I have an opinion that changes because every day is a different day. I'm not a liberal or a conservative. I'm not like that. With Reagan, some things he did were terrible, some things he did were great. Most people tend to take a president and say...he does one thing you really don't like. Like he builds excessive amounts of warheads or something. So you write him off completely. Which I think is completely stupid. And I think, is very narrow minded."

In 1989, Young would eviscerate the political cant of the first Bush administration in "Rockin' in the Free World": "We got a thousand points of light, for the homeless man / We got a kinder, gentler, machine-gun hand." One can see the Young of "Ohio" in this song, but it's harder to reconcile him with the author of "Hawks & Doves" or of the September 11 tribute "Let's Roll," in which he sings: "Let's roll for freedom, let's roll for love / Goin' after Satan, on the wings of a dove." This is the kind of stuff that keeps his biographers up at night.

More recently, Young has been critical of the second Bush administration. His multimedia project *Greendale* assails the Bush administration's war on civil liberties in the name of homeland security. In a 2003 interview with the *Guardian,* in which he was aptly described as a "professional contrarian," Young sounded anything but Republican: "The U.S. is like a baby with a bomb...And this big deal about Bush landing on an aircraft carrier? Talk about a six-year-old kid with a Tonka toy—we got it here...It's a robust time, probably the most fertile time for the underground and for revolution since Nixon. I'm not talking about political overthrow; I'm talking about just general cultural revolution. Bush has polarized the country and is creating this breeding ground for an opposition. In the next couple of months, they'll probably make it unpatriotic to be Democrat."

Bob Lee, a Los Angeles Rustie, sees a little of his own nonpartisan politics in Neil: "Like Neil, I don't really identify as Democrat or Republican, I just have a strong humanitarian sensibility, and it's not just a single ideology that drives me. I make decisions about things based on what I know and how I feel, and I don't have anything to say about someone else's political beliefs. I'm not a Reagan supporter myself but I think some of the venom directed at people who are is misplaced. As for that little prick in the White House today, hell, yeah, we should *all* be angry with his ass."

Lee's reaction to Young's conservatism reminds me of a passage from Christopher Ricks's *Dylan's Visions of Sin*. Writing about critics of Dylan's short-lived fascination with evangelical Christianity, Ricks makes this observation: "Most Dylan-lovers are presumed to be liberals, and the big trap for liberals is always that our liberalism may make us very illiberal about other people's sometimes letting us down by declining to be liberals...You can believe whatever you like so long as it's liberal."

\\|/

CHAPTER

NINETEEN

ACCORDING TO the (otherwise useless) guidebook I'd brought with me, Cleveland had once been nicknamed "The Mistake by the River," the funniest anti–town motto I've heard since "Buffalo: City of No Illusions." In 2004, Cleveland was named the biggest poor city in the U.S., with a 31 percent jobless rate. Entering the city core, we found clean streets and high rises, but ominously few people outside so early on a Thursday evening. Very little traffic, either. It was as if a giant game of hide and seek was being played in the city. We wound around the city center, eventually stopping at the only place that looked open, a small, dark bar on the ground floor of an office building across the street from a federal courthouse.

There were a handful of empty tables in the Sidebar. At one end of the establishment, by a kitchen that was closed for the day, stood a jukebox. Above it, fixed to the ceiling, was a television. There were only half a dozen people inside, most of them gathered at the bar. On the TV, there was a news report about the forged documents relating to Bush's military service. We took seats at one end, where a customer named Donna, who was watching the program, began to rant about Bush. She caught Dave laughing.

"What?" she asked. "Don't tell me you guys are Republicans."

"No, Canadians," Dave said. "We're from Vancouver."

Donna scrunched her face in puzzlement.

"It's north of Seattle," Dave told her.

She looked surprised. "Really. Why are you here?"

"It's a long story."

"But it's true, right, how you guys don't lock your doors"—a reference to the Michael Moore film *Bowling for Columbine*—"and have free health care?"

Dave smiled into the bottom of his glass. "I never lock my door. And I pay fifty dollars a month for my medical insurance."

"I love Michael Moore," Donna said. "I buy DVDs of his movies and give them away to friends."

Somehow—perhaps to interest Dave or Mark, who were, as noted, irresistible to women of all ages—it came up that Donna had worked for Larry Flynt in the seventies and been asked to pose for *Hustler*. Post-Flynt, she'd become a malpractice lawyer. She was proud of her work, battling negligent HMOs on behalf of the poor. She bought us a round of drinks. Next to Donna was her friend, Gary, a notary and a registered Republican who was disillusioned with the current president. "I used to be as progressive-liberal as anyone," he told us.

"We still like Gary anyway," said Donna.

Another round of drinks came our way, from someone whose name I no longer remember. With every round, Tammy, the bartender, would hand each of us a card that was redeemable for one domestic draft. The cards went rapidly back and forth across the bar as strangers, spreading cheer, bought one another drinks. We bought the next round, although as the designated driver I sat that one out. The cards were creased and had a worn-out, velvety texture. In theory, you could take a card home and redeem your drink later, but I doubt, in practice, that the cards ever left the place.

Tammy asked us where we were going. We mentioned our winding route back to our part of the world but nothing about Neil.

"Why are you in Cleveland?" she asked.

"We're going to the Rock and Roll Hall of Fame tomorrow."

"Oh, there's a lot to see. They've got Janis Joplin's car—you'll love it."

Donna chopped her finger in the air. "There's a theme to your trip," she said, her lawyerly skills of deduction in full effect. "That's why you're in Cleveland. What's the theme?"

"It's about a Canadian rock star," I told her. "He was inducted into the Hall in the nineties."

"I give up." She didn't try very hard.

"He was at Woodstock."

"Ooh—I don't know."

"He was in the movie *The Last Waltz* with an air-brushed cocaine booger."

Donna reached for her cell phone to call her daughter, who was away at college but had spent the summer as an intern at the Rock and Roll Hall of Fame. She got voicemail. "It's your mother, I need to know the name of a Canadian rock star in the Hall with a cocaine booger—"

"Dee Snider," another guy at the bar suggested.

"Uhhhhhhhhhhhhh," I said, pretending to consider the lead singer of Twisted Sister. "I don't think he's Canadian."

"Okay," the man at the bar said, scratching his chin. "The Four Lads."

Weren't they a doo-wop group? "Nope."

"How about—Dee Snider?"

"*No.*"

I walked across the room to the jukebox, found a copy of *Déjà Vu,* and selected "Helpless."

"This is a clue, right?" Tammy asked.

"I know these guys," Donna was saying as the song approached its first chorus. "Crosby, right?"

I swallowed my incredulity. "Close."

"Neil Young!"

The four of us started cheering. Gary told us that he'd been at Kent State the day before the four student protesters were slaughtered by Nixon's tin soldiers. Donna bought us another round of drinks before her other daughter, stern-faced, arrived to drive her home. Gary hung around for another beer, then left himself. I gave my fuzzy drink card to Geoff and put some more money in the jukebox. Scrolling through the CDs in the machine, I found *Led Zeppelin IV*. I was hoping to play "Going to California" as a tribute to our eventual destination, but I must have punched the wrong numbers, and "Stairway to Heaven" started instead.

"This song reminds me of high-school dances," Dave informed us. Mark nodded along. "It would be a couple minutes before midnight and you'd be looking around the gym floor for someone you wanted to make out with."

Tammy started laughing.

I turned to Geoff, who was sitting beside a video poker machine. "I always forget how much I enjoy Led Zeppelin." It used to be a guilty pleasure, back in my indie-rock days when I still had guilty pleasures.

We got to the part of the song where the drums start kicking in.

"By now," Dave was saying, leaning across the bar so Tammy could hear him, "my hands would be going to the small of her back—"

Tammy laughed again as she poured Mark a beer. "You guys are hilarious."

Robert Plant had stopped singing and Jimmy Page was playing that part with the ringing chords, just before the solo. "This would be the point of no return," Dave was telling us. "You would have to make your move—"

"Before the fast part," Mark added, reaching across the bar for the beer.

Dave nodded. "Yeah. You needed to be making out before the fast part. Because when the song gets all fast and heavy—"

"It's confusing," Mark continued. "You don't know whether to keep slow-dancing or to, you know, mosh—"

"Exactly."

We stayed at the Sidebar until closing time and posed for a group picture with Tammy, who wished each of us good luck on our travels with a hug. Before he left, Gary the notary had given us directions to the Days Inn where he was a permanent resident. The motel was across the Cuyahoga River. When we arrived, the clerk told us that Gary had not only reserved a room for us, he'd also paid. What we'd heard was true: Cleveland rocked.

IN 1986, Cleveland won the highly contested distinction as the official birthplace of rock 'n' roll because it had been home to Alan Freed, the deejay eventually ruined by the payola scandal who had first popularized the term "rock 'n' roll" in 1951. That and $65 million of local funding ensured its selection as the site of the Rock and Roll Hall of Fame and Museum. (The glitzy induction ceremonies, full of teary speeches and tuxedoed all-star jams, are still held in New York.) The Hall, which opened in 1995, is located at the northern end of the city, by Lake Erie and to the right of Cleveland Stadium. We parked our car next door in the Great Lakes Science Center parking lot.

"Look, we get a discount from the science center if we validate our ticket," I told my companions. "How rock 'n' roll is that?"

The Rock and Roll Hall of Fame is a geometrically shaped building with a glass and steel pyramid designed by I.M. Pei, the architect who also built the entrance to the Louvre. Out front, on a concrete plaza shaped like a turntable, are dozens of colorfully painted sculptures in the shape of Fender Stratocasters. We entered the multilevel complex. To our right were the gift shop and record store. Upstairs was a performance space advertising an upcoming Stiv Bators tribute and a cafeteria, where I'd later buy an "Asian" chicken wrap that came with both a fortune cookie and a pickle. Having paid eighteen bucks apiece to get in, we first took an escalator downstairs to the basement area where the exhibition hall began.

Elvis Costello once complained that rock 'n' roll is now known simply as "rock." For him, this signified how a shifting and fluid art form had become a self-regarding institution. Manner had hardened into matter. We were definitely in the house of rock, and the rock nerd in me was getting off. Guitars, outfits, fan paraphernalia, and juvenilia were displayed in exhibits devoted to inductees or entire musical eras like California rock or the punk scene. We saw John Lennon's report cards, Diana Ross's sequined gowns, Jon Bon Jovi's motorcycle, and the childhood drawings of Jimi Hendrix, whom Young had inducted into the Hall. Hendrix's and Mick Jagger's flamboyant outfits—including a very gay-looking baseball player's costume—wouldn't have been out of place in a figure-skating hall of fame. And there were guitars: Stephen Stills's Gretsch, Kim Gordon's bass, Kurt Cobain's Fender Mustang, one of Jimi Hendrix's Strats.

"It's kind of depressing," Geoff said to me, looking at the guitars in their glass cases.

"Free the guitars!"

"It's not like a museum of anthropology, where you see a tool from the past that's obsolete. A guitar is a functional piece of equipment. Once it's put behind glass it'll never be used again."

"Kind of like Bon Jovi's motorcycle," I said, with a level of bonus flippancy. "On that steel horse he rides no more."

Ignoring me, Geoff shook his head: "I didn't know rock 'n' roll was dead until I went to the graveyard."

Some of the items exhibited were painfully intimate, like the long letter singer Jeff Buckley had written to a fan about his tortured relationship with his musician father Tim Buckley, who'd died when his son was only eight years old. Jeff Buckley's life would also be cut short. Other wisely selected items helped illustrate the gleeful madness that drives music, like the hate letter from a schoolboy in Fiji to the Rolling Stones that began:

Just wanted you to know, me and my friends with nearly the whole school, HATE you. Because you don't look like men, are nothing but ANIMALS and smell like them too.

The Hall of Fame strove to present rock 'n' roll as part of a continuum. A multimedia exhibit linked rock 'n' roll artists with the bluesmen and country artists who'd influenced them. Another set of screens offered up five hundred songs, chosen by a panel of worthy experts, that "rocked" the world. I put on a pair of sweaty leather headphones and listened to Hüsker Dü and Mott the Hoople.

Among the items in Neil Young's exhibit were a copy of his Kelvin yearbook, an early track-listing of *After the Gold Rush,* the original lyrics of "Rockin' in the Free World" on a white marker-board, and a Ragged Glory tour jacket. Given Young's interest in documenting his own career, it made sense that he'd been an early supporter of the Hall and was the artist who'd inducted Woody Guthrie, the Everly Brothers, and Hendrix. Young himself had been inducted twice—first as a solo artist in 1995 and then as a member of Buffalo Springfield in 1997. He boycotted the second event, complaining that "it was a VH-1 show, edited for television and the adult contemporary market served by VH-1. Cheapened forever."

Down the hall in the folk-rock exhibit was Young's fringed buckskin jacket. Man oh man, it was *ugly*. It was a dark, heavy, oversized poncho, and it was as hard to fathom as foot-binding or bloodletting—that there was a point in history in which wearing thirty pounds of poop-colored suede was an acceptable, voluntary fashion decision. How could people-loving people let this happen? On the Rust List, someone had posted a joke made by a stand-up comic about a slobbish friend who "dressed like Neil Young on laundry day." And yet the flannel shirts and jeans Young has been wearing since the seventies are a vast improvement over this monstrosity of a jacket from the sixties.

Across from the Beatles exhibit were the oversized mike and one of the huge amplifiers that Young first used in his 1979 concert tour for *Rust Never Sleeps*. Standing up close to the amplifier, I could see through the silk-screened fabric to its steel frame. When I first saw Young play in 1991, his stage was crowded with giant amps like this one. Equally giant road cases had been hoisted from the stage to reveal them. Once Young had finished his final set, the road cases came down like a curtain falling over a playhouse stage. When he returned to the stage minutes later for an encore, the road cases went up again. I cheered along with the rest of the crowd. In the original Rust Never Sleeps stage show, Young used these oversized props to portray himself as the child he used to be, a naïf who was born into rock 'n' roll. I was fifteen when I saw the concert, a cynical, wise-assed teenager, but I still fell for this bit of stagecraft.

The solo acoustic song "My My, Hey Hey (Out of the Blue)" opens *Rust Never Sleeps*. The song's opening couplet, "My my, hey hey / Rock and roll is here to stay," is followed by one of the most contentious lines in rock 'n' roll music: "It's better to burn out / Than to fade away." A variation of this line comes in a later verse: "It's better to burn out / Than it is to rust." The amped-out electric version of the song, "Hey Hey, My My (Into the Black)," has yet another take on burning out, borrowed from a slogan coined by Mark Mothersbaugh, an ex-copywriter and leader of the New Wave band Devo: "It's better to burn out, 'cause rust never sleeps."

Young's talk of "burning out" has often been criticized as a shallow romanticization of suicide. Even John Lennon, who should have known better than to take words out of context, was prompted to comment: "I hate it. It's better to fade away like an old soldier than to burn out. I don't appreciate worship of dead Sid Vicious or of dead James Dean or of dead John Wayne." The line became a flashpoint when Kurt Cobain quoted it in his suicide note. Young was rattled by Cobain's death, and in his speech at his first Hall of Fame induction, he would mention the newest dead rock star: "I'd like to thank Kurt Cobain for giving me inspiration to renew my commitments."

Defenders argue that Young—while no doubt aware of other possible interpretations, even going so far as to acknowledge the allure of the short, tragically truncated life—was speaking about "burning out" as a musician, taking artistic risks and tempting commercial oblivion rather than becoming a lounge-lizard parody of oneself, churning out the hits at casinos and corporate motivational seminars.

It's hard to believe that Young would choose a tragic, twenty-seven-year-old's death over rust, given how the musician, ever the contrarian, also seems to embrace rust as a badge of pride, as he does his laugh lines or the patches on his jeans, even as he warns himself against it. Perhaps this is why Young's fans have chosen to call themselves Rusties. It isn't so much the physical signs of aging that are to be feared but the corrosiveness of complacency, the airless entropy of one's own legend.

WE WERE DONE at the Hall and we still had a couple of hours to kill. Downtown Cleveland was sunny, if still remarkably pedestrian-free. Being unambitious, we decided against exploring the city's other worthy attractions in favor of the familiar and arrived at the Sidebar in time for the happy-hour buffet. Tammy the bartender wasn't there, but people had heard about "the Canadians" and more of those fuzzy drink cards came to us courtesy of a lawyer–sports agent whose family used to own the building we were in. On our way out, we bumped into Gary the notary, who was looking a little hungover.

We thanked him for the motel room.

"It was nothing," he said. "The least I could do."

"Did you get our present?" Dave asked. He'd bought an eighteen-pack of Busch and left it for Gary at the front desk. Dave always thought of the perfect gift.

"Yeah," Gary said, with a weary nod of his head. "I woke up a little on the rough side and that was the last thing I wanted to see." We shared a laugh. "But, you know, it was a nice touch, guys." He headed inside to begin work on tomorrow's hangover. We headed for the Great Lakes Science Center, where our car was still parked.

\ | /

WE LEFT THE CITY along the I-90, then Route 57, following the directions we'd been given. We passed a string of motels in Elyria, a town notable for being the place where Sherwood Anderson went nuts. Anderson was thirty-six and running a successful paint factory there. On November 27, 1912, while dictating a letter to his secretary, he stopped midsentence and announced to her: "I have been wading in a long river and my feet are wet." He walked out of the factory; when he was found four days later, he was taken to the hospital for exhaustion. Only after snapping did Anderson find the courage to pursue his dream of being a writer.

As we came to Amherst Township, a semi-rural area where houses were separated by large fields, I was reminded of the outer suburb of Vancouver where I spent my childhood. I squinted at my own handwriting; it was indecipherable even to me. "If we come to the Church of the Open Door," I told Geoff, just before we saw a huge church with that name, "we'll have gone too far."

We made a U-turn from the next left-turn lane, then turned left again onto a side road, driving until we came to a house on a large property, behind a field of soy. We pulled up the driveway to a barn filled with musical equipment. The entrance, a huge garage door, was open. There were people inside drinking beer and eating fried chicken in lawn chairs, and *Greendale* was playing loud. Curt Vigg approached us in a floppy brown hat and a shirt that said "Faded Glory." Curt's Neil tribute band was named Ragged Glory, and when he heard on the Rust List that we'd be passing through, he'd organized this impromptu Rust Fest.

"Too bad about the hearse," he said, looking at my brother's Suzuki.

"I know."

Curt was the sole constant in the various configurations of Ragged Glory. The band had been together since 1995, performing in bars around northeastern Ohio. The first time Curt had heard Neil was after *Live Rust* was released. "They played the whole album on the radio, maybe WMMS in Cleveland," he'd told me in an e-mail. "Didn't know who it was at the time, but I thought it was incredible. I turned on the radio and didn't know they were playing the whole album and I didn't even know who I was listening to. I just knew it was great and kept listening because it got my attention right away. I was about eleven years old and listened to it on a little clock radio with my ear against the speaker. I had the radio as loud as it could go, and I had a pillow over my head so my parents couldn't hear. I truly believe that's how I blew out my right ear. To this day I have a hard time listening out of it."

Between the garage and the house was a yard with a place for a fire. A couple of dogs yapped from behind a fenced area. Mark set up the tent, then he, Dave, and Geoff went to buy some beer and food to barbecue. I whipped out my MiniDisc recorder and began chatting up Ragged Glory. Bill, the drummer, has dark blond hair and a goatee. Because he has muscular dystrophy, he uses a wheelchair to get to his drum stool.

"How long have you been playing drums?" I asked.

"Since I was fifteen. I've played with a blues band, a punk-rock band, everything."

"And have you been a Neil fan for long?"

"I've always been a Neil fan. I was in sixth grade when 'Heart of Gold' came out."

"How would you describe Ohio?"

"Well, it's like a cold North Carolina."

"It's a swing state—"

"Swing state?"

"You know, with the election. Are you interested in the election this year?"

Bill laughed. "That's a little deep for me, man."

"What Neil song do you like playing the most?"

" 'Like a Hurricane.' "

Also inside the garage were Rusties Kris Bournay and her husband, Dan, who'd made the three-hour drive from Michigan. They'd brought the KFC chicken that everyone was eating. Kris, a slender woman with glasses and a tie-dyed Neil Young concert shirt, has been a Rustie for four years. Before Neil, she and her husband had been to see the Moody Blues play a hundred times. "It's just watching him play," she said about Young. "To see him play is so special. To watch him move, to feel what he feels— it's unbelievable."

"You have a favorite Neil Young album?"

"No, I would have to pinpoint it down too much. I like the Crazy Horse stuff the most—"

"How has being a Neil Young fan affected your life?"

"It's really increased the debt on my credit card," she said, laughing. "A lot of concerts, travel, gas. A lot of T-shirts."

Jeff, Ragged Glory's bass player, lived in the house across the yard, which was owned by his girlfriend, Barb. Barb, who'd studied at Kent State and recently retired as a teacher, seemed used to having loud music and loud musicians at her place. She was a gracious host who would, on a couple of numbers, sing back-up. Jeff is a small, wiry man who at gigs played up his passing resemblance to his counterpart in Crazy Horse, bassist Billy Talbot, with the fedora he wore—just like Talbot. The hat had been lying around the house and when Curt first saw Jeff wearing it, he flipped out.

Like everyone else in the band, Jeff is generous, funny, and completely unpretentious. I asked him if I could use the bathroom.

"Well, if you only need to take a leak, you can just go anywhere behind the garage."

"Well, uhhhhh."

"Ohhhhhhhh, you need to take a dump."

"Yeah, well, you see it's the Kentucky Fried Chicken." With KFC or Taco Bell, it's as though you are *renting* food.

Jeff nodded in understanding. "I don't know what they put in that stuff."

When I returned, I spoke to Deb Navickas, who'd driven two hours from Pittsburgh to be here. Deb, a fun-loving redhead festooned with various Neil-related buttons, has been to at least fifty Rust Fests. This number includes her trips to *irf,* or the International Rust Fest, which started in 1997 in Saratoga Springs, California and is a four-day event centered around Young's Bridge School benefit concerts, which are held annually in the Bay Area. "We camp out in the redwoods," Deb was saying. "We probably had thirty people the first year, and it's grown to a hundred or one-fifty. They come from literally all over the world: Australia, Germany, Canada, and all over the U.S. I can go to every state in the union, any country in the world and find a friend I know there. Being a Rustie has been one of the best experiences in my life. It's a whole community, a lot of caring people."

"How long have you been a Neil fan?"

"Since 1970. I went to a friend's house. He sat me down in front of his brand-new stereo, put a doobie in my hand, and said, 'Listen to this.' It was *After the Gold Rush.* There was something about the voice and the album cover. It got inside me, I couldn't let it go."

"What's your favorite Neil album?"

"*Zuma.*"

"Me, too!"

"I have a ten-month-old grandson—my first. The first time I held him, he was ten minutes old, and after I said hello to him, the first thing I did was sing 'Barstool Blues' to him. And that's our song now."

Deb's first Neil Young show wasn't until 1991, but she's been to see Neil play two or three times every year since. She owns a couple of Young's set lists and a guitar pick, but unlike Steve Cross, she said, "I haven't cut a piece of his hair off."

"Would you take it if you could?"

"Hell, yeah!" She laughed.

Deb actually met Neil during his 1999 solo tour. "I went to three shows, the first in Akron and two Chicago shows." She'd had backstage passes for all the shows; she exchanged words with Neil in Akron and saw him again in Chicago. "Neil was over in the corner by himself. So I went over to Neil and said, 'Neil, would you fulfill a thirty-year fantasy for me?' And he put his arms out and we had a full-body hug. That was the crowning moment of my life. I can die happy now."

"What is Neil like?"

"It's like meeting the pope. Neil is rather intimidating. I'm not a small person myself, but it's the authority he brings with him. And he's got these eyes that *look like he knows*. They're navy blue, and he just looks at you and they pierce at you right through the center. He seems very gentle, he's got the softest hands of anyone I've ever known in all my life. I was so surprised by that."

"And he's not really that tall?"

"I think he's maybe five-eleven."

I shook my head in disbelief. "In my mind, he's fifty feet tall and made of gold."

"Well, up on stage, maybe, he looks that way. But standing up to me, he wasn't all that much taller. I didn't have to reach up to hug him."

"Could it be Old Man Shrink?" That was the speculation I'd read in a back issue of *Broken Arrow*. In old photos, Neil looks like a giant next to Stephen Stills and Dewey Martin, who, in fact, were pretty short. Still, it was hard for me to get my head around Neil's non-superhuman dimensions.

"Yeah, maybe, but I don't think too much."

"Who's the biggest Rustie you know?"

"Besides me?" She laughed.

Rusties have "handles," online identifiers taken from Neil Young song titles and biographical snippets. For instance, Sharry Wilson's online handle is "Up in T.O. Keepin' Jive Alive," a line from "Ambulance Blues." There are 1,655 registered Neil Young handles, and all the obvious ones have been taken by longstanding Rusties. Like "Cortez" or "Powderfinger," even Neil's guitar "Old Black," and many different variations on the theme of rust.

Deb got her handle, "Rewriting the Rules," after she had returned home from the first International Rust Fest. "I just knew I had to make some changes in my life. I was listening to *Lucky Thirteen,* and the song 'Depression Blues.' There's a lyric that goes: 'Goin' back to school / Savin' up my tuition / Gonna rewrite all the rules / On the old blackboard.' And somehow or other it made sense to me."

"So you're telling me life doesn't end at thirty?"

"Hell, no! Oh gosh, honey, I just turned fifty a year ago and I think it's getting better and better."

I was intrigued. "What can you do now that you couldn't do then?"

"I had a family back then, so I couldn't really travel that much. I wasn't free to spend money on music. I fell into the young suburban matron routine when my kids were young, and I gave up a lot of things to be a mom. They got a little bit older, I got a little bit older, and all of a sudden my life is my own again. And the doors are all open. They say that life really begins at forty, and it does, because you almost become ageless. It doesn't matter anymore. The body might age, you might wrinkle and sag, but inside you feel the spirit of a seventeen- or twenty-year-old or whatever it is. Neil is a muse to me. I like his attitude in life—"

"And what's that?"

"I think he's a little bit selfish, and he lives to make himself and his loved ones happy, and he really doesn't worry about what the rest of the world thinks about him or what he does or doesn't do. I like that, and I'm beginning to adopt that."

By now, my friends had returned with some chicken, hot dogs, and American beer. Dave handed me a can of Busch and cracked one open for himself.

"This stuff goes down fast," Dave said, as we watched Ragged Glory adjust their amps, mikes, and cymbal stands. "It's like water."

I took a sip. "It's light, even for American beer."

"I got to say, I like it." Dave is fairly agreeable about most beer. He's no premium-brand beer snob; he's a volume drinker. "It's so light and perfect for summer. Just sit out in a lawn chair and drink this stuff all day."

I pointed out that he did the same thing—drink all day, at least on vacation—with Canadian beer.

Dave nodded. "I guess I do."

"How does Lyn feel about it?"

"Oh, the same way she did when I used all the butter in the house to make those space cakes. She just shook her head."

I looked up at my tall friend and shook *my* head. "Lyn must have whiplash."

Laughing, Dave dropped a hand on my shoulder and squeezed me against him until I started squirming. "Oh, Kevin. You're my little sass-monkey."

Ragged Glory was ready to perform. Curt announced that he'd begin his show, as Neil often did with Crazy Horse, with a short solo set. "This is a tune I wrote," he said, taking a seat in front of a microphone. "I always do it as a warm-up." I didn't know how intentional it was, but to my ears, Curt even spoke like Neil, in a flat drawl that bore traces of Ontario, the Prairies, and California. Curt is the youngest of seven children, and though he's now in his thirties and makes his living supporting computer systems for northeastern Ohio schools, there's the glint of a little brother in his eyes and in the baby fat on his face. "I was always the shadow," he'd told me, "so this is me crying out saying, 'I'm here—I've got something to say.'"

When Curt started to play, the Neil Young influence was obvious in his sweet, whining voice. His guitar shuffled just like Neil's, and his harmonica honked. "Don't want to be no superstar, how lucky you are," he sang, with a quiet smolder that gathered intensity, "just want to play guitar and be with you." Young has often sung about the simple things and the complications of stardom, and the wistfulness of this song reminded me of him. But you could argue that Curt was practicing the simple life that Young—a millionaire rock star—could only preach. Curt wasn't trying to be a superstar, and yet in his music, he'd come up with a small, good thing.

"Neil is in my blood," he told me later. "He's true, honest, and beautiful. I have this thing—I also like Abe Lincoln. I liked him before I liked Neil, about when I was in second grade. Abe was a self-made man, and that's how I envisioned Neil, just coming out of nowhere and making something for himself. His music is so heartfelt, so human, so fatherly."

"Fatherly" is not a word often used to describe Young's music. Curt, however, considers Young his surrogate dad: "He's been with me throughout my life, ever since I was a kid. Because my father didn't do much with me at all. Neil represents the dad I would want, always there for me, leading me, seeing things more clearly, working hard, understanding others' feelings, putting words into music to express a deep-down feeling. I'm not his son, but he's my father."

After a few of his originals, Curt strapped on his electric guitar—like Neil's, a black Les Paul, with a Bigsby whang bar—and was joined by his band. Ragged Glory started playing "Hey Hey, My My," and it got very loud. I was amazed by how much Curt sounded like Neil, how much he played guitar like him. Curt even moved like Neil, hunched over with his back jerking as though he were hoeing a field. Rusties call it Neil's "knife in the back" move.

Ragged Glory wasn't a perfect band, but then again, they weren't a tribute to the Alan Parsons Project, either. Every flubbed note and accidental shift in tempo made them sound more like the gloriously ragged Crazy Horse, who'd once modestly dubbed themselves "the third best garage band in the world," perhaps to leave room for improvement. At one point, Curt, Jeff, and Brad, the rhythm guitarist, huddled together in front of the drums and began rocking—just like Crazy Horse.

"I always knew I would do this," Curt told me later. "Even when I was playing air guitar to Neil, I felt I could get to that same place he does when he performs. I wanted that 'peace-of-mind zone' he gets, when everything just goes away and it's just the music and the creativity and the sense of brotherhood." Over the evening, the band would play excellent renditions of all Neil's hits, plus lesser-known songs like "Eldorado" and "Crime in the City" from *Freedom* and an excellent version of "Sun Green" from *Greendale,* with a real-life police siren.

"I know of other tribute bands," Curt told me. "There's a real good U2 tribute band called Zoostation. There used to be a Neil cover band called Powderfinger, saw them once and didn't think it was Neil. The guy never touched the Bigsby once, can you imagine that? I've had my dad and brother and some other people suggest I do other stuff, like the Eagles. I tried it once with a friend rehearsing down in the basement at my old house and I said, 'Enough of this shit, I don't want to play "Margaritaville," "American Pie," or "Brown Eyed Girl."' People can get that stuff any day of the week, wherever they are."

Ragged Glory is obviously Curt's baby. Since the band's formation, there have been, by his estimate, ten different bass players and ten drummers. "I'm trying to find the right people who can fit the role. They usually don't last long. I take them how I can get them and I try to mold them into something." In his determination to achieve the right sound, Curt's ruthlessness resembles Neil Young's. "If it doesn't work out, they're gone. I rotate. This is the best group of guys I've had in a while. My last drummer was really out there. He had a double-bass pedal"—used on many heavy-metal records, but never by Neil Young—"and I couldn't take it anymore."

Ragged Glory played three sets. When they finished, Deb had to drive home to Pittsburgh, and Chris and Dan headed back to their hotel. The rest of us sat outside by a fire that Dave had started with Jeff the bassist's son. Jeff's son was about twice the size of his father. He owned two cars and was graduating half a year early because of his home-schooling. He was a little envious that we were heading to Las Vegas.

"What's your game?" I asked him.

"I like poker. Texas Hold'em."

"Cool," I said, nodding in approval. "I watch it on TV, like everyone else in the world." I looked across the fire to Brian, who was a friend of the band's. "Is it me or does Brian looks like Chris Ferguson?"

Both Brian and Chris Ferguson, a professional poker player on TV whose nickname is "Jesus," have long dark hair, narrow faces, and beards. Brian is also in a wheelchair, because he had the misfortune of being in the wrong place at the wrong time when someone started firing an AK-47.

After hearing about the precautions we'd had to take crossing the border, he gave Mark and Dave a big-assed bag of weed.

"You know," Mark said to me, "I'm still skeptical about this country, but I can't say I've ever met nicer people. And we're strangers to them."

While we sat outside, Curt was still in the garage, playing Neil Young songs. A bassist friend had dropped by and wanted to jam, and they played songs like "Old Man," "Harvest Moon," and "See the Sky about to Rain." Curt just loved to play. Another hour passed before he came out and sat down in a lawn chair next to his wife. I thanked him for organizing the Rust Fest and having us out. We sat around for a while longer drinking beer. Dave put some chicken and hot dogs on the hibachi. It was two in the morning by the time we crawled into our tent. We were late risers, we told Barb. There was no need for a wake-up call.

\\|/

CROSSING THE UNITED STATES along Route 66, Neil Young
was terrified that Mort Two would suffer the same demise as its name-
sake. While the rest of the car was high on Bruce Palmer's weed, Young
was jacked up on speed and obsessed that the other drivers—Jeanine and,
depending on who's telling the story, Tannis or Judy—were running the
hearse too hard. They survived on fast food, though on one occasion they
were invited to dinner by a gas station attendant in Indianapolis who
confused Neil and Tannis for Sonny and Cher.

Young was growing increasingly paranoid. When he should have been
sleeping, he lay awake in the back of the hearse listening to the transmission. Eventually, he would insist on doing all the driving. Jeanine Hollingshead would tell Johnny Rogan: "He only let me drive when he was
completely exhausted. Even then, he would scream at me from the back,
'Don't lug my car!' It wasn't my fault. The thing had never been out of
second gear in its entire life."

They were all getting annoyed with one another. Neil was crabby
and suspicious; the women were too interested in having a good time
to realize that Neil and Bruce were on a mission. As they neared Albuquerque, Young pulled over and removed everyone's luggage from the
car. "He just basically said, 'Out, out, everybody out,' and he just tore out

everything, threw it all out on the ground. He just emptied the hearse," Jeanine said in *Shakey*. "I think at one point Neil was considering leaving us and everything there and driving away. He just stood there with his shirttails hangin' out, his eyes all bloodshot, lifted his arms to the gods, screamed to the ozone, 'AAAAGGHHH!' and got over it." A state trooper arrived and told them to get moving. By the time they approached Albuquerque, both the hearse and Young had started falling apart.

WE'D HAD a coffee in Barb's driveway before we packed our tent and returned to the highway. Stopping at an Elyria gas station, we picked up some breakfast. I used to be a connoisseur of junk food. As a kid on road trips into the States, I loved Milk Duds and the tuna fish that comes in vacuum-sealed plastic. In Elyria, Dave and I each bought two maple breakfast sausages for ninety cents.

"These are pretty good," Dave said, biting into a sausage. We were standing outside the store and looking out at the thrumming interstate, our steaming cups of coffee atop a waste bin. Mark was running a squeegee across the windshield of the car; Geoff was using the restroom. "My dad used to love hot dogs. When he was in his twenties, before he met my mom, he and his roommate would come home from a night of drinking and split a twelve-pack of wieners."

I laughed. "Do you remember, when we were teenagers, how they used to keep chili as a condiment at the 7-Eleven? You had to push down on a lever to pump out the chili, which came out of a spout, just like the ketchup. You'd buy a Slurpee and two hot dogs and load them with chili."

"These really are good sausages," Dave said again.

I totally agreed. Why didn't we have maple breakfast sausages in Canada? Not only was this variation of probably the most efficient vessel of energy delivery in human history imbued with the native flavor of our cherished homeland, but the buns came, steamed and individually wrapped, from a drawer below the heat lamps. I'm not being a smart-assed Canadian when I say that these sausages are one happy by-product (made up, no doubt, of actual by-products) of American ingenuity. The bun-steaming drawer, too. I inhaled my maple breakfast sausages.

Climbing back into the car and following the signs for the on-ramp, we started for Vegas, nonstop. I'd spent the past couple of days staring at my map book, tracing the red lines that showed the approximate driving distances and adding up the times between cities. It was cruel math. We'd be driving for at least forty hours. I'd known all along that this would be the most brutal leg of the trip. It was a Saturday, and because of my scheduling stupidity, we had only two days to get from Ohio to Las Vegas. Geoff was hoping to fly out of Vegas on Monday and needed to be back at work on Tuesday. I took the first shift driving, knowing that fatigue would catch up with me by nightfall.

An hour into our drive an accident stalled westbound traffic on the highway. We sat idling for a half-hour before I turned off the engine and Mark felt it was safe to leave the car and empty his bladder on the side of the road. Another fifteen minutes passed before traffic began to move.

"Do we have time for Memphis?" asked Dave. "Pippa at the hostel in Toronto said it was pretty cool."

"Well, it doesn't look like we have the time—"

"Come on, we'll be driving forty hours anyway. What's a little detour?"

I turned around to see if he was serious. Of course he was.

"*We* can do it," said Mark. "We're Team Crazy Horse. We can do anything we put our minds to."

"That's just what they told you at school. They were lying." I shook my head. We weren't going to Graceland. It would add another four hours to our trip. We'd get there in the middle of the night. We wouldn't have any time to spend there. And yet I felt strangely guilty. This was an anything-goes kind of trip, and the course and logic of it already defied practical considerations. I hated having to say no to any dumb-assed suggestions.

At four in the afternoon, we stopped for a buffet, another road-trip ritual, at an Indiana truck stop. The sick-making selection included, bafflingly enough, chunks of dried-out shepherd's pie and sweet and sour pork that looked as though it were dredged in Yuletide candle wax. Mark had two helpings of fried chicken. At the table next to us, a man who was maybe six feet tall and at least 350 pounds sat down with a heaping plate, looking at us. The cheeks of his ass spilled out from the sides of his chair. "The drive sure builds up your appetite, doesn't it?" he said to us. We nodded. We were full.

I felt crusty from a night of campfire smoke and back-yard camping. In the restroom next to the restaurant, I took a shower. At the register, the cashier gave me a key, a towel, and a face cloth. The showers, which were free, a courtesy to truckers, were institutional, yet lavish. I expected a closet-sized stall, but the shower room was spacious: there was a sink and a sort of powder room with a bench next to the actual shower stall, which had a beige tile floor and a hand-soap dispenser. Having bathed and deposited my towels in a bin by the cashier, I checked my e-mail. If I'd wanted to, I could also have lounged in the TV room and bought ornamental mud flaps. We returned to the road.

It was Geoff's turn to drive, and he took us on and on into the dusk. The highway took us into the outskirts of Indianapolis. We needed to stop to ask for directions back to the highway. We were given roundabout directions that took us through a couple of tough-looking neighborhoods, and by the time we were back onto the interstate it was nightfall.

"I know a guy," Geoff was telling us, "who broke up his band because he was the only one of them who could drive."

"How many guys were in the band?" I asked him.

"Three. They toured across Canada two or three times, and he'd have to do all the driving on his own. They'd get to a gig and this guy who'd been driving would be totally wiped. The other guys would be completely rested and didn't understand why he was so tired and so cranky." Geoff laughed. "Can you imagine how crazy you'd get?"

"You're dead weight on a road trip if you don't drive."

The highway was a happily faceless place—built on uniformity, interchangeable chains of motels, gas stations, and burger huts—that almost encouraged you to ignore it. Not only did you forget where you were, and not only did you forget where you'd come from, you also forgot who you were when you left.

In the dark, traveling had become a blurry experience. Moving along amber-lit roads, we sat listening to music in near darkness, occasionally gaping at the bursts of highway strangeness. As we drove through southern Illinois, there was a huge sign on the highway advertising "The Porn Superstore" right next to another huge highway sign with the urgent message "Pornography Destroys Lives." And it was around this time that we saw the first of at least three giant crosses on our journey. This one seemed at least ten stories high and was lit from the ground.

We definitely weren't in a godless part of the country, and the god foisted on us was not only merciful and wrathful, but he was also on the move. Between CDs, we listened to a Christian radio station. In a scripted infomercial, a teenage girl was testifying about a boyfriend who was pressuring her for sex. She looked to her faith to resist temptation: "I told my boyfriend that I was breaking up with him for a guy who respected my boundaries: Jesus." Her boyfriend had been cockblocked by Christ.

During this stretch of driving I was especially glad that Jim Fitzgerald's hearse had broken down before we left Vancouver. Who knows what would happen if we got stranded here? We'd have to hide out at the Porn Superstore. I whipped out my MiniDisc recorder.

"How are you liking the Midwest?" I asked Geoff.

"The roads are in pretty good condition," he said. "The restrooms seem to work pretty good. That seems to be about all I can say."

"What did you like about Cleveland?"

"The pants. I saw a lot of famous people's pants."

"You mean, at the Rock and Roll Hall of Fame? Whose pants did you like the most?"

"Al Green had some cool pants—Curtis Mayfield, too. TLC had TV screens on their pants."

"Do you find that there's been a parade of smells since we've been in Illinois?"

"I'd say about every fifty miles or so there's a new smell. There was a smoky urine smell, then there was a skunky smell for a while, and then a really bad shit smell."

"The manure from an hour ago?"

"I guess that's a shit smell, too. But then there was more of a human shit smell."

"The last smell was of rotten eggs."

"Yeah," Geoff said, sounding unsure. "Did you smell skunk?"

I didn't think I had. I turned to Dave in the back seat. "How are you enjoying the drive?"

"Right now? It's getting a little bit squirrelly. I'm starting to really hate this car."

"Whom do you hate most in this car?"

"Right now? You, for putting that mike in my face."

"Whom do you hate least?"

"Myself."

"What do you miss about home?" I asked everyone in the car.

"My girl," said Dave.

"My girlfriend," said Mark.

"I'd have to say my family," said Geoff. This was the first time I'd heard him use the word "family." I wondered where he'd been—at work, or at the breakfast table, or in bed—when the word became normal for him.

"What about you, Kev?" Dave asked, with a crooked smile. "What do you miss—your dog?"

I nodded. "Yes, my dog."

"He really has nothing to go home to," said Geoff.

"That's true. I'm just going to keep driving once I drop you guys off. Then I'll probably pick up a drifter and kill him for sport."

In fact, I missed my apartment, my bed, my half-dead spider plant. I missed the sanity of my routine, my Thursday night at the Legion, my diner lunches. I missed working. And I did miss my dog.

Finally we caught a glimpse of St. Louis and its arches. Traffic slowed down as we approached an upturned car on the grassy median. The farther into the Midwest we went, the lower the gas prices fell. Filling up in Missouri, Geoff switched places with Mark, and as we headed toward Springfield and the center of the heartland, I passed out and missed the world's biggest McDonald's. Dave was still talking about it when I faded back to waking. "We saw the sign first," he was telling me with awe and rapture in his voice. "There was a McDonald's on either side of the highway and then a huge overpass above the highway that was also a McDonald's."

I was in a groggy delirium, unable to sleep for more than a few consecutive minutes. I got out at the next gas station, long enough to buy a donut and a bottle of water, before passing out once more. Dave bought a cup of "Rev," a blend of coffee designed especially for truckers, which gave him a stomachache. We drove through the Ozarks at night, a place I knew of only through Woody Guthrie songs. I was too weary to regret not being able to see those mountains. I was determined to get to more sleep; it was my turn to drive next.

1 *Next to the Rock and Roll Hall of Fame is Cleveland's Science Center, where they keep a machine that shrinks humans. Later that night, I slept in a thimble.*

2 *I really have nowhere to go. I just keep driving— going from town to town, solving mysteries and reuniting estranged families, like the Littlest Hobo. The whole world is my home. (Photo courtesy of Dave Yellowlees.)*

3 *Deb Navickas, fun-loving Rustie from Pittsburgh. For Deb, meeting Neil was like "meeting the pope."*

4 *Curt Vigg, leader of Ragged Glory, rocking out in northeastern Ohio.*

1

2

4

3

CHAPTER

TWENTY-TWO

WHEN I WOKE NEXT, it was just before sunrise. On the car's vent windows were greasy head-shaped smudges where we'd nodded off. Geoff said the smudges looked like spray-on snow, the kind of stuff they put on storefronts around Christmas, and it was a freakishly accurate description. Dave had finished driving the red-eye shift, and we were outside Oklahoma City at yet another truck stop. This place had a chapel room, and in the restroom where the hand dryer would normally be found there was some kind of cologne-dispensing machine. For twenty-five cents, you could take a pigeon bath in Drakkar Noir.

"Let's just stop," Dave said, his voice desperate with fatigue. He pointed to a knoll of yellowing grass beside the air and water pumps that separated this gas station from the next one. "We can lie down there for a while."

"Dave," I said to him, "that's a hump of grass."

"I don't care."

"They'll call the cops on us. We're not hoboes, Dave."

Dave let out a cry. "I can't drive anymore."

"I can drive," I told him.

I'd slept maybe two or three hours in the back, and either I was feeling refreshed or I was too delirious to realize the extent of my exhaustion.

Probably the second. Dave and the rest of us reluctantly returned to the car, and we turned back onto the highway. Facing us was the arid prairie landscape. All the green had been stripped from this oil-rich part of the world. I had driven for an hour and a half, approaching the Texas border with the emerging sun on our backs, when Dave insisted, again, that we stop.

"I can't take it anymore," he told me. "I need to stretch my legs."

I pulled over at the next rest stop. Sitting at a covered concrete picnic table, I watched as Dave laid out his long legs on the lawn. He was only there for a moment before he jerked upright with a yelp. His back was covered with little cacti. I picked thorn balls from his shirt. We brought out the hibachi and the cooler and made some chicken and hot dogs.

Mark returned from the restroom, where he'd splashed water on his face. "I called my dad yesterday," he said, when he saw the meat on the grill. "I said America was making me fat. He had a laugh."

"I stopped worrying about it after our fiftieth hot dog," I said, biting into one of the jalapeño peppers that Barb had given us in Ohio. "I also stopped caring about whether we'd get salmonella from the chicken, or whether we're driving on enough rest. I mean, we've gotten this far—what else is there? We're invincible." I was crazy. "Think about it. This will be the longest drive any of us will ever take in our lives, if we're lucky, and the journey's more than halfway over. We can do it. We're *going* to live *forever*."

Mark threw on his wraparound sunglasses. He just looked at me and smiled sympathetically.

"Geoff, do you want a hot dog?" Dave asked.

Geoff gave no answer. His reserves of good cheer had been exhausted and there was an ornery expression on his face as he lay passed out on the unwelcoming lawn, his hat covering his eyes. If Geoff wanted to sleep, even a bed of thorns couldn't discourage him. He was a stubborn bastard.

A pale dude in a white "wife-beater" and black track pants approached us. He had a thick silver band in each ear and was clutching a cell phone. "You fellows want to give me a ride to Amarillo?" he asked in a rough, slurring voice.

"Sorry," Dave said. "Car's full."

"Fuck," this guy said. "I hitched from Tulsa, told the last car to drop me off here. Figured it would be easy to get a ride. Been here two hours already." He stared at his phone. "Don't get any reception here."

"Wish we could help," Dave said.

"You have a smoke?" he asked.

Dave gave him one of his Kools.

Geoff rose from the dead to have a piece of chicken and a wiener. Then we piled back into the car. I took my time, settling behind a truck moving at the speed limit, following it until it turned at an exit, then finding another truck to glom onto. As we headed into Texas, the sky pressed down and the landscape grew brown and flat. Across a strip of grass, running parallel to the I-40, was Route 66. Every hour or so, a sign would announce another turn-off onto the historic highway that Neil Young had taken four decades earlier. Young would tell Jimmy McDonough: "Route 66 was a gas. I just loved traveling. I got hooked on those kind of trips when I was five, six, years old when my dad used to drive us down to Florida. The highway bug, long thin lines through the desert, goin' into these towns, the gambling, all the neon lights. I went, 'Wow, this is so wild!' Pretty far out." The empty two-lane highway sat there preserved in the open air, lined with rickety telephone poles, white like exposed bone, that slung silky black cables. Fence posts, crooked like bad teeth, were threaded together with rusting wire.

I pulled onto it at the next turnoff. I announced to the car, "I want a taste of history."

There were only patchy, unconnected stretches of Route 66 remaining. We got three blocks' worth of road before coming to a dead end. So much for history.

"How was your journey through the past?" Geoff joked. He was riding shotgun. "Did it blow your mind?"

"Oh yeah," I said.

"Let me drive next. I'm the reason we're on this nonstop ordeal."

After filling up in Amarillo, I relinquished driving duties to Geoff. We gawked at Amarillo's world-famous steakhouse—a flashy place that has its own gift store—where you can eat a ninety-six-ounce steak for free if you do it in under an hour. Having finished my shift, I immediately crashed. It might have been for ten minutes, it could have been two hours. By the time I woke up, Albuquerque had started to appear on road signs.

As we chipped away at the miles, I put on *Tonight's the Night,* the crown jewel of the Ditch Trilogy, Young's personal favorite, and the favorite of many fans.

"Every time somebody close to me passes away," Rustie Bob Lee would tell me, "it's one of the records that ends up getting pulled out at two AM. It pulls together the emotions, from grief to falling-down-the-stairs chaos. To me, it's the whole picture."

It certainly wasn't an upbeat album. As Young told Cameron Crowe: "If you're gonna put a record on at 11 in the morning, don't put on *Tonight's the Night.* Put on the Doobie Brothers." It was Sunday morning by now, though we could have made the case that it had been one long Saturday night.

The album that Young dubbed "the first horror record" was made at an L.A. rehearsal studio in August 1973, after long nights of tequila-fueled partying. It went unreleased for two years. The story goes that right before the planned release of his now-apocryphal *Homegrown,* Young played his album of break-up songs at the home of Rick Danko of the Band. They also listened to *Tonight's the Night,* which happened to be on the same reel. After hearing both albums, Danko urged Neil to release the rawer album instead.

"He was kinda rebelling against everything," guitarist Nils Lofgren told McDonough, who wrote extensively and rhapsodically about *Tonight's the Night* in *Shakey.* "I remember talkin' to him and he said, 'Hey, I've made records where you analyze everything and you do it three thousand times and it's perfect. I'm sick of it. I want to make a record that's totally stark naked. Raw. I don't wanna fix any of it.'"

Young would tell Bud Scoppa in *N.M.E.:* "I think what was in my mind when I made that record was I just didn't feel I was a lonely figure with a guitar or whatever it is that people see me as sometimes. I didn't feel that laid-back—I just didn't feel that way. So I thought I'd just forget all that and...be as aggressive and as abrasive as I could." With *Tonight's the Night,* Young wanted to snap-shoot himself at rock bottom, raging over the drug-related deaths of friends like roadie Bruce Berry and original Crazy Horse guitarist and collaborator Danny Whitten, who, the year before, had overdosed using money from Young, after Young fired him from a recording session. "I'm sorry. You don't know these people. This means nothing to you," Neil wrote in the liner notes.

On the album, Whitten appears back from the grave, singing on a 1970 recording of "Come on Baby Let's Go Downtown," essentially a country-rock version of the Velvet Underground's ode to scoring drugs, "I'm Waiting for the Man." "Tired Eyes" is Young's fictionalized rendition of a real-life drug deal turned homicide. "Well, it wasn't supposed to go down that way," he mumbles, "but they burned his brother, you know, and they left him lying in the driveway." Young's voice soars, gloriously raw and off-key, for the refrain: "Please take my advice. Open up the tired eyes." His plea for self-awareness seems especially bitter because you feel he's singing to people who can no longer hear him. Usually you close a dead person's eyes.

"I'm singing this borrowed tune I took from the Rolling Stones," he sings, setting his burnt-out anguish, strangely enough, to the melody of "Lady Jane," the Rolling Stones' unintentionally comical ode to Arthurian legend, "alone in this empty room, too wasted to write my own." In songs like "Speakin' Out" and "New Mama," Young also brought to the album the uncertainty he was feeling about relationships and fatherhood.

Even the lighthearted ode to smoking weed, "Roll Another Number (For the Road)," contains a verse in which he distances himself from the idealism of his past: "I'm not going back to Woodstock for a while, though I long to hear that lonesome hippie smile / I'm a million miles away from that helicopter day"—an allusion to the helicopter CSNY flew on to get to the festival—"No, I don't believe I'll be goin' back that way."

I was playing *Tonight's the Night* mostly for the eighth track on the album, "Albuquerque." It's another song in which Young seeks escape on the road, yet in this case, he seems to have realized the open road can also grow wearisome. "Well, they say that Santa Fe is less than ninety miles away," Young half-speaks, his fuzzed-out guitar leavened by Ben Keith's weeping, angelic steel guitar, "And I got time to roll a number and rent a car." During the refrain, he stretches out the first syllable of "Albuquerque": "Oh-oh, Al-al-al-ah-alal," he wails, before the thudding "—buquerque."

It's entirely conceivable that the spent and wasted tone of this song was inspired by the unplanned pit stop Young made in Albuquerque in March 1966 on his way to California. He was exhausted from days of driving and restless anxiety, and as soon as the hearse arrived in Albuquerque, he fainted. Jeanine Hollingshead drove him to a hospital emergency room, where a doctor told Neil he was suffering from fatigue and shock. The first symptoms of Young's epilepsy appeared here as he rested.

"We were originally staying in a motel," Jeanine had told me, "then we made friends with some people in the university coffeehouse area, including Brian [Moniz]'s dad, and he put us on to a vacant student-housing place and a kind woman, Jean Something, who let us crash in her big empty house. I don't remember paying any rent. We helped with the groceries." Young spent three or four days convulsing on a mattress on the floor, attended by Palmer. He would wake up for soup or water, then promptly return to sleep in his borrowed sleeping bag. After Young had rested, he, Palmer, and Mack continued their trip, leaving Neiman, Hollingshead, and Gallagher behind.

By the time my friends and I arrived in Albuquerque, it was about five PM and bright-white hot. If we hadn't been so exhausted I might have made an attempt to locate the address of the Igloo, which, like so many addresses we'd visited, was probably occupied now by something else. As it was, with reheated oatmeal for brains, we picked a random exit to pull off the highway and drove around a residential area of the city looking for somewhere to eat. "So I'll stop when I can," Young sings in "Albuquerque," "find some fried eggs and country ham / I'll find somewhere where they don't care who I am." Between blocks of ranch-style homes with rock gardens in their front yards, we came upon strip malls full of fast-food outlets, barbecue places, a lot of Mexican restaurants, but no likely destination for a late-afternoon breakfast. At last, we settled for a Denny's.

We ordered from the breakfast menu. Along with eggs and ham, I had a side salad (an act of penance for all those hot dogs) and a cup of coffee.

Geoff didn't look too happy. I asked him how he was enjoying his breakfast.

"It's quite good, although we could go to a Denny's in Vancouver and have the exact same meal," he said. "But that's my bad attitude."

"We're almost there," I told him. "We'll get you to Vegas on time."

The four of us ate without much conversation; the nine or ten hours' worth of driving still ahead weighed down on us like a collapsed house. Then again, maybe the heat made everyone brain-dead. Our waiter resembled a lobotomized surfer dude; every request we made—for an extra set of "silverware," for water—was followed by five seconds of dead silence before comprehension finally dribbled across his face. It took us a while to get our bill. As we waited, we chatted with the busboy, who asked us where we were heading. We must have looked like people passing through. He was a man in his twenties with the kind of thatchy beard most often sported by Appalachian minstrels.

He was impressed by the time we were making. "You guys should be in Vegas by two in the morning."

"You go there often?" I asked.

"Yeah, in the past. I used to drive a lot." His eyes bore down on you when he spoke. They were gray and girlish, heavily lashed, and had a spook in them. "I drove for a year or two, went everywhere. This was a few years back. I lived in my car the whole time."

I asked him why he'd been driving around.

"It was a period in my life. I didn't want to work. I didn't want responsibility. I wanted to see what it would be like to have no money. I wanted to be really poor and just live on what I could find. I wanted to see how far I could go and throw myself to fate." He let out a sigh. "I did some things I regret, things I'm ashamed to think about. I got tired of it after a while, that's why I have a job. But you know what? I'm thankful for it. It made me appreciate the value of money. How much a tank of gas costs, the price of a loaf of bread."

His answer was sensible to me, at least in principle. Perhaps anything would have seemed reasonable in that heat and with so little sleep. He wished us a good journey as we stumbled outside into the swelter.

CHAPTER
TWENTY-THREE

ACROSS THE STREET from the Denny's, we stopped to fill our tank. Mark was next to me, in the driver's seat, ready to turn into traffic.

"Maybe you should get a ticket home," Dave suggested to Geoff once again. He hadn't mentioned it in a couple of days, and I thought he'd given in to Geoff's wait-and-see approach. "If we looked around, we could find an internet connection—"

Geoff's eyes were heavy, from either the fatigue or the meal, and the corners of his mouth drew back in a wide, bitter grin. "Maybe you should get off my ass," he told him.

Dave tried to laugh it off. "I'm just trying to help."

"You've been on my ass the whole trip."

Dave moved to the offensive. "Why didn't you buy a ticket when we were in Toronto?" he asked Geoff. "I would have lent you my credit card."

"I didn't know if we could get to Vegas by Monday."

"Look at us. We're almost there. If you got a ticket for Monday now, we would get you there on time."

Geoff stared out the rear driver's-side window as we pulled onto the highway. "I'm going to call the airline the minute we arrive in Vegas."

"Don't you know how much same-day tickets cost?"

"I think I can get a standby ticket."

"You *think*."

In the rearview mirror, I watched them fuming at each other. Dave was right, but it was hard for me to be angry at Geoff. It would have made more sense for Geoff to leave for Vancouver from Toronto. And yet, if he wanted to be completely practical, he wouldn't have come on this trip to begin with. He was undertaking the journey to Las Vegas because he wanted to be on the road with us for as long as he could.

Up front, Mark and I stared out into the open road, each of us discreetly averting his gaze from the back seat like a limo driver on prom night. As we left Albuquerque, we were moving steadily uphill.

"I'd love to see the Grand Canyon," Mark said. "We'll be passing it at night."

"It's worth seeing," I said. "Maybe next time."

"When I get back home, I'm going on a hike. Sophia will be on a canoe trip, and I'll have a few days to kill. I want some time away from cars, from other people. I just feel so gross."

"When I get home," I said, "I'm going on Slim Fast."

I kid. Mark, on the other hand, is someone who spends his free time digging out cross-country skiers from under avalanches. The year before, he'd taken a forty-hour bus ride to Mexico, doping himself on sleeping pills to get through the monotony, in order to go mountain-climbing. If I've given him short shrift in the course of this narrative, it's only because I don't know him as well as my other two friends. Mark is a quiet fellow who, like Dave, could get along with anyone in the world, in spite of his overpoweringly stinky feet. He was the youngest in the car, at only twenty-six, which nevertheless is late middle-age for tree-planters.

"I want to travel next year—maybe South America," he was saying. "First, I'd have to convince Sophia. But I have this other plan. I could get a crew together and work around the world. There are trees that need planting in Scotland and Australia—everywhere. And because Canada is the leader in the tree-planting industry, they basically look to you to show them how it's done. You can work slowly, so that you don't kill yourself, and tell them that's how we do it at home and still get paid nicely. We'd work in one place for a couple of months, then take a month off and travel. It's such hard work, we'd need to rest up. Then we'd fly to the next place and plant trees."

We'd forgotten to clean our windshield at our last stop, so our view was veiled in bug-splatter, each white speck holding light in its blotchy grip. We were halfway between Gallup and Flagstaff when the sun began to tumble down the huge huge sky. The tension in the back of the car had faded as the miles passed.

"I know this is corny," Dave said, "but when I look at the sky, I can understand why so many people believe in God in this part of the world."

The sky was swollen and heavy; the mesa framing the horizon was flattened like a penny on a railroad track. Dave was right. This was why I kept him around. And he wasn't even high—not yet. Dave brought out the weed that Brian in Ohio had given us, and the three of them smoked up. Around this time, a police car sped by.

"I don't feel comfortable with all this weed in here," Mark said. "We were lucky with that car. The next patrolman will notice our Canadian plates and pull us over. They'll just assume the car is full of potheads."

Dave laughed. "They'd be right."

"It's cultural profiling," I suggested.

Mark wasn't amused. "I think we should throw it out. If we got caught with weed we could do jail time in the States. Is it worth it? We'll be meeting more Rusties. Chances are, if we're hanging out with them, they'll have more weed. And in another week, we'll be back in Canada where we can smoke all we want."

"I don't think it's such a big risk," Geoff said. "But, I mean, whatever's cool with you—"

Mark turned to me for support. "What do you think about this?"

"Well, I don't smoke pot—"

"But you'd be affected."

"I guess." I shrugged. It was the risk I assumed when I traveled with my friends.

Mark's pot hysteria had somehow fused with the patriotic feelings a Canadian exhibits only when he is away. "I just know that I'm proud," he was saying, "to be from a country where I can smoke dope and not worry about it, and I can't wait to get out of the States. It's not worth the risk."

Mark's paranoia won over.

"Such a waste," Dave said, shaking his head as he rolled down the window and let the plastic bag fly out of it. "I hope some convicted shoplifter scooping roadkill from the highway finds this."

At Flagstaff, Dave bought a can of Red Bull and took the late-night shift once more. We drove into the ascending darkness. We passed the exit for the Grand Canyon. We took a state highway into Nevada that was under renovation and wasn't allowing trucks. The road was dark and empty without the big rigs. Actually, Nevada was dark except for occasional gigantic bursts of light; the flashing marquees of the monster casino complexes along the highway, trying to lure travelers away from Vegas, brayed on about cheap lobster dinners and bettor-friendly odds. Hoover Dam was enormous and elegant and lit with a sepulchral glow. The overpowering shine of Las Vegas was visible from half an hour's distance.

At last we entered Vegas. Even in the middle of the night, the city was aglitter. We squinted as we turned into downtown Vegas. The older casinos in the core were nestled among newer places, like the casino for Jimmy Buffett. Who's next, Tony Danza? Out on the edge of the strip were new theme-park-sized casinos.

We had a discount coupon for the biggest Super 8 Motel in the world. By the time we got there, it was Monday morning, three AM, Pacific time. We'd left Ohio on Saturday at noon, Eastern, meaning that we'd been on the road for forty-two hours. I checked in with a clerk who managed the difficult feat of being perfectly polite and yet completely hostile. His brow was clenched in a frown, and his eyes seethed as he handed me the pass cards for our room.

"Enjoy your stay," he spat out with contempt. He was in his forties and had a blond brush cut and a meaty face the color of ground pork.

Moments after entering our room, Dave and Mark passed out on one bed. Geoff started calling airlines from the motel phone. I realized that I didn't have any clean clothes. I treaded down to the front desk. The clerk's eyes rose from his desk. When they alighted on me, they gave the impression that he wanted to sever my head from my body with a letter opener.

"Where's the laundry room?" I asked.

"It's on the second floor," he growled.

I started for the elevator, then turned once more. The clerk's face had reddened with rage.

"Can I *help* you?"

"Uh, you don't happen to sell detergent—"

He let out a breath, and his eyes grew beady with the determined rage of a pit bull whose jaws are locked on a fluffy white terrier. He came back with a small box of Tide. "That'll be a dollar twenty-five, please," which was translated by his demeanor into, *"I can't believe I work at this shit-hole and have to deal with chunks of corn-studded turd like you."*

The world's biggest Super 8 was a perversion of what Vladimir Nabokov describes, in *Lolita,* as "the Functional Motel—clean, neat, safe nooks, ideal places for sleep, argument, reconciliation, insatiable illicit love." This gargantuan motel had swollen to hugely dysfunctional proportions. It consisted of four interchangeable three-story wings with at least two elevators each. After walking around in the maze of the second floor—where leggy women emerged from rooms giggling and huge, thick-necked dudes covered with tattoos loitered menacingly around the ice machines—I deposited my laundry in the washer. I returned to our room and showered; in the mirror, I found hives along my neck. They had returned.

I got lost on my way back to the laundry room, then found it again. I picked out my wet laundry and placed it in the dryer. I realized I didn't have enough quarters and went down to the front desk.

"What do you want now, you worthless bag of crap and puke?" the front clerk asked. "Can I help you?"

I held out a five-dollar bill: "I, uh, need more quarters."

"Will four be enough?"

"Mm—yeah."

On the far wall of the front lobby was a bank of blinking slot machines. I'd been to Vegas before, and I was surprised they didn't have video poker terminals in toilet stalls. I thought of Burton Cummings playing video poker on the crapper and started giggling.

"Are you okay?" Geoff asked me. He was sitting at a computer with an internet hook-up next to the coffee machine and a stack of Styrofoam cups. The burnt coffee was free, but use of the computer came at a larcenous fee—five dollars for fifteen minutes.

"Oh," I said. "I didn't see you."

On the screen of the computer was a travel website showing prices for one-way flights to Vancouver. "The airlines I spoke with wanted six hundred U.S. for a one-way flight. Do you mind if I borrow your credit card?"

"Of course." I gave him my credit card.

"I'll give you cash back."

"Um, yeah, I'll need your money."

"Do you want to use the computer?"

"I'm in no rush."

I went upstairs, fed the dryer, and returned to the lobby. Geoff was putting another five dollars into the payment slot.

I scratched the hives along my neck. "What's the matter?" I asked him.

"This site won't take a credit card with a Canadian mailing address."

He tried buying the ticket once again and got the same request for an American mailing address. I was internet-savvy from years of web research and cyber-stalking women I'd never gotten over. I didn't want to be a back-seat browser, but I suggested a couple of other travel websites I knew. Geoff tried them out, but he wasn't the fastest typist in the world and his internet time was about to expire. None of the sites had any reasonably priced flights, anyway.

"Try the airline's website," I suggested.

The airline's website also asked for a U.S. mailing address.

"Click on the 'contact' link," I said. There was a 1-800 number, which Geoff wrote down just as his time on the computer ran out. He went back to our room to make the call. I waited by the computer. Geoff returned with the address of the airline's Canadian website. He put another five dollars into the computer, bought a ticket for an afternoon flight, and then decided to go for a walk around Vegas.

Scratching my neck again, I checked my e-mail in the lobby, picked up my laundry, and tried to sleep. I couldn't sleep. Why couldn't I sleep?

I lay on one side of the motel-room bed. (I hate box-spring mattresses.) I didn't know if I could do it. I didn't know how I was going to do it.

Scratched my neck. We were in Vegas: why were we here? This had nothing to do with Neil Young. What if I couldn't write this book? Who wanted to read about this part of my journey? I wasn't even in a hearse. What if people looked at this book and held their noses? What if I delivered another steaming turd, like the novel I'd spent three years writing, into which I carved a chunk of myself—of everything I knew and felt? What would I do then? I should have been sleeping. I didn't need to be thinking about this right now. I was tired; this was a fact. I would have to drive Geoff to the airport in seven hours. Six hours. Scratched my neck. Five hours and forty-five minutes. How could I trust that I was doing the right thing? I didn't know what was good. What I thought was good no one liked. Even Neil Young had had trouble putting out his records with David Geffen, but (a) I wasn't Neil Young, (b) those albums weren't that great, and (c) I wasn't Neil Young. I was a failure. Four hours. What had I gotten myself into? I started twitching. Three hours. Scratched again. Two, one.

When Geoff returned at six in the morning, he fell next to me on the double bed and slept for an hour.

"Do you want to go for breakfast?" I asked him.

"Sure."

On our way to the casino next door, in the parking lot, we passed a war memorial on wheels: the names of all the soldiers who'd died in Iraq were on the side of a truck with what looked like a huge doghouse for a canopy. We found the casino restaurant and had some surprisingly good steak and eggs for only three dollars and change. The waitress knew we were Canadian because we asked for brown bread instead of whole wheat.

"What were you doing all night?" I asked.

"Just walking around, getting my bearings," Geoff said. "Thinking."

He handed me some money for the flight. "I'm sorry to be bailing on you guys," he said.

"I'm glad you could come. I know how hard it was to leave your family. I feel like we kidnapped you for a couple of weeks. It's been nice," I said. "Are things okay with you and Dave?"

"Oh yeah, we got things out in the open. Then we were okay. It's good to have friends who'll call you on your shit."

"Good."

"How are you feeling about this book?" he asked me.

"I'm feeling okay about it," I lied. "You know me, I'll pull something out of my ass. I'm a champion ass-puller."

Geoff laughed. "Well, I'm looking forward to reading it. I think it'll turn out just fine."

"Thanks."

"It's been fun. A lot of interesting places, and it was nice to get out of Vancouver. Gives you perspective."

"Yeah. I can't believe we drove forty-two hours straight. For some reason, I feel extraordinarily proud that we managed to make it here."

"We were determined—"

"We've still got it."

"Right."

"It Must Have Been Love" by Roxette was playing on the casino sound system, a piece of lachrymose soft rock from Sweden that perfectly captured the peculiar, pungent sadness I felt about my friend going home. It wasn't as though I wouldn't be back in Vancouver in another week. Yet, I was sad. I hiked my thumb into the air, as though pointing to the music.

"I wrote this song for you."

After delivering Geoff to the airport, the three of us spent the afternoon walking around Vegas and drinking thirty-six-ounce margaritas for a buck and a quarter. We played nickel slots at Circus Circus. At around eight, I ended up back at the motel, where I finally slept. I passed out for twelve hours, waking only briefly when Dave and Mark returned to the room at four in the morning. Their only-in-Vegas night out had involved, in no particular order, mud wrestling, go-go dancers, Dave singing Devo at karaoke, a hooker who tried to tempt them with a twofer rate out by the pool, an all-you-can-eat barbecue, a guy who offered to loan them his girlfriend. I was glad to have slept through it.

By the time we checked out, I was feeling much better. I approached the front desk with our room cards. The homicidal dude who'd checked us in was at the desk again, and the corners of his mouth dropped when he saw me. He took the room cards and ran our room through his computer.

"I would shoot myself," he said, *"if I could play blackjack in the after-life. My savior, unfortunately, doesn't make those types of promises.* Do you want to charge this room to your credit card, *fuck-boy?"*

I could no longer help feeling that the deep, bowel-impacted loathing in his squint was directed solely at me. I replied in kind: "Is it all right if *you remove your thumb from your tushie and* I pay with traveler's checks?"

He canceled the credit card deposit slip and gave me a pen to validate the traveler's checks. *"When you were sleeping I entered your room and defiled myself all over your feet,"* he said with a brisk, tight smile. "Thanks very much and have a good trip back."

CHAPTER

TWENTY-FOUR

WE LEFT VEGAS around noon. The dirt devils prowled across the Mojave Desert as we drove out; past them, in the distance, lay puddles of silvery water. We filled up at Barstow, where our lives were profoundly, irrevocably altered after seeing the world's biggest thermometer. Well—it *was* a big-assed thermometer.

We were listening to *Zuma* with California on our minds. However much it really matters, *Zuma* is not just my favorite Neil Young album but my favorite album of all time. I acknowledge those who claim *Tonight's the Night* as Young's greatest achievement, his most unflinching, raw, nakedly despairing work—his own ragged truth taken to its uttermost—but it's like formalwear: only for special occasions. *Zuma* is, in contrast, like a cherished flannel shirt: it can be worn anywhere, anytime. The album ranks as my favorite because it's rare that a couple of weeks pass when I don't listen to it.

In interviews before the album appeared, Young had originally spoken of an album about time travel and lost civilizations. This idea was scotched for a collection of fuzzed-out guitar songs like "Don't Cry No Tears" and "Stupid Girl" and wistful ballads like "Pardon My Heart" and the CSNY outtake "Through My Sails." Recorded in a rented Malibu house, *Zuma* marks the end of the period chronicled in the Ditch Trilogy. Not that there aren't any notes of darkness. "Danger Bird" recounts a tale of soured love and infidelity at a dirge-like tempo. Young lends some confusion to the song by throwing in two different sets of lyrics for the chorus, the first-person accusations of a wronged lover merging with the cryptic third-person account of a man who "cracked...long ago in the museum with his friends." The verses are about the symbol-freighted danger bird itself. For this allegorical creature, the freedom of flight has become a millstone, as his wings "have turned to stone." In his solos, Young's guitar squawks like a scavenger bird circling the meat of a dead love. If *Zuma* is, as Jimmy McDonough put it, "daybreak hitting the water," then the darker songs like "Danger Bird" and "Cortez the Killer" lend it gravitas.

On the whole, however, the mood of the album is one of exuberant melancholy. The opening track, "Don't Cry No Tears," is addressed to a tearful ex-lover, presumably girlfriend Carrie Snodgress—but coming after three self-lacerating albums it also could also be mistaken for a pledge by Young not to bum everyone out. By the time *Zuma* was recorded, Young seems to have traced his problems to the fairer sex and joyously sends women on the road in rocking kiss-off anthems like "Stupid Girl" and "Drive Back" (yet another driving song). "Lookin' for a Love" shows Young in a more tender, optimistic mode, with the male bravado rolled back. "Lookin' for a love that's right for me, I don't know how long it's going to be," he sings. "But I hope I treat her kind, and don't mess with her mind, when she starts to see the darker side of me."

The reformed Crazy Horse on this album sees Frank Sampedro replacing Danny Whitten, and Whitten's funky white soul is replaced by Sampedro's earthier, bottom-heavy playing. Young's guitar sound in "Don't Cry No Tears" and "Cortez the Killer" has a tube-distorted sweetness, and his playing has moved beyond the piercing one-note riffs and bent-note shrieks of his first few albums to more melodic lines that draw on his earlier years of playing guitar instrumentals. One is practically bathed in guitar listening to "Barstool Blues," a drunken, mid-tempo soliloquy: "If I could hold on to just one thought, for long enough to know / Why my mind is moving so fast, and the conversation is slow." Young apparently wrote this song after a night at the bar, and his repetitive mutterings clutch the threads of coherence long enough to tug at truth. Noting how self-deception and desire feed on each other, Young sings: "I have seen you in the movies, and in those magazines at night / I saw you on the barstool when you held that glass so tight." The song's soaring guitar solo seems to suggest the hope and, in its weeping vibrato, the eventual disappointment of barstool yearning.

The album's masterpiece has to be the epic "Cortez the Killer," a guitar classic noted for Young's sad, aching solos, and the one song remaining from his original concept for the album. There's an obvious duality here between Cortez's rapaciousness, "with his galleons and guns," and the paradise of the Aztec world, where "hate was just a legend, and war was never known." And yet there's also beauty in Cortez, as he comes "dancing across the water," or at least there's beauty in his voyage. Young is so confident of his ability to place the listener in his own cluttered mind that he abruptly shifts the song to first person, becoming Cortez and turning him into a lovesick Ulysses in the final verse: "And I know she's living there, and she loves me to this day / I still can't remember when or how I lost my way."

Young identifies with the conquerer and the journey he takes because he knows that to find someplace new, you have to first get lost. The act of discovery requires a loss of innocence—like leaving in "Sugar Mountain" or giving up the illusion of a perfect love—but it's necessary, and not only because that's the nature of things. To fully appreciate paradise, Young seems to be singing, to fully experience the condition of blissful torment in which paradise is lamented, you first have to see paradise burn.

AFTER STEPHEN STILLS'S ARRIVAL in Los Angeles in 1965, his early collaborators included a friend from Greenwich Village, Peter Thorkelson, in a duo called Three Gorillas Minus One Buffalo Fish, and a former child star and aspiring lyricist named Van Dyke Parks, who'd soon be writing lyrics for the Beach Boys. Stills befriended Dickie Davis, the stage manager of a popular club called the Troubador, and Barry Friedman, a former clown and fire-eater turned publicist. But, still, he had no band.

In September of that year, Stills came across a casting call in *Variety:* "Madness!!! Auditions—Folk & Roll Musicians—Singers for acting roles in new TV series. Running parts for four insane boys, age 17–21." Years later, Stills would continue to tell any interviewer who asked that he wouldn't have accepted a place in the Monkees if he'd known he wouldn't be able to perform his own music. And while he was reportedly turned down for his bad teeth and thinning hair, the friend Stills had recommended to the show's producers—Peter Thorkelson, under his nom de rock, Peter Tork— would make the cut.

Having bought Stills's story about the great band he was playing in, Richie Furay arrived from New York that winter to discover the band consisted of the two of them. Yet Furay saw enough potential in Stills's songwriting to stay. They learned each other's songs, including Furay's version of "Clancy." Stills was unable to make contact with Young early in 1966, while the Mynah Birds were still in flight, but he was able to sweet-talk Young's old bandmate, Ken Koblun, away from his steady gig as the bassist for the folk group Three's a Crowd. Having seen Stills's unformed group and been quickly disabused of any notions of stardom, Koblun flew back to Toronto and the security of his old job.

Young was on his way to California. He, Bruce Palmer, and Judy Mack arrived in L.A. on April Fool's Day, 1966. Mack almost immediately called home for money and returned to Canada by bus. Young and Palmer slept in their hearse for a few nights before briefly crashing with a folksinger Young knew from the Winnipeg 4-D. They used their hearse as a limousine and chauffeured people around the Sunset Strip. Young was hoping to find Stills, but he had no address.

It is fitting that the pivotal moment of Young's career was spurred not only by a car, but by Young's unique taste for hearses. On April 6, after five days of asking around, Young and Palmer planned to go look for Stills in San Francisco, where his mother lived. According to everyone involved, Stills, Furay, and Friedman were in a white van on Sunset Boulevard, stuck in traffic. Someone—depending on whom you ask, it could've been any of the three men in the van—noticed a black hearse with Canadian license plates going in the opposite direction. There was some screaming before Young noticed Stills at the window. They pulled over and continued their reunion in a parking lot.

Soon, Stills and Furay were playing their electrified version of "Clancy" for Young. Given the accidental nature of the band's formation, it was suitable that the name of their group came to them offhandedly and with little deliberation. "They were resurfacing Fountain Avenue," Friedman told John Einarson in *For What It's Worth: The Story of Buffalo Springfield,* "and we pulled up in front of the house behind a steamroller. It had a sign on the back that said 'Buffalo Springfield'. We said, 'That's it.' So we took the sign off the back of the steamroller and took it into the house, stuck it on the wall, and that was that." Friedman became the band's de facto first manager and was a big help to the band early on, letting them stay at his place, finding them the right contacts, including the managers of the Byrds, and landing them a drummer named Dewey Martin. Martin was another Canadian, born in Chesterville, Ontario, in 1940. Several years older than the other guys, the new drummer was a seasoned pro who had toured with Patsy Cline, the Everly Brothers, and one of Young's idols, Roy Orbison.

Buffalo Springfield debuted at the Troubador on April 11, five days after Young's hearse was spotted on the Strip. This was their first show, not, as long claimed, their opening slot for the Byrds on April 15 at the Swing Auditorium in San Bernardino. Later that month, they opened for the Byrds at a dozen shows in the Los Angeles area and up the coast. Though they were still sharing rooms in a motel and living on hot dogs, the band would pile themselves and their gear into Young's hearse, drive to the office of the Byrds' management, and take the Byrds' limousine to their concerts. "One day," Young recalled, "we got into the hearse and the back end fell out. It needed a U-joint, but we couldn't find one so we just left it there."

About three weeks later, Scott Young got a call from the Ontario Provincial Police, following up on an enquiry from California state troopers about an abandoned hearse that was registered to his address. "At the time of the phone call," the elder Young would recall in *Neil and Me,* "I still didn't know for sure whether Neil was in Los Angeles, whether he owned the hearse when it was abandoned, or *anything.*" His son would call a few weeks later: "Didn't want to call until I was sure this is real, but it's looking good, Dad. Got a group and the managers have a place for us to live and cars for us to drive around in. (Laugh) No money to spend, but everything else is great. Best of all, we're doing our own material."

"CITY IN THE SMOG, city in the smog," Young sings in "L.A.," on *Time Fades Away,* "Don't you wish that you could be here, too?" While Los Angeles is where Young got his start and his first taste of fame, it's also the source of his most apocalyptic work. There's a verse in "L.A." in which he sings of meeting a lover, "when the suppers are planned and the freeways are crammed / And the mountains erupt and the valley is sucked / Into cracks in the earth."

In "Revolution Blues," Young does a convincing job of impersonating Charles Manson (an acquaintance whose brimstone charisma he initially found appealing enough to recommend to his record company): "Well, I hear that Laurel Canyon is full of famous stars, but I hate them worse than lepers and I'll kill them in their cars." (Years later, in jail, Manson would have few good words for the celebrities he mixed with—except for Young, who had bought him a motorcycle.)

We arrived in Los Angeles late in the afternoon, through its dense mesh of highways. Though we weren't in a hearse, we found Sunset Boulevard and cruised past the shops, dingy motels, and bars of the Strip, gawking at the expensive rides, until we found the Whisky a Go-Go. I'd been told that the Whisky was nothing like it used to be back when Buffalo Springfield played, that it was now mostly for hard-rock bands. The club hadn't yet opened for the evening, but there was music playing inside. The doors were unlocked, and I stepped inside. On a small stage to the side, I watched a Caribbean rap group run through a sound check. A small taste of the club was all I needed.

Dave, Mark, and I found a pizza place on the Strip with a banner that advertised two-for-one New York pizza and ninety-nine-cent beers. We each ordered a small pizza and the beer special.

"You can't have the beer special with whole pizzas," the waitress said. Her blonde hair was tied into a ponytail, and her face glistened with moisturizer. "You can only get it with slices."

We decided to get a couple of slices each.

"But the two-for-one rate doesn't apply if you also get the ninety-nine-cent beer."

"Okay, sure," Dave said.

I'd been paying enough attention to news back home to know that the World Cup hockey final between Canada and Finland was taking place, and when our pizza and beer arrived, we asked the waitress to switch the channel from the televised poker that was on.

"I need to talk to my manager first," she told us. She pointed to a burly man on the street talking to friends. "He's outside smoking."

She picked up a phone behind the counter, and we watched as the man outside answered his cell phone. After they spoke, the waitress pulled out a remote control and switched the channel. I left my friends there watching hockey with their frosty beers and wandered down the block to meet Ian Rosen, an L.A.-area Rustie whom I'd arranged by phone to meet in front of the Whisky. Rosen works as a children's librarian, and he speaks with a gentle singsong cadence.

"I think the scene is a lot more splintered now," Ian told me as we stood outside the club. "There's a lot more cliques, different people who like different music. It's not the unified movement it used to be. And it's a lot more fashion-conscious"—I would say that Comanche war shirts and buckskin jackets belonged to an era in a fashion coma—"than it used to be. People are more jaded now. It doesn't have the same grassroots quality as it used to have. I think MTV has co-opted anything that's interesting and made it more mainstream. And the Sunset Strip is a really good example of that."

The Whisky a Go-Go opened in 1964 in a renovated bank building under the management of a former Chicago policeman. At the time, clubs, all-night restaurants, boutiques, and health-food stores had followed the young people to the newly formed mecca of youth culture. The leading groups on the Strip were the Doors, Love, and Iron Butterfly. As a man with long hair, Young would run into trouble from hostile police. He was taken to the station for a few unpaid parking tickets and roughed up by a cop whom he'd lipped off. In November 1966, Stephen Stills was inspired to write his classic "For What It's Worth (Stop, Hey What's That Sound?)" by the unnecessary brutality of L.A. police enforcing a ten o'clock curfew.

After a recommendation from the Byrds' Chris Hillman, Buffalo Springfield played their first show at the Whisky on May 2, 1966, and they would become the club's house band for six weeks. With go-go dancers flailing around, the Springfield opened for the Doors, Love, Captain Beefheart, and the Grass Roots. According to music historians, Buffalo Springfield played with an intensity never equaled on their studio recordings. Furay was the band's front man, prancing around onstage like Mick Jagger. At opposite ends of the stage, trying to out-duel each other on guitar, were Stills and Young, who was still content to be only a songwriter and lead guitarist. Palmer, the mysterious musician's musician, remained in the background, with his back to the audience, facing drummer Dewey Martin, who'd sing on the band's cover of Wilson Pickett's "In the Midnight Hour." The shows sold out, with lineups going around the block. The band adopted a Wild West image, in keeping with the "Buffalo" in their name. With the $125 a week he earned at the Whisky, Young bought his first fringed jacket and was known early on as "Neil the Indian." Blond-haired Stills was the cowboy in his Stetson and jeans.

The outfits and the music were enough for the band to win the attention of women. Young's song "Mr. Soul," written in the fall of 1966, was "respectfully dedicated to the ladies of the Whisky a Go-Go and the women of Hollywood." The song, propelled by a riff that resembles the Rolling Stones' "Satisfaction," touches on Young's displeasure with fame, in lines about how his "head is the event of the season" and "the clown who is sick does the trick of disaster." It's also about opinionated female fans who flummoxed Young with their attentions and misconceptions of him, when "any girl in the world could have easily known me better." Yet in his oblique lyrics, Young isn't so much trying to be known better as to jam the signal. "Mr. Soul" might be one of the earliest examples of how Young's reluctance to offer himself for mass consumption becomes itself an offering—a teasing fan dance for his fans.

On July 25, about a month after their engagement at the Whisky, Buffalo Springfield would play in front of nineteen thousand people at the Hollywood Bowl as the warm-up act for the Rolling Stones. The band fired their unofficial manager, Friedman, and replaced him with Sonny and Cher's managers, Charlie Greene and Brian Stone, whom they went with, in large part, for the posh limousine the managing team rode in. Soon the band began courting record offers, eventually going to the highest bidder, Atco.

(Like Colin Kerr with the Mynah Birds, Greene and Stone were creative in their attempt to get the new band noticed. In one famous instance, they sent a young woman to seduce David Crosby, a notorious poonhound. As a member of the Byrds, Crosby had recently toured Europe, where he'd met the Beatles and been given an advance copy of "A Day in the Life." When Crosby woke up the next day, both the woman and his Beatles tape were gone. A local radio station, KHJ, was already playing the song alongside the songs of Buffalo Springfield, whom they agreed to promote in exchange for the scoop.)

Buffalo Springfield would produce three albums, plus a legendary non-release called *Stampede*. Their efforts would yield only one top-ten single, Stills's "For What It's Worth." Young produced a handful of gems, including "Clancy," "Mr. Soul," and the stoner classic "Flying on the Ground Is Wrong." Young's "Expecting to Fly" was a breathtakingly lush orchestral number produced by composer-arranger Jack Nitzsche, an early champion of Neil's work and the producer of his first album.

Young and his bandmates were overwhelmed with free love, and the band became teen-magazine heartthrobs. When interviewed by *TeenSet* in April 1968, Young offered readers tips on wooing him: this man needed not a maid, but a human day-planner—or maybe a personal assistant. "I don't think I'll ever be organized until I get married," Young said. "Then I'd have someone to keep me organized...you know, regular meals, making sure I get a piano when I need it...that sort of thing. I'd like to marry a girl who likes and understands my music but doesn't keep telling me how groovy it is, you know? I don't know if I'll ever find someone like that, but I guess it won't be too terrible if I don't."

And yet Buffalo Springfield would never live up to their hype. Their greenhorned decision to use Stone and Greene as producers of their first album resulted in a work the group disliked. Palmer's deportations for marijuana possession set in motion a revolving door of bassists, including Jim Messina and, once more, Ken Koblun. The engorged egos of certain band members, addled by drugs and the attentions of worshipful groupies, would also get in the way. Young and Stills battled for control of the band using their favorite weapons: Stills was brash and obnoxious about his ambition; Young, who soon became adamant about singing his own material, would deal with conflicts by withdrawing.

In the fall of 1966, Young's epilepsy began to worsen, resulting in grand mal seizures during which he'd convulse and go unconscious. (Some critics have suggested Young's convulsions were an influence on his herky-jerky guitar leads.) When he blacked out onstage, many fans thought it was part of the act. Some of his bandmates harbored the same suspicion. "We thought he used to stage some of those whenever there was a good-looking girl in the audience," Dewey Martin told John Einarson. "And he'd end up with his head in her lap and a wet cloth on his head, the girl wiping his brow." Years later, in *Shakey*, Young would admit that some of his seizures were indeed faked: "I would think I was gonna have one, and then I'd get myself kinda into havin' one—'Oh, I'm gonna have one'—and then I wouldn't...the seizures were an escape hatch." Young did manage to get his epilepsy under control and hasn't had a seizure in over thirty years.

Rather than ceding control of Buffalo Springfield, Young was willing to sabotage its prospects. In 1967, he quit (briefly) before an appearance on *The Tonight Show* that could have made the band's career. Later, David Crosby would have to fill in for him at the Monterey Pop Festival. ("David Crosby did not replace Young at Monterey," I was told by Einarson, who is also the author of *Mr. Tambourine Man: The Life and Legacy of the Byrds' Gene Clark*. "Doug Hastings from the Daily Flash replaced Neil a few weeks earlier. Crosby simply sat in with them at Monterey because they needed another voice—Hastings didn't sing, unlike Neil—and Richie Furay had a sore throat. It's a longtime myth that my Buffalo Springfield book dispels.") By the time the band played its final show on May 5, 1968, Young was angling for a way out. His move to secure

Elliot Roberts as his manager was a perfect demonstration of the sadistic cunning that would later characterize his artistic and business decisions. Roberts, newly hired as Buffalo Springfield's manager, was fired by Young for daring to play a round of golf. Then, a week later, at one in the morning, Young showed up at Roberts's house to tell him that he wanted Roberts to manage him as a solo artist instead.

"He's a really different character," John Einarson told me, speaking about how his portrayal of Neil Young changed between his book on the Squires and the one on Buffalo Springfield. "The Buffalo Springfield book, even though it's a companion piece to *Don't Be Denied,* is not as appealing a portrait of Neil Young. He was in and out of the band, he couldn't deal with the fame and success. And he couldn't deal with the fact that it wasn't his band. That was the problem from the beginning."

Over the years, Young's affection for Buffalo Springfield and his desire to revisit the past has competed with his control-freak tendencies. On the couple of occasions the group has come close to reuniting in public, including at the Rock and Roll Hall of Fame induction ceremony in 1997, each time it was Young's absence that killed the attempt. (On October 1, 2004, bassist Bruce Palmer would die of heart failure at the age of fifty-eight.) And yet, it was Young who was behind the handsome four-disc boxed set that was issued in 2001. "It's interesting to see how Neil has positioned himself as the leader of the band," Einarson told me about the boxed set. "His photo is first, his bio is first. He spearheaded the creation of the whole boxed set, paid for it. He's rewriting history a little bit there."

"Neil Young has made me a much more happy person," Ian Rosen was telling me as we joined my friends for a slice of pizza. "His music shows me what beauty life can be capable of. And I can't say that about many people."

I introduced Ian to Mark and Dave, who were on their third beers.

"Canada won the game," Mark told me. Poker was on the restaurant's TV again.

When our waitress came to the table, Mark and Dave ordered another round. "I forgot to tell you guys that there's a three-beer maximum on the special," the waitress said.

"I thought that was three drinks per slice," Dave said.

There was a pause; the waitress worked it out in her head. "Yeah, but you got the two-for-one special."

Dave looked puzzled. "But I thought we couldn't get the two-for-one special if we ordered the beer special."

"Let me call my manager."

I turned to Ian. "You just get whatever you want. I can expense it." Ian ordered a slice of pizza and a Coke, and we spoke about Neil and the Rusties I'd met until it was time for Dave, Mark, and me to find a place to camp by the beach. I settled the bill without closely examining it. I was outside before I realized we'd been charged for the fettucine that someone at the table next to us had been eating.

1

2

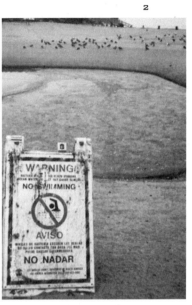

3

4

1 *Whisky a Go-Go on Sunset Boulevard. I had time for neither whiskey nor go-gos. Sigh.*

2 *This sign at Zuma warns you to beware of discarded breast implants and rhinoplasty leavings. (Photo courtesy of Dave Yellowlees.)*

3 *Zuma Beach, Malibu.* Zuma *is still my favorite Neil Young album, though the beach in September was a bit of a letdown.*

4 *Neil Young, the man, at Farm Aid 2004. (Photo courtesy of Paul Tomita.)*

\\|/

CHAPTER

TWENTY-FIVE

WINDING THROUGH BEL-AIR as it grew dark, we followed the street signs directing us to the Pacific Coast Highway and continued north. We couldn't find the campsite recommended in the guidebook, so Mark asked for directions at a gas station, and we found a campground north of Malibu. The idea was to spend the next day around Zuma Beach, for which we had high hopes.

We were drinking the beer that we'd bought in Ohio. Dave turned to me with a big, drunken smile. "So, Kev, what's it like to be single?"

I shrugged. "You wank a lot."

Dave laughed. "We *all* wank."

Mark nodded agreeably.

I tried to give a more thoughtful answer. "Well, I get to do what I want, and I don't have to answer to anyone. I like that. And every once in a while you meet a special, sleazy someone to make it worthwhile." I shrugged again. "I don't know how you guys do it. Sometimes I envy my friends for being such grown-ups, but I don't exactly want to trade lives with them. Anyway, I'm happy you're happy."

"I love you, too, Kevin."

"Thanks, Dave."

With a few beers left in the cooler, we just waited for our overpriced bundle of firewood to die before we went to sleep. We woke up late the next morning, packed the car, and turned south on the highway. Driving through Malibu in daylight for the first time, we ogled the gorgeous cliffside houses with their wall-sized panel windows overlooking the ocean. Young has lived in a number of Malibu places, including a house reputed to have been F. Scott Fitzgerald's hideaway for trysts. Zuma Beach was one of Los Angeles' largest public beaches, and I was carrying in my mind a verse from "Lookin' for a Love": "Where the sun hits the water, and the mountains meet the sand, there's a beach that I walk along sometimes / And maybe there I'll meet her, and we'll start to say 'hello' / And never stop to think of any other time."

Since we had arrived on a cloudy September morning, though, what we got was more *On the Beach* than *Zuma*. There was no one on Zuma Beach to start saying hello to, except perhaps the seagulls, who clustered peacefully as the gray waters of the Pacific Ocean lapped their feet. Signs warned us that swimming in the ocean could have harmful consequences, especially if we were pregnant. We spent maybe ten minutes walking along the cold sand.

Dave was driving. Before we headed back to Hollywood, I asked him to turn off the highway and take the exit to Topanga Canyon, listening to the album it inspired, *After the Gold Rush*. Originally inhabited by the Chumash people, Topanga was first homesteaded in 1865 and was a popular hunting destination at the turn of the past century. In the forties and fifties, jazz and folk musicians began to inhabit Topanga—including Woody Guthrie, who owned nine acres of property and wrote "This Land Is Your Land" while living there. In the late sixties, musicians residing in Topanga included Joni Mitchell, Stephen Stills, and David Briggs, Young's longtime collaborator. On March 20, 1968, a drug bust at Stills's ranch landed Young, Eric Clapton, and several others in jail.

Young had taken the advance for his first album and bought a house next door to actor Dean Stockwell. (One promotion for Young's first solo album offered free Topanga dirt; like the album, the promotion wasn't much of a success.) Around this time Stockwell was working on a script called *After the Gold Rush,* about an apocalyptic flood. Young would record his 1970 album of the same title in his house next door. While working on it, he kept himself happy with a marijuana-based delicacy called honey slides. In a widely bootlegged 1974 show from New York City's Bottom Line, he offered his recipe:

> [You use] poor grade marijuana, worse than you get on the street. And you take it and you get your old lady, you know, if you got one, to cook it up on the stove, you know, put that stuff in the grinder, get it real fine, in a frying pan, put it on the stove, turn the heat up a little, wait 'til the grass just starts to smoke, just a little bit, take it off the heat, don't want to burn it too much, then you take the honey, you know, get a half a glass of honey about this big—I hope you ladies are listening to the recipes tonight—just heat that honey up until it's slippery, you know, and mix that grass with it, you know the fine grass that you've cooked up just until it started to smoke and you took it off, mix those together and you get a spoon you know.
>
> I think you should eat it after that. Just eat a little of it, you know, maybe a spoonful or two, you'll be surprised, it just makes you feel fine. That cheap grass is great. You know, in these times, you have to think about prices and things like that.

After the Gold Rush is probably my second favorite album of all time. Young was living with his new wife, Susan Acevedo, and the album has a domesticity to it, in its spare production and in the songs themselves. You feel as though you've crawled into Neil Young's laundry hamper when you hear him singing, "I was thinking about what a friend had said, I was hoping it was a lie." "I Believe in You" is, like "A Man Needs A Maid" and "Everybody Knows This Is Nowhere," one of those Young songs with a deliciously double-edged title. You're in Young's head, repeating an old lover's quarrel, when he sings, "Now that you made yourself love me, do you think I can change it in a day? / How can I place you above me? Am I lying to you when I say, that I believe in you?" There's the folk-pop romanticism of "Tell Me Why" and the nursery-rhyme waltz of "Only Love Can Break Your Heart." Even the short songs that close out each side of the album—"Till the Morning Comes," a one-line tune, and "Cripple Creek Ferry," an evocative fragment set on a riverboat—are perfect miniatures, brilliant throwaways.

As we drove up the canyon, the Santa Monica Mountains bookended our view. "All in a dream, all in a dream," Young was cooing on the album's title track, "the loading had begun / They were flying Mother Nature's silver seed to a new home in the sun." As Young's extraterrestrial environmentalist classic played, the soft steep curves of the mountainside, covered with gray-green weeds, reminded me of an alien planet on the original *Star Trek* series.

On July 2, 1992, an article entitled "UFOs over Topanga" appeared in the *Messenger,* "the Santa Monica News and Arts Publication." A couple of weeks earlier, various people had called to report seeing intense white lights "traveling south-to-north very fast in a horizontal path." A couple from West Hollywood, who'd been out for a drive, showed up at the police station. "Officer," they said, "we were driving through the Canyon, where the Canyon gets deep, and we noticed a bright light in the sky." This light was following them. "Suddenly it was over us, we lost control of the car and it lifted us up in the sky, lifted us up off the ground." The couple lost consciousness for a couple of minutes, and when they woke up they were back on the ground. Realizing how farfetched the story was, they told the policeman that "we don't drink, don't take drugs and have no history of psychological problems." Perhaps, then, Neil Young wasn't *that* stoned. The article concluded with a quote from Preston Dennett, author of a book entitled *UFOs Over Topanga,* who estimated that this was "at least the sixth encounter in the Canyon."

Judging from all the health-food stores and restaurants we passed, Topanga still seemed to be occupied by hippies, albeit rich ones. An electric car whizzed by us as we wound slowly along Topanga Canyon Boulevard. Eccentric houses lay deep in their lots, hidden behind oak trees. One house used a railroad storage car as a bridge over the ditch running between the road and the property.

"I think Neil used to live on a street called Skyline Trail," I told Dave and Mark.

"I don't care," Dave said. "I'm starving."

"Well, there's that organic bakery down the road—"

"I think we passed a Taco Bell on our way here."

Dave turned the car around. After we'd eaten, Dave picked up a glossy real-estate listings magazine where we found a picture of Young's old house with the listing: "Musical History Echoes Through This House":

> Neil Young, Bernie Leadon & Patti Davis Lived here. As Patti said in her autobiography, there are so many windows it's like living outside. Every room in this house has a stunning view. There is a broad entertainment deck off the living room and dining room, and a short trail that leads to a lookout point with a big deck, hot tub, and a romantic hide-away you can sleep in. There is a two-room studio tucked in below the house where some incredible music has been written. It has a million-dollar view for only $899,000.

What a bargain. If every Rustie on the listserv put in three hundred bucks, we could buy the place and use it as a time-share. We'd each have a day every ten years.

We returned to Hollywood and found a room in a motel. By the afternoon it was hot and muggy, so we spent the afternoon watching HBO and drinking Mexican beer we'd bought at a supermarket across the street that had an amazing selection of chili peppers. That night, I was supposed to meet up with some friends who'd moved to L.A. from Vancouver and with another Rustie, Bob Lee. Mark decided to get some sleep, but Dave said he'd come along.

In the car, Dave slipped in some LL Cool J. As we drove down Sunset Boulevard, he turned up the volume until the car was rattling. "I've always wanted to listen to LL Cool J in Los Angeles," he said, yelling over the music.

The Cat and Fiddle was an English-themed pub and restaurant located at the end of a long and very non-English kind of courtyard. Bob, whom I'd met online, had suggested this place because the courtyard had been used in the filming of the video for "Over and Over" from *Ragged Glory*.

Dave and I stood at the bar with our beers, looking out for yet another stranger.

"He told me he looks like Stephen King," I said to Dave, scoping the room. "Do you see anyone like that?"

Dave pointed to someone who resembled the horror writer. "How about that guy?"

I looked at that guy and tried to make eye contact. He looked in my direction and I smiled. I felt kind of gay. It was at this moment that Bob Lee tapped me on the shoulder and introduced himself.

Bob is originally from New Jersey and, like Neil Young, an L.A. transplant. "One of the things that really influenced my life and made my decision to move out here a lot easier was that a lot of the bands I liked were from here," he said as we got talking. "From about sixteen on, I was really into everything I heard coming out of California and from SST"—a punk record label—"Black Flag and Hüsker Dü and the Minutemen."

Back in the 1970s, when punk rockers first emerged, Young's contemporaries poured scorn on them. "It's dumb," David Crosby told Rogan. "There is no New Wave. Punk is just people trying to get attention. They'll do anything to get attention if they figure they can win that way. . . I know that Devo is shit and Rickie Lee Jones is pretty good."

While never exactly a punk, Young himself was inspired by the movement's directness—its fierceness, its lack of polish, its irreverence. "The whole rock establishment, they're so carried away with themselves," he told journalist Mary Turner, "and now they're there and everything and it doesn't really mean anything anymore." New groups like Devo and the Ramones "are much more vital to my ears than what's been happening in the last four or five years."

"Did Neil attend a dozen punk shows? Study the complete oeuvre of the Germs?" Jimmy McDonough wrote. "I doubt it. But in a sidelong glance he got the picture: out with the old guard, in with the new. A bunch of upstart kids were spitting at rock dinosaurs, and Neil Young was the one elder reptile cheering them on."

Bob Lee was only a casual Neil Young fan until the release of *Weld* in 1991, which made him "a true fan and collector." He added: "When I think about what I want out of punk or why I got into punk, I was really interested in bands that were irresistibly their crazy-assed selves, a uniqueness of vision that had to be brought out regardless of commercial standing or accessibility to the public. When you think about it, that description applies to Neil Young, because if you take a cursory look at the guy's work, this isn't Jackson Browne we're talking about. I can't think of anybody whose records have veered so crazily from one sonic extreme to the other. I've never put on a Neil Young record and felt like he's trying to sell me what people are buying today."

Around this time, my friends Robyn and Sarah appeared. Robyn is a film student at USC and Sarah, who was originally from Los Angeles but moved to Vancouver as a teenager, is a registered nurse. While I spoke with Bob, my L.A. friends chatted with Dave. It turned out that the three of them had grown up in the same part of Vancouver.

Sarah squinted at Dave. "Did you have a goatee when you were younger? And work at a place called the Saskatchewan Restaurant?"

"How do you know?" Dave asked.

"You dated a friend of mine!"

Dave gasped. "I remember you. I snuck you into a club."

"It was the first time I was ever in a bar."

Dave asked about Sarah's friend from high school. "What ever became of her?"

"She's doing well. She's now dating women."

"I'm glad to hear that," Dave said, laughing. "I never got very far with her."

Originally, Bob and I had planned to visit the Studio Instrumental Rentals (SIR) rehearsal studio, where *Tonight's the Night* was recorded. But SIR had long since moved, to a location a few blocks away from us on Sunset. Neither of us knew where on Santa Monica Boulevard it used to be, and Bob needed to take back some fish and chips for his wife at home. Dave and I were still exhausted from the drive to Vegas. It had taken all our energy to get here, and now we were toe-tapping Los Angeles.

Though he now works full-time for a medical-device company, Bob still plays with a couple of local bands. In the past, he'd toured with punk bands like Clawhammer and with Minutemen bassist Mike Watt's solo band. Bob was in one of Watt's videos, and he told me that his claim to fame was an appearance on *Beavis and Butt-Head*.

"Watt recorded with a friend of mine in Vancouver last summer," Dave said to Bob. "My friend's band e-mailed him and Watt said he'd do it for the price of a plane ticket."

"Mike mentioned something about that to me," Bob said. "That story sounds familiar."

"They stopped him at customs because he didn't even bring a change of clothes. The only thing he brought was a toothbrush. 'I'm just a dirty punk rocker,' he said to the border guard, 'not a terrorist.' They eventually let him come through."

Mike Watt, Bob told us, was currently playing bass for Iggy and the Stooges, who'd recently reunited after thirty years.

I know this is a book about Neil Young, but to be honest, I was more excited to be talking with Bob about Iggy Pop. Not only had Bob seen the Stooges play, but he'd met Iggy backstage and nearly got a picture. I love Iggy, not only for his music and his persona, but because he answered a fan letter I wrote him when I was seventeen. His reply came a year after I'd written him, on hotel stationery from Munich. Iggy told me how much he still enjoyed skanky girls (he'd written about them, with respect and deep admiration, in an issue of *Sassy* magazine, and I'd asked him about it) and said he'd take another listen to *Raw Power* on CD. (I'd told him that it sounded a little brittle. A few years later, a remastered version of the album appeared; I'm not saying I had a hand in it, but I'm not saying I didn't.) I'd also sent him my band's sticker, and he told me that he was putting it on his suitcase.

"I'm glad my music makes you feel less dumb," Iggy wrote, "or at least distracts you from that condition."

Iggy Pop is definitely another of my rock 'n' roll heroes, someone I got into around the same time as Black Flag, Fugazi, Hüsker Dü, the Replacements, Led Zeppelin, Lou Reed, and Neil Young. At some point, all these bands fit together in my world. All of them made me feel less dumb, or at least distracted me from the condition. They answered every letter I sent them. They still do.

\\\|/

CHAPTER

TWENTY-SIX

WE LEFT L.A. late in the morning. The last twenty-something hours of our driving was going to be the most predictable. I'd gone up and down the I-5, which runs between California and Washington, maybe half a dozen times before, a few of those times with Dave. And, with the exception of Mt. Shasta in northern California, this big, multilaned highway bypasses anything remotely picturesque in favor of yellow fields and evergreens. Driving past farm equipment dealerships and huge billboards stuck in muddy cow patches—some, this time, in support of an anti–gay marriage initiative—you begin to daydream about how your next trip down the coast will be on the much more scenic Pacific Coast Highway. Of course you never take that trip, because the I-5 is ugly but fast.

Our businesslike mood suited the route. Our last night in Hollywood had been restful, and we were neither cranky with fatigue nor as excitable as we'd been earlier on. We embarked on this final leg of the journey as though we were cleaning up the morning after a party. With relief and a little sadness, we knew our adventures were almost behind us. There was one more stop—Farm Aid—and then we were done.

Somewhere north of Sacramento, we put on *Greendale,* Young's most recent album (also a film, a stage musical, a book, a model railroad set, and a website). Young has called *Greendale* a "musical novel": there are characters who cross over from one song to another, but unlike in a rock opera, Young sings all the parts, narrating mostly from a third-person perspective, even doing bits of dialogue. Greendale is a small fictional town in northern California not too different from the places we were now hurtling past. Cloaked from the highway by evergreens, these were communities with a Main Street, a couple of taverns, a hardware store, maybe a Chinese buffet.

Greendale's story concerns an extended family, the Greens, whose lives are changed when one of them, Jed, kills a policeman named Carmichael. In the *New York Observer,* Lucas Hanft described the Greens as a family who "have resigned themselves to pursuing a communal harmony solely within their family; they've realized that their old change-the-world psychosis can only be achieved in a vacuum." From his rocking chair, Grandpa Green, the family patriarch, offers his version of homespun wisdom, an ornery sentimentalism not unlike Young's: "It ain't an honor to be on TV / And it ain't a duty either / The only good thing about TV / Is shows like 'Leave It to Beaver.'" In the news-media frenzy following Jed's arrest, Grandpa dies of a heart attack. Sun Green, the youngest Green, is moved to action. She becomes an environmental activist, "a goddess in the planet wars," until FBI surveillance forces her to leave for Alaska to save "Mother Earth."

I'd heard bits and pieces of *Greendale* and found it underwhelming at first. Many of the songs are a little dull, full of heavy-handed symbolism, and Young overreaches by throwing together so many issues—environmental activism, anti-drug laws, tabloid media, the invasion of civil rights—only tenuously connecting them. And yet, for me, *Greendale* was a grower. I began to like its open sound, its raw and uncluttered production. Stripped of all frills to reveal Young's strange, sometimes awkward creations, the album is affecting because of the sincerity of—the determination behind—this mess, and how this messiness ultimately encapsulates the ideas and themes and humanity that run through Young's entire career.

If only by accident, Young's musical novel fulfills the standard set by John Irving: "A good novel is at once sophisticated in its understanding of human behavior and utterly rebellious in its response to the conventions of good taste." Young displays a deep sympathy for his fictional creations. "Carmichael," for instance, a song about the policeman killed by Jed Green, describes how, at the cop's funeral, his affair with a woman named Lenore is uncovered but not revealed to Carmichael's wife, who stands at the gravesite speaking to her dead husband about the time they met Wayne Newton.

I thought of what Geoff had said about *Greendale:* "It's like 'Powderfinger,' but over an entire album." He'd gotten tickets for Young's show in Vancouver earlier that year as a Christmas present and hadn't been sure what to expect. Young had played the entire album, Geoff told me, as his friends and family acted out the parts on crude sets. An even more crudely made video show played in the background. "Sarah hated it because it was so hokey," Geoff had said. "But Neil is hokey. That's what makes him Neil."

The critical reaction to *Greendale* was mixed. Most reviewers seemed intrigued enough by Young's audacious move into narrative to reach a "nice-try" or a "genius misfires" verdict, and many were willing to concede *Greendale* surpassed Young's previous album, the feeble *Are You Passionate?* Writing in *Salon,* Shannon Zimmerman placed it with *Re*Ac*Tor* and *Trans* as "one of Young's career-defying left turns, a screw-it-all foray into the man's wacky, fractured imagination."

The most scathing criticism of Young I'd seen recently was a Greendale tour concert review by Judith Lewis. In the fall of 2003, writing in *L.A. Weekly,* she railed against not so much *Greendale*'s lyrics or musicianship as its politics. She noted the irony—hypocrisy—of Young's performance of his environmentalist musical at an amphitheater that was raffling off a Humvee and lashed out at his audience for not recognizing the contradiction. Young's anti-corporate libertarianism—he is the man who once sang, "I ain't singing for Pepsi / I ain't singing for Coke / I don't sing for nobody / Makes me look like a joke"—was hard for Lewis to ingest when she saw a billboard appear onstage with the name of the show's sponsor, Clear Channel, and the slogan "Support Our War": "Enthusiastic cheers erupt from the crowd, and *Greendale* becomes a metaphor for all that's wrong with America." Ultimately, Lewis suggested "Young's politics, like most of the country's, are as incoherent as *Greendale*'s plotline."

Her argument is hard to refute. Young's politics *are* convoluted—his words not always reconciled with his actions, his iconoclasm supported by big record conglomerates. All I can say, in Neil's defense, is that political righteousness isn't an all-or-nothing deal dividing the world into eco-warriors and seal-hunters.

My favorite song from the album is "Bandit," the tune that best stands alone outside of the song cycle. The acoustic number begins with a rattling bass string; the kind of noise that other musicians might conscientiously wipe from their recordings is precisely the sound Young painstakingly embellishes. "The buzzing bass string in 'Bandit,'" noted novelist Madison Smartt Bell in the *New York Times,* "captures the unstrung quality of the mind of Earl Green." Earl, Sun's father, is a Vietnam vet whose paintings don't sell until the Devil (another character in Young's song cycle) cleans the vet's glasses.

"Bandit" is a soliloquy, a mumbled transcript of Earl's mumbling mind: "Wrappin' up dope in a paper bag, talkin' to yourself, takin' a drag / Who are you kidding / With what you say? / What does it matter? / They'll never hear it anyway." Spending the night in a motel, he comforts himself with the refrain "Someday, you'll find everything you're looking for." Young growls this line after the first two verses, going into his whiny falsetto halfway through the final two choruses. Amid Greendale's calls for political action and the machinations of its loopy narrative, Young manages to squeeze in another contrary voice: an achingly intimate song about someone gazing into his navel to find the comfort and the resolve to bear his wounds. When I hear a song this beautiful, I don't care about Neil Young's politics.

Dave, Mark, and I camped in southern Oregon on our second-to-last night, and the difference in climate between here and our last stop, Los Angeles—and the change in season from the beginning of our trip to its end—was hard not to notice. I was comfortable in my sleeping bag only after I'd put on my jacket. Mark slept soundly at the far end of the tent, in his sub-zero sleeping bag, which was made for snowstorms. The sleeping bag I'd brought had been scientifically designed to withstand basement rec-room temperatures and pillow fights. The next morning, I lay in the tent half-awake, too cold to get up. I'd just opened my eyes when Dave rolled over and smiled.

"Morning, gorgeous."

I yawned in his face: "Morning."

Dave put his arm around me. "You're my favorite to snuggle with, you know that?" Because our trip was almost over, we'd been getting all sentimental. "You put up a fight at first, but eventually you let me put my arm around you. Plus, you're warm."

I smiled; I love a compliment. "When we were in Toronto," I recalled, "you smelled like an orange grove. It was great."

"That was probably a good day."

IT WAS POURING RAIN. We stopped in Eugene, Oregon, where there is no sales tax, to do a little one-stop shopping at the Fred Meyer. We bought some chicken to grill on the hibachi; Mark, who'd left his hiking shoes in our motel parking lot in Vegas and was wearing his sandals, bought some new footwear; I picked up Kermit the Frog underwear and some cheap CD-RS. At Taco Bell, I stood in line for the restrooms with a woman wearing a Bush-Cheney button.

"Isn't Dick Cheney in town?" I asked. I'd seen local newspaper headlines about the vice-president's campaign stop in Eugene.

She lit up with a big smile. "My husband greeted him at the airport."

I nodded politely. She seemed like a perfectly decent conservative.

We crawled through Portland during rush hour. At this rate, we wouldn't be at our next Rust Fest until ten PM. I wasn't even sure there would be anyone still awake. By the time we approached Mike Heinz's house in Tacoma, it was black outside except for the streetlights and an orange glow coming from Mike's back yard. The rain had subsided— temporarily.

Mike was hosting a Rust Fest for fans from across the Pacific Northwest and the rest of the States who'd traveled to see Neil the next day at Farm Aid. We parked the car on the street and approached the light of the campfire and the sound of acoustic guitars. At the other end of the large back yard, half a dozen tents had been pitched. It was a Rustie shanty-town. Harry, the Seattle Rustie I'd met with Sharry at the beginning of the summer in Toronto, waved from beside the fire, where he sat strumming his guitar. Harry had just been to see Young play in Berkeley.

Rusties were catching up all around us. Most of them knew one another from other Pacific Northwest Rust Fests or the International Rust Fest. A guy named Kevin had come the farthest, all the way from Buffalo. We joked that we had taken the long cut to Tacoma, turning what would have been a three-hour drive from Vancouver into a 120-hour journey. A couple of people knew about our trip and had read my intermittent postings from the road.

There was a lot of music that night, some beer, and, as Young puts it in "Pocahontas," a pipe to share. For many of the Rusties here, it would be their first time attending Farm Aid, a benefit concert for family farmers normally held in the Midwest or the eastern U.S.

Jim Dickie, who'd grown up on a farm in New Brunswick, would be attending his first Farm Aid show. "I lived in eastern Washington," he said. Jim now lives just across the B.C.-Washington border in Blaine. "I drove through a gazillion miles of factory farms. Corporate farming is huge." He'd come down to Tacoma in his vintage Chevy van with his wife and has been a Neil Young fan for thirty-five years, and his favorite album is *Tonight's the Night*. "It's just the best—late at night. It's an album you can listen to by yourself, and with really close friends. It's not an album you play at a party." *Old Ways* is another favorite of his: "There's a song called 'My Boy,' about Neil's son Zeke. It's pretty special if you've got a boy. There's the song 'Bound for Glory,' about hitch-hiking the Trans-Canada Highway. I hitchhiked the Trans-Canada three times. It's not bad, as long you're not stuck in the north end of Ontario or anywhere east of Thunder Bay." When I asked Jim if being a Canadian living in the U.S. has affected his view of Young, he quickly shot me down. "Neil's just Neil."

Paul Tomita, a Seattle architect, has been a Neil Young fan since the early 1970s. His first Neil Young show was the one on the Rust Never

Sleeps tour at the St. Paul Civic Center. "Neil Young helped a lot when I was going through puberty," he told me with a laugh. *"Tonight's the Night* I put on whenever I got really down, and it helped me get through those times."

"By making you *downer?"*

"By making me realize it couldn't be that bad."

Mike Heinz and his wife, Margie, were being gallant hosts. Their back yard was overrun with Neil Young fans, many of them strangers, and yet Mike had a beatific expression on his face. His first Neil Young concert had been the famous four-hour CSNY show in Seattle on July 9, 1974; it was the first stop of the band's reunion tour, and they blew out their voices on the first show. Mike had seen Young play about thirty times since. When asked to choose, he said his favorite album was *Ragged Glory*. He quickly added: "I have to say *Harvest Moon* also has special significance to me. At certain points in your life, Neil's there and it just seems to click with what you're going through."

"Has Neil Young affected your outlook on life?" I asked him.

"I'd have to say yeah, because he dominates quite a bit of my life. His music is part of my soul."

"Come look at our home," Margie interjected. "Because we have more pictures of Neil in our house than we do of our children."

"Is that a bad thing?" Mike asked, laughing. "I don't think so."

I went inside to see for myself, and Mike's wife wasn't exaggerating by much. The pictures of Neil on their walls were interspersed with family portraits and photos of the kids. It was as though Neil was a favorite uncle who played guitar.

"I remember back in the early to mid-seventies, when friends of mine used to give me a hard time about Neil," Mike told me. "They would actually give me shit about Neil and his voice and one-note solos. But that's what I loved! For years, I thought I was alone. I knew I wasn't. There had to be others who felt the music the way I did." He looked around the yard full of Neil Young fans with his foot-wide grin. "I was right all along."

Around two in the morning, the rain started up again and we all crawled into our tents. By the time we were bundled inside, water had gotten through the tarp Mark had diligently laid under the tent and through my sleeping bag and clothes. I ran back outside, shrieking like a goatherder on the night of his arranged marriage. In the car, I started shivering. I turned on the engine periodically to run the heater and pulled my new Kermit the Frog underwear over my head to block the glare of the streetlights. An hour later, Mark came to the car soaking and took the seat next to mine. Dave slept, without incident, on an inexplicably dry patch of lawn.

CHAPTER

TWENTY-SEVEN

IN THE WEEK leading up to Farm Aid, Neil Young had done two other benefit concerts. On September 15, he'd played a set in Berkeley to benefit "an Oakland youth anti-violence program, a Bay Area youth program for Native Americans, and a Canadian 'conscious radio' network." And the night before Farm Aid, on September 17, Young had appeared onstage in Duncan, B.C., to support Randy Bachman's efforts to fight a pulp mill. Later that fall, he would play his annual benefit concert for the Bridge School and appear at a Los Angeles fund-raiser with Paul McCartney to support efforts to abolish land mines.

The benefit concert is one of rock's mixed blessings—an opportunity to support a good cause, but also an occasion for self-congratulation and group-hugging. At least, a benefit allows musicians to endorse a cause without writing a tedious song or album about it. Young's attempts at "message rock"—in songs about the environment ("Mother Earth" and "Be the Rain"), commercialism ("This Note's for You"), or racism ("Southern Man")—have yielded so-so results. "Southern Man" was a staple of CSNY sets and is a classic-rock chestnut, and "This Note's for You" began the second wind of Young's career in the late 1980s. Songs like "Mother Earth" and "Be the Rain," on the other hand, are flat-footed sermons only partially redeemed by the depth of Young's convictions.

"Respect Mother Earth and her giving ways," Young intones in the former, "or trade away our children's days."

The most spirited response to Young's politicizing came from southern rockers Lynyrd Skynyrd, who took issue with Young's white-liberal posturing in songs like "Southern Man" and "Alabama." "Well, I hope Neil Young will remember," Ronnie Van Zant sings on their spirited rebuke, "Sweet Home Alabama," "A southern man don't need him around anyhow."

(Evidently, the "feud" between Young and Skynyrd was lighthearted. Young loved the song, which appealed to his perverse sense of humor. And Ronnie Van Zant was such a big fan of Young's that he wore a *Tonight's the Night* shirt onstage and on the cover of Skynyrd's *Street Survivors* album. Young even offered Skynyrd a couple of his songs, including "Powderfinger," for them to record before Van Zant's death in a 1977 plane crash. A few weeks after the crash, Young paid tribute to him by playing a medley of "Alabama" and "Sweet Home Alabama" at a concert in Miami. It's been rumored that Van Zant was buried in his *Tonight's the Night* shirt.)

Farm Aid was conceived during the peak of the benefit concert craze in the mid-eighties, and with the exception of 1988, there's been a Farm Aid involving Willie Nelson, Young, and John Mellencamp every year since 1985. Farm Aid 2004 would be held at the White River Amphitheater on the Muckleshoot Indian Reservation, about a half-hour's drive east of Tacoma in Auburn, Washington. I wanted to arrive a few hours before the show to attend the press conference, so Dave and Mark dropped me off at the concert ground and then went for breakfast.

By the time I collected my credentials, an information package, and a loot bag—with family-farm products like raisins and chocolate soy milk, moisturizer and nail polish, as well as a glowing pen from the Muckleshoot Casino—all the seats in the longhouse-style conference room had been taken.

The audience sat facing two long tables—the first draped with a Farm Aid banner, the second on a platform—as a wild, weird assortment of people took their places onstage. There were rock stars, musicians in cowboy hats, the Reverend Jesse Jackson, organizers, sponsors, a cluster of tribal representatives festooned with headbands and bright feathers, and Dave Matthews. I had been hoping to meet up beforehand with Lou Cheffy, a Rustie from Florida who was taking photos for *Broken Arrow,* but I had no idea who to look for. I found a place to stand by one of the PA speakers, as close as I could get to the front of the room. Lou had been to the Farm Aid press conference the year before, and he'd told me that each person onstage would give a statement but there wouldn't be any opportunity to ask questions.

Young sat next to Willie Nelson, front-row center. His face was be-jowled, and his famous sideburns, now graying, looked more like strips of bacon than muttonchops. A floppy white safari hat shadowed his navy blue eyes. I knew I wasn't going to try to meet or speak with him, but it was scary enough to be fifteen feet away.

A tribal elder welcomed Farm Aid before the organization's executive director, Carolyn Mugar, made a statement. Farm Aid supports family farmers through financial and legal aid, but it also lobbies for fair farm and trade policies and provides information on the genetically modified food produced on corporate farms. Farm Aid president Willie Nelson spoke next about biodiesel, a less-polluting and renewable fuel made from vegetable oil that could be made by family farms, and even the old oil produced by fast-food outlets. A long, hooting round of applause came after his asser-tion of biodiesel's potential to reduce the country's dependence on foreign oil, one of several allusions he made to the Iraq War and the Bush admin-istration. (Later, Jesse Jackson would get a big laugh about the weight he'd lost on his "no-CARB" diet: "No Cheney, No Ashcroft, No Rumsfeld, No Bush.") Today's event was being powered by a biodiesel generator, as was, it had been recently reported, Young's newly retrofitted bus.

Young spoke after Nelson. "Thanks for coming to Farm Aid eighteen, I think—something like that, it's close," he joked. "It's too bad we're still doing this, even though it's great to see everybody. Just to put everything in perspective, we're being pretty upbeat, but how many family farms are we losing a week right now? Three hundred and thirty family farms a week are going down in America. The numbers keep changing, but it's accumulated, and it's had a huge effect on America and its roots. I just want to bring that up, just for a backdrop. Look, take an extra minute, try to find a market with a lot of local stuff or at least organic—something that sets it aside. That's usually where you find this kind of food that we're trying to get out there and support. Find the markets, get familiar with it. Life can be a lot more fun just by going out and meeting the people who grow the food. It's a huge country, a lot of people live in cities, and it's easy to lose touch with where everything's coming from. It's an education for you and your family—especially for your children." In the audience, I recognized Young's wife, Pegi, and his younger son Ben.

As Young extolled family and tradition, I was reminded of the traditionalism he espoused in his *Old Ways* period. And yet, as he continued with his brief statement, the different facets of his worldview came to light. Young went on an anti-government riff: "You see a lot of supermarket food and it doesn't tell you what it is. There's laws against having it labeled. The government does not want us to know where everything comes from and what's in everything."

Young seemed unfazed by the contradictions that biographers and critics see in his politics. After voicing this suspicion of the government's motives, he offered a lucid, if broad-reaching, explanation of the connections between personal decisions and world events. One's food choices, he suggested, are an expression of "a much greater struggle going on...It's control of what we're eating, how we're living, the information that we're using, and of our civil rights. All these things are tied together with the control of food markets worldwide, using food for power. Using food to control Third World countries, making them grow cash crops and selling them cheap food. Now we're supplying their food. That's what's happening around the world, and farmers are paying for it because our government wants to sell food so cheap that our farmers can't make any money at these prices."

Like Nelson, Young offered a slice of utopia in the form of biodiesel. "If you've got a diesel truck, if you're a farmer, give this stuff a try. If you've got a boat, it's perfect marine fuel. If you dump it in the water, nothing dies. If you dump it out on your lawn, nothing dies. You can put it right beside your house in a plastic tank—two hundred, three hundred gallons—and just fill it up yourself, if you don't have a gas station nearby. Willie and I do this all the time—we just feel good. We're not polluting." (Biodiesel's main drawback is that, without the established infrastructure of the fossil-fuel producers, it presently costs about twice as much as conventional diesel.)

The crowd that began applauding was obviously partisan, and it was hard for me not to get caught up. Here was somebody with lava in his belly, someone whose politics might not be entirely consistent but who was still pitching himself against complacency, who had buffeted his idealism with practical solutions and everyday choices. I bought it. Young was still my hero, even if I was well past the age for role models. And I was relieved.

"It's American-grown fuel," Young was saying into the cheers. "It doesn't damage anything. This is so obvious."

"Also, too, Neil," Willie Nelson quipped, "if you back it into the garage and leave the motor running and go to sleep, you'll just gain weight."

IT WAS NOW PAST NOON, and concert security staff were beginning to allow people through the gates. I ran into Dave and Mark out front, and we went back to the parking lot so I could drop off my tape recorder and the cumbersome man-purse in which it came. Dave and I already had tickets, but not Mark. The three of us pitched in and bought an extra ticket from a pack of Dave Matthews fans.

Lou Cheffy called my cell phone to say he was still in the conference room. The line at the gates now stretched back to the portable toilets by the parking lot.

"You go ahead," Dave urged me, taking a spot in line. "We'll see you inside."

"Should we choose a place to meet up?" I asked.

"Nah," Mark said. "We're tall."

Flashing my press pass at security, I returned to the conference room, which had been remade into a media center. By the entrance were sign-up sheets for fifteen-minute interviews with Steve Earle and Tegan and Sara. Farther back, on a long table, a dozen laptops hummed. At the other end of the room was a table full of bag lunches from Farm Aid sponsors. There were a couple dozen reporters and photographers picking at their lunches, loading film, scribbling notes.

"Lou!" I started screaming. "Lou!"

A man in a Farm Aid shirt from a couple years back waved me to his table. "Neil is, by far, my favorite performer, but I cannot tell you why," Lou had written in an e-mail. "I was not as exposed to the Dead, growing up in a very rural Ohio community. Lennon is great, as is Dylan, and I've thoroughly enjoyed the music of both, but there is no comparison to Neil for me. He is the rare artist that grows more and more on me every time I hear him. His lyrics are just accessible enough. We can relate to something in them, and yet they are so full of imagery and hard to interpret that we can all interpret them to fit our desired perception. His lyrics say what we want to hear, but we have no idea what the hell he is talking about."

Lou had come all the way from Florida, and he'd been to the show the night before in Duncan, he told me. In order to get here in time for the press conference, he'd taken a plane.

"What did Neil play?" I asked innocently.

"Same as Berkeley," he said, with a shrug, "but without 'Heart of Gold.'"

Rusties usually post set lists and concert reviews within hours of a performance, and they speak in a hyper-abbreviated language that takes for granted a pathological obsession with Neil. The scary thing was that I knew exactly what Lou was talking about. I had seen the set lists for Berkeley and Duncan already and read the Rustie reviews. I had become one of them.

It was Lou's first visit to the Pacific Northwest, and we were chatting about the Mariners game he was planning to see the next day when he was called away with the other photographers. I finished my lunch and walked around the concert grounds. The show had just begun, and lines had yet to form to the restroom doors. It had been some time since my last festival event—probably Lollapalooza 1992. The covered seating area of the open-air amphitheater was maybe a quarter full as the warm-up acts played. Attendants handed out flimsy plastic ponchos to those who were sitting on the damp lawn: men in cowboy hats and boots, middle-aged women in tie-dyes, vegan punk girls, bespectacled volunteers from the college radio station, guys in Harley Davidson T-shirts, clean-cut Dave Matthews fans.

The concession stands were doing good business, offering teriyaki chicken bowls, loose barbecue-pork sandwiches, and pretzels. Farm Aid T-shirts and jackets were also popular, bearing slogans like "Get Fresh with a Family Farmer!" and "Stop Factory Farms!" (written in white over a red stop-sign logo). The T-shirts were produced by American Apparel, a garment company based in Los Angeles that pays its workers a living wage—between thirteen and fifteen dollars an hour.

There were three beer gardens on the site, but, as Mark had suggested, it wasn't hard to find him and Dave. Under the tent of one garden, I spotted them towering over a group of female admirers. I'd brought them a baguette sandwich to share from the conference room, and they tore into it like a pair of hounds.

"So, you're the writer?" a woman named Lynn asked me.

"A poor miserable writer."

"Let me buy you a beer." Lynn said she was more of a jazz fan, though she did like Dave Matthews. She was here with her adult daughter and a few of her daughter's friends.

I started talking with a woman from Renton who'd been grabbing the asses of both Mark and Dave. "You should meet my friend," she said about another woman. Apparently the other woman's mother was a friend of Jean M. Auel, the author of *Clan of the Cave Bear.* "You should shake her hand, so the good luck rubs off on you for your next book."

The ass-grabber called over the friend who knew Jean M. Auel and I shook her hand. What harm could it do? I needed all the luck I could find.

I turned to Lynn's daughter, who wanted to know if I was going to interview Neil Young. Sipping the beer Lynn had bought me, I told her I had no plans to. "I wouldn't know what to say."

"You'll know," she replied. "I once played backgammon with Keith Richards."

"Wow." I mentioned seeing Mick Jagger's tiny outfits at the Hall of Fame in Cleveland. She nodded and made two circles with her thumbs and index fingers: "Keith's legs are like tent poles."

"How did you meet Keef?" I asked. She said she had a friend working at a Los Angeles hotel who knew the Stones had booked some rooms there. Lynn's daughter and another friend flew to L.A. and stayed there, too. She ran into Richards in the lobby, and he invited her to his room to play backgammon. "He was a perfect gentleman. We were listening to Howlin' Wolf in his room, and for every game I won, he would lean over and give me a peck on the cheek. I mean, rock stars are just people. That's all I'm saying. Just try talking to them. Look at me. I've done it."

"It helps to have boobs," Dave cracked.

"Well, yeah," Lynn's daughter admitted, laughing. "That's true."

\ | /

CHAPTER

TWENTY-EIGHT

I WAS IN AND OUT of the amphitheater for much of the afternoon and evening. Dave and I had seats in the lower bowl, but to the side and rear, by a cameraman on a crane. We had no idea where Mark was. Geoff had left a message on my phone. He'd been planning to come down to the concert with Sullivan, but he had caught Sully's cold, and both of them were laid up for the weekend.

The Rusties from the night before were clustered in the front rows, in the middle. I wandered over and was introduced to Karen Schwarz, who was from back east and had spent the week following Neil along the west coast, and Fred Tenisci, a Rustie from Trail, B.C., who had recently retired from railway work. I'd exchanged e-mails with both of them.

There was some fun onstage. Willie Nelson joined country band Trick Pony for a song. Lucinda Williams sang like a peroxide-streaked angel in denim. And I hadn't known how good Steve Earle was, especially his newer, more political work. There was a brash recklessness behind his songs against political injustice, a thoughtfulness and poetry that informed and elevated his polemics against imperialism. Before a song called "The Devil's Right Hand," Earle admitted that it wasn't originally intended as a gun-control song. But he'd changed his mind about the meaning, and he believed, he said, unlike the sitting president, that it was "a sign of strength to change your mind."

Though it should be admitted that I've never given him a fair chance, I fled the concert area as soon as Dave Matthews appeared. By the backstage entrance, I ran into two Rusties I'd met the night before, Cosmo Spada and Cathy Harris.

When I'd first introduced myself to Cosmo, he told me he had read—and enjoyed—my first book. Which was frankly dumbfounding, because *no one* has read my novel. Cosmo, a farmer, had come to the concert from Oregon. "Growing up on a family farm, I know how important it is to preserve a way of life. And I thoroughly support the mission of Farm Aid. If it goes the way it is, the family farm will be gone. It's about preserving a tradition. Neil Young likes the Old Ways, you know—values and traditions."

Cosmo was wearing a green baseball cap with "NY" on it.

Somebody passing by us was inspired to yell out: "Yankees suck!"

"But Neil Young doesn't!" Cosmo yelled back.

Cathy Harris was wearing a T-shirt with "More Barn!" written on it. The inspiration for the T-shirt was a story Graham Nash liked to tell about Neil: "I once went down to Neil's ranch and he rowed me out into the middle of the lake—putting my life in his hands once again. He waved at someone invisible and music started to play, in the countryside. I realized Neil had his house wired as the left speaker, and his barn wired as the right speaker. And Elliot Mazer, his engineer, said 'How is it?' And Neil shouted back: 'More Barn!'"

For many fans, Nash's anecdote is a perfect distillation of Young's music and personality: the volume, the pastoralism, the eccentricity, the humor, the intensity. The shirts—below "More Barn!" is a cartoon depicting Young and Nash in a rowboat—are produced and sold by Rusties, with the proceeds going to the Bridge School.

Cathy is originally from Texas, though she'd recently moved to Tallahassee, Florida, for a new job. Unlike a lot of people here, she was a Farm Aid veteran. "This is my sixth, but my fifth in a row." On her way back to Florida, she told me, she was going to stop in Dallas. "I'm gonna see my grandbabies and give them smooches. They start at twelve, then almost three, almost two, and two months." I loved the twang in her voice, especially when she said "grandbabies" and "smooches."

Dave Matthews had just ended his set when a woman approached Cosmo, Cathy, and me. She was in her early twenties, boyish with light-colored hair cut to her ears, wearing a red T-shirt with the comic-book hero Flash's insignia: a yellow lightning bolt on a white circle.

"I need to get a message to Dave," she told us.

Maybe she had seen my press pass or the backstage pass Cathy had gotten from a friend. Whatever the reason, the woman seemed to think that we, people who had stepped away from our seats to deliberately avoid Dave Matthews, were her key to the modern-rock star.

"I have a friend in a coma," she told us.

We started to explain, but she didn't seem to understand.

"It's actually a really sad story. He's been in a coma for six weeks."

"None of us knows Dave Matthews."

She was undeterred. "He fell off a scooter. The helmet he wore had been recalled in 1989."

"We'd like to help but—"

"And I know if I can get my message to Dave that this is going to choke him up."

It was getting cold by the time John Mellencamp began playing, and I was wearing only a thin jacket over my shirt. Deciding to conserve my energy for Neil, I watched Mellencamp perform on the closed-circuit TVs in the media center. I'd seen a VH-1 biography on him and knew about the massive heart attack that had prompted him to *cut down* his smoking. Mellencamp performed an acoustic set sitting in a chair, taking occasional drags from a cigarette; evidently he had chosen smoking over standing. During an extended solo, he got up and started shimmying to the fiddle. Then, twelve bars later, he sat right down again.

After Mellencamp's set, I returned to my seat. Outside the amphitheater a woman came toward me in a garish leather jacket with an American flag on the back. She stopped and, without pausing for introductions, started complaining to me.

"I paid one hundred bucks," she said, "and I didn't even get 'Jack & Diane.'"

"You came just to see the Cougar?" I asked, before willing the incredulity from my expression.

"Uh-huh. I've never seen him play before and I came all this way to see 'Jack & Diane.'"

I told her I was sorry. "At least he played 'Pink Houses.'"

"He could have played 'Cherry Bomb.'"

"The first CD I ever bought was *The Lonesome Jubilee*," I started saying, straining to commiserate. Actually, the first CD I bought was *Whitesnake*. "'Paper in Fire' is a great song—"

She had taken her moping elsewhere before I could finish.

THE CONCERT STAFF checked Dave's and my ticket stubs as we entered the lower bowl. Mark's ticket was for the upper bowl, but we were going to sneak him down. Harry, a veteran concert-goer, had told us about the art of "stubbing." Two people go into the lower bowl; one of them leaves with both ticket stubs and, using the second stub, returns with a third person. I gave my stub to Dave, and he went to town, stubbing not only Mark, who had been lingering in the beer garden, but Lynn's daughter and one of her friends.

Once Mellencamp's set was over, all the Rusties had risen to their feet, filling the center aisle and pressing toward the stage. A short video featuring Young and his involvement with Farm Aid was playing on monitors on either side of the stage. At the back of the platform were Young's pianos and a pipe organ that gave the stage a faintly churchlike atmosphere. In the middle of the stage half a dozen guitars stood circled reverently around a chair. Willie Nelson came out to introduce Young, who then appeared in his safari hat and a white jacket with Navajo-style designs. Picking up a guitar, he began thumping its strings with the heel of his palm.

"Aurora borealis, the icy sky at night," he started singing, as the crowd cheered in recognition. "Paddles cut the water, in a long and hurried flight." He continued thumping his guitar through the first verse of "Pocahontas," before he began strumming his twelve-string and the sound of paddling overtook the beating war drums; the Indians had escaped the marauders. This was only the fifth Neil Young concert I'd attended, and each time I quickly grew lightheaded, as though his voice picked me off the ground. I forgot how cold I was, and how tired I'd made myself. I broke out of my trance long enough to see everyone turned to the man onstage. Even the strange woman in the Flash T-shirt who'd wanted an audience with Dave Matthews: she was holding her cell phone up above her shoulder, as though flashing a badge, her gaze fixed on the stage. Together, we moved from herds of buffalo and slaughter on the open plains to a penthouse from which tiny taxis ran along our feet, and we ached for Pocahontas.

Young went next to another crowd-pleaser, "Harvest Moon." With its schmaltzy guitar opening, "Harvest Moon" was gassed by Jimmy McDonough as being "more synthetic–Neil Young than America's 'Horse with No Name.'" Maybe so, but you look at Young, and you see he's not so youthful, and you hear his voice crack as he sings about his love for his wife, and these objections seem trivial—an excess of good taste.

When the song had ended, Young told the audience that we could thank him in "a special way...just go and buy some food grown by family farms. Grown by some people and not by some factories. Grown by some families, not some board of directors. Grown by people living in a house, not at the top of a building in Chicago. Thank God for love."

As Neil sang "Journey Through the Past," his journey seemed more arduous than when he first recorded the song, his lament for the past deeper. And yet his performance of "On the Way Home" retained the song's misty-eyed optimism; he played it on piano, transforming a song recorded as a jaunty white-soul number with Buffalo Springfield into a reflective ballad. The tune is about the confusion that follows when stardom comes as quickly Young's did: "When the dream came, I held my breath with my eyes closed / I went insane, like a smoke ring day, when the wind blows." Now, when Young sang the line "Though we rush ahead to save our time, we are only what we feel," he seemed to be rushing because, in middle age, there's still much he wants to do.

Between songs, Neil repeated his pleas for the family farmer. At one point, tinkling the piano, he told the audience: "We live in a strange time, where people who speak their mind may alienate half the country. Even though some of us may say things, especially in this election year, that you may not agree with, it's because we have the right to speak our minds, and that's what makes America so great." He was likely alluding to his participation, later that year, in the Vote for Change tour, which was meant to target younger, unregistered voters, presumably Democrat, in swing states. Coming from someone who'd been so unapologetic about his political statements and beliefs, this comment was disarmingly humble. "If I say something in the next couple of months or do something that really aggravates you or makes you upset, don't take it out on Farm Aid. Don't give up on this."

Young went on to play "Cowgirl in the Sand," and on acoustic guitar the minor chord progression of the verse had a sinister snap. About this enigmatic song Young once said: "This is a song I wrote about beaches in Spain. I've never been to beaches in Spain." I had happened to be in southern Spain the year before, on an artist's residency, and I remember I heard the song in my head on a day trip along the coast. We'd gone to see a couple of Moorish outposts with views of the Mediterranean. The sea changed from an iridescent middle-blue in the afternoon to blue-purple early in the evening. As we drove, the color of the hills changed, from brown to a broccoli color and then to an almost-red. I realized now, singing along with Young, that I knew exactly what a "ruby in the dust" must look like.

"Don't Let It Bring You Down" came next, then "Birds" on piano, in the order they do on *After the Gold Rush*. For "Human Highway," Young brought out his wife, Pegi. "I come down from the misty mountain," Young sang. "I got lost on the human highway / Take my head refreshing fountain, take my eyes from what they've seen." Then he picked up his banjo and played "Old King," a song about his old dog Elvis. Earlier in the summer, I'd known there was too much Neil Young in my head when I was able to name five different dogs that he'd owned: Skippy (from Omemee), Winnipeg (on the cover of *Everybody Knows This Is Nowhere*), Art (who'd run onstage during the 1974 CSNY tour), Elvis, and his current dog Bear. During an instrumental passage, Young added a couple of convincing sniffs and woofs.

Young finished his set with "Four Strong Winds," the Ian and Sylvia song he used to listen to on the jukebox at Falcon Lake. "Four strong winds that blow lonely, seven seas that run high," Neil and Pegi sang, "All those things that don't change, come what may."

He was singing about inevitable things: things that don't change, things that gain truth with every passing year. In the song, fall would soon be winter. Before our eyes, on that cool September night, summer was turning to fall.

WE LEFT THE AMPHITHEATER after Willie Nelson's crowd-pleasing set and the all-star gospel rave-up that ended the evening. By the time we got to the rocky field where the car was parked, cars stretched along the road back to Tacoma. We got in line for the exit.

"Park the car again," Dave suggested after a few minutes. "I'm hungry."

"So?"

"Park the car," he repeated. "We're not going anywhere soon. Besides, what's the hurry?"

He was right; there was no hurry. I pulled out of line and turned off the engine. We still had chicken legs in the cooler and some barbecue sauce. Dave brought out the hibachi for one last meal. A security person on horseback approached our impromptu cookout, started laughing, and moved along.

"I'm going to miss you," Dave said.

"Thanks, Dave."

"I'm talking to the hibachi," he said, patting the hibachi lightly with his fingertips. "Maybe you were right in Ontario. Maybe it's more about hanging around you, Mark, and Geoff. But I do really miss this hibachi. If it had a tongue, I'd kiss it."

We watched the lot and concert grounds completely empty out. We were like the guys at the party who don't want the party to end.

It was around one in the morning by the time we left, and the roads were empty on our way back to Tacoma. We stopped by Mike and Margie's house to pick up our still-soaking tent. Our hosts had gone to bed, but there were Rusties still gathered around the fire. Of the six Farm Aid concerts she'd been to, Cathy claimed this was the best one. Cosmo's favorite part of Young's set was "Four Strong Winds." Paul's highlight was seeing Young and Steve Earle singing from the same mike. Dave and Mark had one last smoke before we started back home.

As we were leaving, Cathy approached me and put some money in my hand.

"Take it—it's a donation," she said. "So you can come to *irf.*"

"It's okay," I said. "I've got a wedding to attend in New Jersey next month. And I have to write this book."

"There's nothing in the world like *irf.*"

"Next year, I promise."

She reluctantly took back her money. I thanked her anyway.

"Does anyone want to drive?" I asked with a yawn. Sleeping in the car last night was finally catching up with me.

"Sorry," Mark said. "I'm stoned out of my mind."

"Me, too," said Dave.

It was pouring rain as I took the exit back to the 1-5. As we plowed through the storm, waves of water spouted from each side of the car. I clutched the steering wheel so tightly that my fingers went numb. Don't fall asleep, I told myself. Don't fall asleep.

We passed by the Tacoma Dome, which reminded Dave of the time he saw the Grateful Dead with his friend Tyler.

"Tyler had smuggled a quarter in his boot and we bought some acid in the parking lot that we forgot about until halfway through the show," he was saying. "The acid started working by the time the show was over. We went to the parking lot and sat there. We were really high. We were fucked up. The parking lot was emptying. A cop came up to us and told us to leave the parking lot. Tyler told him he was too high to move. The cop said we had to leave the parking lot anyway. So we drove onto the highway and got off at the first exit. We spent the night passed out in an alleyway."

"So. Not much has changed." I kept looking at the clock every five minutes, shaking my head quickly to stay alert. I was ready to pull into the nearest alleyway myself.

Dave laughed. "Not really."

"We don't do acid anymore."

"Yeah, that was a high-school drug."

Outside downtown Seattle, I saw a sign for an exit. "I'm going to pull over. I'm so sleepy, I might end up killing us."

"I'll drive," Dave said. "Why didn't you just let me drive in the first place?"

"I thought you said you were baked."

"So?" Dave looked at me and shook his head. "Since when has that ever bothered you?"

"Good point."

We switched over, and Dave turned us back onto the highway. It was quiet the rest of the way. Dave wanted to catch the early ferry home to Victoria, even if it meant waiting an hour at an empty terminal. Mark was going to crash at my place before heading to his parents' the next day. He wasn't sure whether he'd be taking a bus home to the Interior or snagging a ride from his folks, who were planning a wine tour of the Okanagan later that week.

I dozed off in the back seat. When I woke up, two hours had passed and we were already at the border. The Canada Customs official asked a couple of perfunctory questions before waving us through.

I'd fallen asleep many times on our trip, but I'd never been so disoriented. I felt the way I had as a ten-year-old when my brother and I accompanied my mother to her mah-jongg games, which always went late into the night. When her game ended, she would drag me and my brother from the couches we'd passed out on, pile us into the back seat of that car, and take us home. Slouched deep in the back seat of this car, absolutely wasted, I felt like a child again. I could hardly wait to grow up.

\ l /

A NOTE ON

SOURCES

THE TRIP I TOOK traced Neil Young's apprenticeship as a musician in Canada and the hearse trip he made to Los Angeles. Young's journey is detailed with great care and devotion by John Einarson in *Don't Be Denied,* an essential read for all fans interested in Neil's white-buck days. I would never have conceived of my book without first having read *Don't Be Denied.* John's book on Buffalo Springfield, *For What It's Worth,* co-written with Richie Furay, was also very helpful in my research on Young's early years with Buffalo Springfield.

Before the Gold Rush, Nicholas Jennings's intelligent and entertaining chronicle of the Yorkville coffeehouse scene, provided me with an illuminating overview of the freewheeling, often sublimely ridiculous world into which Young was briefly absorbed.

While writing about Young's childhood in Omemee, I turned to *Neil and Me* by Scott Young, a loving and affecting account of the changes and reversals that occur between a father and a son over a lifetime. As well, Scott's descriptions of the hand-to-mouth lifestyle of a freelance writer in *Neil and Me* and in his autobiography, *A Writer's Life,* were both fascinating and eerily familiar to me.

When writing about Young's work and life from the 1970s to the present day, I consulted Young's two major biographies: Jimmy McDonough's

Shakey and Johnny Rogan's *Zero to Sixty*. McDonough's book is Young's sort-of-authorized biography: there were legal firebombs exchanged before McDonough was allowed to publish this book. *Shakey* has a fair number of factual errors (Young, for instance, didn't stop in Ohio in 1966, though I did in 2004) that probably irk someone trying to write a book about Neil Young more than they would readers, who will enjoy McDonough's pistol-whipping prose and the pages of Young's own voice transcribed—including repetitive verbal tics like "heh heh" and "innaresting"—at length.

In contrast, *Zero to Sixty,* which was published in the U.K., is written with a more even-keeled, critical approach. (While its tone is dry, *Zero to Sixty* features the most, um, theatrical author photo I've ever seen in my life: Rogan is pictured bare-chested wearing only a dark, untrimmed, nipple-length beard. The author stares directly into the camera, his fingers splayed across the side of his face; the nails on his fingers are so long that they curl. In the jacket biography, readers are told that he works "in complete and extreme isolation, often writing for years through long nights without human interruption, usually in laborious longhand, after which he touch types thousands of pages and amended notes before moving on to the next project." Uh yeah, I do that, too.) Unlike McDonough, who writes with great passion and insight about Young's work with Crazy Horse and on *Tonight's the Night* but almost seems to wish a lobotomy on himself when discussing Young's work with Crosby, Stills, Nash, & Young and on *Harvest Moon,* Rogan doesn't skimp in his discussion of Young's less incendiary material. Meticulous and gracefully written, Rogan's book should appeal to readers who find McDonough's crash-and-burn style too intrusive.

I also read and deeply enjoyed Sylvie Simmons's concise and compact biography *Reflections In Broken Glass.* While not the most authoritative book on Young, Simmons's biography might be the wittiest. Simmons, for instance, writes of Young's "finger-jammed-in-a-live-wire one-note solos" and likens Nils Lofgren having to tune the guitar of a strung-out Danny Whitten to "the guitar player equivalent of having someone wipe your butt."

The route I've shown Neil Young taking from Toronto to Los Angeles in 1966, on the map at the front of this book, is based on biographical accounts. It remains unclear which roads Young and his friends drove to get from Sault Ste. Marie to St. Louis, where they entered Route 66, so I guessed.

The Neil Young song lyrics quoted throughout the book and the discography have been adapted from an internet song database found on Human Highway (http://human-highway.com), an invaluable research tool and source for Neil Young news. I also found interesting articles and hyperlinks on HyperRust Never Sleeps (http://hyperrust.org), Thrasher's Wheat (www.thrasherswheat.org), Sugar Mountain (http://members. cruzio.com/~tah/sugarmtn.html) and Traces, Michal's Neil Young site (www.angelfire.com/rock2/traces).

I took advantage of Sharry Wilson's collection of *Broken Arrow* fanzines, which are published by the Neil Young Appreciation Society (c/o Scott Sandie, NYAS, Meadowfield Court, South Street, Falkland, FIFE, KY15 7AT, Scotland. Website: www.nyas.org.uk/).

The scenes in this book with the people I met in Vancouver and on my trip are based on tape-recorded interviews. On a number of occasions, I've also quoted from e-mail interviews and exchanges, especially with Neil Young fans I befriended online. There are also several moments in the book—sometimes an entire scene, like my evening at the Sidebar in Cleveland—that have been re-created from memory.

Throughout my book, and especially when writing about my friends in the car, I've often shaped exchanges and bits of dialogue for clarity or comic hyperbole, and, in general, to suit my nefarious purposes.

PRIMARY

SOURCES

Einarson, John. *Neil Young: Don't Be Denied: The Canadian Years.* Kingston: Quarry Press, 1992.

Einarson, John, and Richie Furay. *For What It's Worth: The Story of Buffalo Springfield.* New York: Cooper Square Press, 2004.

Jennings, Nicholas. *Before the Gold Rush: Flashbacks to the Dawn of the Canadian Sound.* Toronto: Penguin Canada, 1997.

McDonough, Jimmy. *Shakey: Neil Young's Biography.* Toronto: Random House Canada, 2002.

Rogan, Johnny. *Neil Young: Zero to Sixty: A Critical Biography.* London: Calidore Books, 2001.

Simmons, Sylvie. *Neil Young: Reflections in Broken Glass.* Edinburgh: Mojo Books, 2001.

Young, Scott. *Neil and Me.* Toronto: McClelland & Stewart, 1997.

SOURCE NOTES

INTRODUCTION

4 *"That's my style"* Available online: www.canoe.ca/JamMusicPopEncycloPagesY/
young.html. Also confirmed by a Rust List member who has a tape of the recording
sessions.

5 *"Is it hard"* From "Tell Me Why" by Neil Young, on *After the Gold Rush* by Neil
Young (Reprise, 1970). Published by Broken Arrow Music.

5 *"Big birds"* From "Helpless" by Neil Young, on *Déjà Vu* by Crosby, Stills, Nash, &
Young (Atlantic, 1970). Published by Cotillion/Broken Arrow Music.

5 *"far richer and more complex ailment"* Thomas Pynchon, introduction to *The
Teachings of Don B.* (New York: Random House, 1992). (Also available online:
http://www.themodernword.com/pynchon/pynchon_essays_barthelme.html.)

7 *"Well, I keep gettin' younger"* From "Crime in the City" by Neil Young, on *Freedom*
by Neil Young (Reprise, 1989). Published by Silver Fiddle Music.

7 *reckless abandon* Jimmy McDonough, *Shakey: Neil Young's Biography* (Toronto:
Random House Canada, 2002), p. 95.

CHAPTER TWO

17 *"largest pants"* Nardwuar the Human Serviette, Gorbachev press conference,
March 28, 1993. Available online: http://nardwuar.com/vs/mikhail_gorbachev/
index.html.

17 *"On the Great Canadian Shield"* From "Winnipeg 64" by the Evaporators, on *I'm
Going to France* by the Evaporators (Nardwuar Records, 1993).

18 *Young having lunch downtown* Kerry Gold, "Interview hound on scent despite
Neil's 'never,'" *Vancouver Sun,* February 27, 1999, D2.

CHAPTER THREE

23 *"With your chrome heart"* From "Long May You Run" by Neil Young, on *Long May You Run* by the Stills-Young Band (Reprise, 1976). Published by Silver Fiddle Music.

23 *"When I came out"* London Times. Quoted in *Neil Young: Reflections in Broken Glass* by Sylvie Simmons (Edinburgh: Mojo Books, 2001), p. 169.

23 *"I'm an Aerostar"* From "I'm the Ocean" by Neil Young, on *Mirror Ball* by Neil Young (Reprise, 1995). Published by Silver Fiddle Music.

23 *"back in Blind River"* From "Long May You Run" by Neil Young, on *Long May You Run* by the Stills-Young Band (Reprise, 1976). Published by Silver Fiddle Music.

23 *"I can't believe a machine gun"* From "Driveby" by Neil Young, on *Sleeps With Angels* by Neil Young and Crazy Horse (Reprise: 1994). Published by Silver Fiddle Music.

24 *"And he left them lyin'"* From "Tired Eyes" by Neil Young, on *Tonight's the Night* by Neil Young (Reprise, 1975). Published by Silver Fiddle Music.

24 *"I had me a Buick"* From "Get Gone" by Neil Young, on *Lucky Thirteen* by Neil Young (Geffen, 1993). Published by Silver Fiddle Music.

24 *"Gettin' in an old black car"* From "Big Time" by Neil Young, on *Broken Arrow* by Neil Young and Crazy Horse (Reprise, 1996). Published by Silver Fiddle Music.

CHAPTER FOUR

34 *"Every time I think about"* From "Everybody Knows This Is Nowhere" by Neil Young, on *Everybody Knows This Is Nowhere* by Neil Young and Crazy Horse (Reprise, 1969). Published by Broken Arrow Music.

36 *"Hello, ruby in the dust"* From "Everybody Knows This Is Nowhere" by Neil Young, on *Everybody Knows This Is Nowhere* by Neil Young and Crazy Horse (Reprise, 1969). Published by Broken Arrow Music.

36 *"The longer I keep going"* Mary Turner, Warner Bros. Music Show radio interview, 1979. Quoted in *Neil Young: Reflections in Broken Glass* by Sylvie Simmons (Edinburgh: Mojo Books, 2001), p. 169.

CHAPTER FIVE

42 *"You knew that when you went out"* John Einarson, *Neil Young: Don't Be Denied: The Canadian Years.* (Kingston: Quarry Press, 1992), p. 97.

CHAPTER SIX

49 *"There was a time, sure"* Cameron Crowe, "Neil Young: The Last American Hero," *Rolling Stone,* February 8, 1979.

50 *"Think I'll pack it in"* From "Out on the Weekend" by Neil Young, on *Harvest* by Neil Young (Reprise, 1972). Published by Silver Fiddle Music.

50 *"I was thinking that maybe I'd get a maid"* From "A Man Needs a Maid" by Neil Young, on *Harvest* by Neil Young (Reprise, 1972). Published by Silver Fiddle Music.

51 *"without any irritable"* John Keats. Quoted in *A Poetry Handbook* by Mary Oliver (New York: Harcourt, 1995), p. 77. (Also available online: www.mrbauld.com%2Fnegcap.html.)

51 *"Neil Young is not one of those folks"* John Mendelssohn, review of *Harvest, Rolling Stone,* March 30, 1972.

51 *"Traveling there soon became a bore"* Neil Young, liner notes for *Decade* (Reprise, 1977).

51 *when Scott Young heard* McDonough, p. 370–71.

52 *"A few minutes later"* Cameron Crowe, "Neil Young: The Last American Hero," *Rolling Stone,* February 8, 1979.

52 *"Unlock the secrets"* From "Transformer Man" by Neil Young, on *Trans* by Neil Young (Geffen, 1982). Published by Silver Fiddle Music.

52 *"not commercial in nature"* The David Geffen Company v Neil Young, C 474373 filed November 4, 1983 in Superior Court of California, County of Los Angeles. Quoted in *Neil Young: Zero to Sixty: A Critical Biography* by Johnny Rogan (London: Calidore Books, 2001), p. 487.

53 *"They said"* Bill Flanagan, interview, *Musician,* 1985. Quoted in *Neil Young: Zero to Sixty,* p. 489.

53 *"People tell us that we play too loud"* From "Prisoners of Rock 'n' Roll" by Neil Young, on *Life* by Neil Young and Crazy Horse (Geffen, 1987). Published by Silver Fiddle Music.

55 *"embraced this marginalization"* Stephen Metcalf, "What's So Great About Wilco?" *Slate.com,* July 15, 2004. (Available online: http://slate.msn.com/id/2103887/.)

CHAPTER SEVEN

57 *"When I was a young boy"* From "Don't Be Denied" by Neil Young, on *Time Fades Away* (Reprise, 1973). Published by Silver Fiddle Music.

57 *"Sometimes I talk to Daddy"* From "Crime in the City (Sixty to Zero, Part One)" by Neil Young, on *Freedom* by Neil Young (Reprise, 1989). Published by Silver Fiddle Music.

58 *"Neil is the 'happy-go-lucky'"* Einarson, p. 33.

58 *"I knew when I was thirteen"* Einarson, p. 46.

58 *"Invariably the girls"* Einarson, pp. 44–45.

59 *"I guess I wanted to play hockey"* Einarson, p. 48.

59 *"drawing amplifiers"* Einarson, p. 53.

59 *"Exams must be upon you"* Letter from Scott Young. Quoted in McDonough, p. 100.

60 *"If she was dealing"* Rogan, p. 29.

61 *"People told me I couldn't sing"* Einarson, p. 76.

64 *"With its drab tarpapers"* Einarson, p. 84.

CHAPTER EIGHT

70 *left on his own* Einarson, pp. 25–27.

72 *"Go and give it a try"* Einarson, p. 92.

72 *"I received my different diplomas"* Broken Arrow 51, p. 47.

CHAPTER NINE

76 *"Memory will rust"* From "Left and Leaving" by John K. Samson, on *Left and Leaving* by the Weakerthans (G7 Welcoming Committee, 2000).

76 *"fiction and rock"* Carl Wilson, "Lit rock is on a roll," *Globe and Mail,* August 14, 2004, R1.

77 *"My city's still breathing"* From "Left and Leaving" by John K. Samson, on *Left and Leaving* by the Weakerthans (G7 Welcoming Committee, 2000).

CHAPTER TEN

82 *"When we got to Winnipeg"* From "Don't Be Denied" by Neil Young, on *Time Fades Away* by Neil Young (Reprise, 1973). Published by Silver Fiddle Music.

82 *"There was nothin' new"* McDonough, p. 62.

82 *named Gary Renzetti* McDonough, p. 62.

85 *"He was a kind of persecuted"* Einarson, p. 156.

CHAPTER ELEVEN

92 *"I used to listen to this song"* Bridge Show Benefit concert, bootleg recording, October 24, 2004.

93 *"Go to the country"* From "Here We Are in the Years" by Neil Young, on *Neil Young* by Neil Young (Reprise, 1969). Published by Broken Arrow Music.

95 *"One can hardly tell"* Einarson, p. 89.

95 *"You're a good guitar player"* McDonough, p. 93.

95 *"Well, I wonder"* From "Don't Cry No Tears" by Neil Young, on *Zuma* by Neil Young and Crazy Horse (Reprise, 1975). Published by Silver Fiddle Music.

95 *"I think he was afraid"* Einarson, p. 89.

95 *"You love me"* Einarson, p. 89.

95 *"Yeah. I'm sure"* McDonough, p. 92.

95 *"Well, I never cared too much"* From "I Wonder" by Neil Young, April 2, 1964 CKRC recording by Neil Young and the Squires (unreleased, 1964).

96 *"mom's biggest tool"* McDonough, pp. 84–85.

97 *"I wanted to play in a band"* Einarson, p. 97.

97 *"I'm not particularly worried"* Rogan, p. 33.

97 *"Because being the unknown"* McDonough, p. 107.

98 *"Well, hello lonely woman"* From "Hello Lonely Woman" by Neil Young. Originally performed by Neil Young and the Squires in 1964, this unreleased song was performed live by Neil Young on the 1987 and 1988 Bluenotes tours.

98 *"And the people would say"* Einarson, p. 102.

98 *"Farmer John, I'm in love"* From "Farmer John" by Don Harris and Terry Dewey, on *Ragged Glory* by Neil Young and Crazy Horse (Reprise, 1990).

98 *"one of my heroes"* John Irving. Quoted in "Artist Of The Year: Neil Young" by Greil Marcus, *Relix,* 1994.

98 *"Now you say you're leaving home"* From "Sugar Mountain" by Neil Young, on *Decade* by Neil Young (Reprise, 1977).

99 *"beauty plus pity"* Vladimir Nabokov, in *Lectures on Literature,* edited by Fredson Bowers (New York: Harvest Books, 2002), p. 243.

100 *"the day John Lennon"* Einarson, p. 121.

100 *"a great time"* Einarson, p. 124.

102 *"Look, when the hearse"* McDonough, p. 667.

102 *"Well, it was back"* From "Long May You Run" by Neil Young, on *Long May You Run* by the Stills-Young Band (Reprise, 1976). Published by Silver Fiddle Music.

102 *"I almost became that hearse"* Broken Arrow 51, p. 47.

CHAPTER TWELVE

109 *"She wore rose-colored glasses"* From "Tannis" by Brian Moniz, from an MP3 sent by e-mail.

CHAPTER THIRTEEN

118 *"member of the younger generation"* Scott Young, "The Hearse Dealer," *Globe and Mail,* June 15, 1965.

119 *"I think the problem was"* Einarson, p. 146.

120 *"Well, I'm up in T.O."* From "Ambulance Blues" by Neil Young, on *On the Beach* by Neil Young (Reprise, 1974). Published by Silver Fiddle Music.

CHAPTER FOURTEEN

126 *"Back in the old folky days"* From "Ambulance Blues" by Neil Young, on *On the Beach* by Neil Young (Reprise, 1974). Published by Silver Fiddle Music.

127 *Public Futilities* Rogan, p. 56.

127 *"Why don't you just pack"* Rogan, p. 57.

127 *"Who's that stomping"* From "Nowadays Clancy Can't Even Sing" by Neil Young, on *Buffalo Springfield* by Buffalo Springfield (Atco, 1966). Published by Springalo Toones—Warner Tamerlane.

129 *"It was like a hockey trade"* John Einarson and Richie Furay, *For What It's Worth: The Story of Buffalo Springfield* (New York: Cooper Square Press, 2004), p. 58.

130 *"He'd come into our dressing room"* Bruce Palmer. Quoted in *Neil and Me* by Scott Young (Toronto: McClelland & Stewart, 1997), p. 55.

130 *"I was so high"* Einarson, *Don't Be Denied,* p. 167.

130 *"we needed something"* Neil Young, to Cameron Crowe. Quoted in *Neil and Me* by Scott Young, p. 56.

CHAPTER FIFTEEN

136 *Ontario Agricultural College* Young, *Neil and Me*, p. 39.

137 *"Did you ever go into a shower"* McDonough, p. 568.

137 *"One week I'm a jerk"* Simmons, p. 127.

138 *"For years I've figured"* Xan Brooks, "The good, the bad and the Shakey," *Guardian,* September 17, 2003.

139 *"a schoolboy on good time"* From "Mellow My Mind" by Neil Young, on *Tonight's the Night* by Neil Young (Reprise, 1975). Published by Silver Fiddle Music.

139 *"Life was real basic"* McDonough, p. 43.

140 *"Omemee life was great"* Young, 17.

140 *"There is a town"* From "Helpless" by Neil Young, on *Déjà Vu* by Crosby, Stills, Nash, & Young (Atlantic, 1970). Published by Cotillion/Broken Arrow Music.

140 *"emotion recollected in tranquillity"* William Wordsworth, *William Wordsworth: The Major Works* (Oxford: Oxford University Press, 2000), p. 611. (Available online: http://www.brysons.net/academic/wordsworth.html.)

140 *"dream comfort memory"* From "Helpless" by Neil Young, on *Déjà Vu* by Crosby, Stills, Nash, & Young (Atlantic, 1970). Published by Cotillion/Broken Arrow Music.

142 *"Writing this now"* Young, *Neil and Me*, p. 24.

142 *"So we waited"* Young, *Neil and Me*, p. 27.

143 *"For most of Neil's childhood"* Young, *Neil and Me*, p. 18.

143 *"What makes you think"* Scott Young, *A Writer's Life* (Toronto: Doubleday Canada, 1994), p. 154.

144 *"The only way"* Young, *Neil and Me*, p. 19.

144 *"I tried to represent"* Young, *Neil and Me*, p. 19.

CHAPTER SEVENTEEN

152 *"an art-school kid"* Rogan, p. 64.

153 *"practically engineered"* McDonough, p. 147.

156 *"By 1966, I knew"* Einarson, p. 172.

157 *"I had to shit on"* Einarson, p. 174.

157 *"revelled in the highjinks"* Rogan, p. 66.

160 *"Fuck off, you fucking pillhead"* Rogan, p. 89.

CHAPTER EIGHTEEN

168 *"I want to come back"* Ritchie Yorke, *Globe and Mail,* 1969. Quoted in Einarson, *Don't Be Denied,* p. 205.

168 *"I've always missed"* Broken Arrow 51, p. 47.

168 *"To me, Canada is"* McDonough, p. 37.

169 *"Now I'm going back to Canada"* From "Journey through the Past" by Neil Young, on *Time Fades Away* by Neil Young (Reprise, 1973). Published by Silver Fiddle Music.

169 *"From down in L.A."* From "One of These Days" by Neil Young, on *Harvest Moon* by Neil Young (Reprise, 1992). Published by Silver Fiddle Music.

169 *"I could live inside a tepee"* From "Sail Away" by Neil Young, on *Rust Never Sleeps* by Neil Young and Crazy Horse (Reprise, 1979). Published by Silver Fiddle Music.

169 *"I ain't tongue-tied"* From "Hawks & Doves" by Neil Young, on *Hawks & Doves* by Neil Young (Reprise, 1980). Published by Silver Fiddle Music.

169 *"Thirty-three years later"* Richard Byrne, "Please Come to Ohio," *The American Prospect Online,* July 6, 2004. Available online: http://www.prospect.org/web/printfriendly-view.ww?id=8066.

170 *"lookin' for Khaddafi"* From "Mideast Vacation" by Neil Young, on *Life* by Neil Young and Crazy Horse (Geffen, 1987). Published by Silver Fiddle Music.

170 *"one of Young's most amusing"* Rogan, p. 538.

170 *"Don't you think it's better"* McDonough, p. 588.

170 *"When Ronnie and Nancy"* From "Everybody's Rockin'" by Neil Young, on *Everybody's Rockin'* by Neil Young (Geffen, 1983). Published by Silver Fiddle Music.

170 *"When I was a younger man"* From "Get Back to the Country" by Neil Young, on *Old Ways* by Neil Young (Geffen, 1985). Published by Silver Fiddle Music.

171 *"The economy was getting"* From "Old Ways" by Neil Young, on *Old Ways* by Neil Young (Geffen, 1985). Published by Silver Fiddle Music.

171 *"There's women and men"* From "Nothing Is Perfect" by Neil Young. This unreleased song was performed at Live Aid on July 13, 1985.

171 *"You go to a supermarket"* McDonough, p. 588.

171 *"Neil Young said"* Justin Mitchell, *Rocky Mountain News,* May 29, 1987. Quoted in Rogan, p. 535.

172 *"I have an opinion"* From a 1989 interview. Available online: http://www.thrashers wheat.org/ptma/reagan.htm.

172 *"We got a thousand points"* From "Rockin' in the Free World" by Neil Young, on *Freedom* by Neil Young (Reprise, 1989). Published by Silver Fiddle Music.

172 *"Let's roll for freedom"* From "Let's Roll" by Neil Young, on *Are You Passionate?* by Neil Young (Vapor, 2002). Published by Silver Fiddle Music.

173 *"professional contrarian"* Adam Sweeting, "Will I be deported?," *Guardian,* May 22, 2003.

173 *"Most Dylan-lovers"* Christopher Ricks. Quoted in "Idiot Wind" by James Wolcott, *The New Republic,* August 8, 2004.

CHAPTER NINETEEN

180 *"it was a VH-1 show"* Rogan, p. 638.

180 *"My my, hey hey"* From "My My, Hey Hey (Out of the Blue)" by Neil Young and Jeff Blackburn, on *Rust Never Sleeps* by Neil Young and Crazy Horse (Reprise, 1979). Published by Silver Fiddle Music.

180 *"It's better to burn out"* From "Hey Hey, My My (Into the Black)" by Neil Young, on *Rust Never Sleeps* by Neil Young and Crazy Horse (Reprise, 1979). Published by Silver Fiddle Music.

181 *"I hate it"* John Lennon, quoted in an article by David Sheff, *Playboy,* September 1979. Quoted in McDonough, p. 534.

181 *"I'd like to thank Kurt Cobain"* Rogan, p. 620.

CHAPTER TWENTY

183 *"I have been wading"* Sherwood Anderson. Quoted in "Quitting the Paint Factory: On the Virtues of Idleness" by Mark Slouka, *Harper's Magazine,* November 2004.

188 *"Goin' back to school"* From "Depression Blues" by Neil Young, on *Lucky Thirteen* (Geffen, 1993). Published by Silver Fiddle Music.

190 *"third best garage"* McDonough, p. 609.

CHAPTER TWENTY-ONE

193 *"He only let me drive"* Rogan, p. 82.

194 *"I think at one point"* McDonough, p. 148.

CHAPTER TWENTY-TWO

204 *"Route 66 was a gas"* McDonough, pp. 148–149.

205 *"If you're gonna put a record"* Cameron Crowe, "So Hard To Make Arrangements For Yourself: The *Rolling Stone* Interview With Neil Young," *Rolling Stone,* August 14, 1975. Quoted in McDonough, p. 433.

205 *"the first horror record"* Bud Scoppa, "Play It Loud and Stay in the Other Room," *N.M.E.,* June 28, 1975.

205 *"Hey, I've made"* McDonough, p. 413.

205 *"I think what was in my mind"* Bud Scoppa, "Play It Loud and Stay in the Other Room," *N.M.E.,* June 28, 1975.

206 *"I'm sorry"* Liner notes to *Tonight's the Night* by Neil Young (Reprise, 1975).

206 *"Well, it wasn't supposed"* From "Tired Eyes" by Neil Young, on *Tonight's the Night* by Neil Young (Reprise, 1975). Published by Silver Fiddle Music.

206 *"I'm not going back to Woodstock"* From "Roll Another Number (For the Road)" by Neil Young, on *Tonight's the Night* by Neil Young (Reprise, 1975). Published by Silver Fiddle Music.

206 *"Well, they say that Santa Fe"* From "Albuquerque" by Neil Young, on *Tonight's the Night* by Neil Young (Reprise, 1975). Published by Silver Fiddle Music.

207 *"So I'll stop"* From "Albuquerque" by Neil Young, on *Tonight's the Night* by Neil Young (Reprise, 1975). Published by Silver Fiddle Music.

CHAPTER TWENTY-THREE

213 *"the Functional Motel"* Vladimir Nabokov, *Lolita* (New York: Vintage International, 1997), p. 145.

CHAPTER TWENTY-FOUR

219 *"cracked...long ago"* From "Danger Bird" by Neil Young, on *Zuma* by Neil Young and Crazy Horse (Reprise, 1975). Published by Silver Fiddle Music.

219 *"daybreak hitting the water"* McDonough, p. 486.

219 *"Lookin' for a love"* From "Lookin' for a Love" by Neil Young, on *Zuma* by Neil Young and Crazy Horse (Reprise, 1975). Published by Silver Fiddle Music.

219 *"If I could hold on"* From "Barstool Blues" by Neil Young, on *Zuma* by Neil Young and Crazy Horse (Reprise, 1975). Published by Silver Fiddle Music.

220 *"with his galleons"* From "Cortez the Killer" by Neil Young, on *Zuma* by Neil Young and Crazy Horse (Reprise, 1975). Published by Silver Fiddle Music.

221 *"Madness!!! Auditions"* Rogan, p. 77.

222 *"They were resurfacing"* Einarson and Furay, *For What It's Worth,* p. 90.

222 *"One day"* Einarson and Furay, *For What It's Worth,* p. 100.

223 *"Didn't want to call"* Young, *Neil and Me,* p. 66.

223 *"City in the smog"* From "L.A." by Neil Young, on *On the Beach* by Neil Young (Reprise, 1973). Published by Silver Fiddle Music.

223 *"Well, I hear that Laurel Canyon"* From "Revolution Blues" by Neil Young, on *On the Beach* by Neil Young (Reprise, 1974). Published by Silver Fiddle Music.

225 *"respectfully dedicated"* McDonough, p. 194.

225 *"head is the event"* From "Mr. Soul" by Neil Young, on *Buffalo Springfield Again* by Neil Young (Atco, 1967). Published by Springalo Toones—Warner Tamerlane.

226 *"I don't think I'll ever be organized"* Broken Arrow 40, p. 34.

227 *"We thought he used to stage"* Einarson and Furay, *For What It's Worth,* pp. 143–44.

227 *"I would think I was gonna have one"* McDonough, p. 177–78.

CHAPTER TWENTY-FIVE

233 *"Where the sun hits"* From "Lookin' for a Love" by Neil Young, on *Zuma* by Neil Young and Crazy Horse (Reprise, 1975). Published by Silver Fiddle Music.

234 *"poor grade marijuana"* From live recording at the Bottom Line, New York City, May 16, 1974 (late show).

234 *"I was thinking about"* From "After the Gold Rush" by Neil Young, on *After the Gold Rush* by Neil Young (Reprise, 1970). Published by Broken Arrow Music.

234 *"Now that you made"* From "I Believe in You" by Neil Young, on *After the Gold Rush* by Neil Young (Reprise, 1970). Published by Broken Arrow Music.

235 *"All in a dream"* From "After the Gold Rush" by Neil Young, on *After the Gold Rush* by Neil Young (Reprise, 1970). Published by Broken Arrow Music.

235 *"traveling south-to-north"* Colin Penno, "UFOs over Topanga," *Messenger,* July 2–15, 1992.

237 *"It's dumb"* Rogan, p. 444.

237 *"The whole rock"* Mary Turner, Warner Bros. Music Show radio interview, 1979. Quoted in *Zero to Sixty* by Johnny Rogan, p. 443.

237 *"Did Neil attend"* McDonough, p. 523.

CHAPTER TWENTY-SIX

240 *"musical novel"* Dorian Lynskey, "Neil Young: Greendale," *Guardian,* August 15, 2003.

241 *"have resigned themselves"* Lucas Hanft, "Young's Old and New Masterpieces Lament His Dashed Hippie Dreams," *New York Observer,* August 25, 2003.

241 *"It ain't a privilege"* From "Grandpa's Interview" by Neil Young, on *Greendale* by Neil Young and Crazy Horse (Vapor, 2003). Published by Silver Fiddle Music.

241 *"A good novel"* John Irving, *My Movie Business* (New York: Ballantine Books, 2000), p. 7.

242 *"one of Young's career-defying"* Shannon Zimmerman, "Return of Rock's Angry Old Man," *Salon.com,* August 20, 2003. (Available online: www.archive.salon.com/ent/music/review/2003/08/20/young/.)

242 *"I ain't singing"* From "This Note's for You" by Neil Young, on *This Note's for You* by Neil Young (Reprise, 1988). Published by Silver Fiddle Music.

243 *"Enthusiastic cheers"* Judith Lewis, "Don't You Get It?," *L.A. Weekly,* September 26–October 2, 2003.

243 *"The buzzing bass"* Madison Smartt Bell, "Have You Heard the New Neil Young Novel?," *New York Times,* November 9, 2003.

243 *"Wrappin' up dope"* From "Bandit" by Neil Young, on *Greendale* by Neil Young and Crazy Horse (Vapor, 2003). Published by Silver Fiddle Music.

CHAPTER TWENTY-SEVEN

248 *"an Oakland youth"* Joel Selvin, "Nobody gets more low-key than Neil Young," *San Francisco Chronicle,* September 17, 2004.

248 *"Respect Mother Earth"* from "Mother Earth" by Neil Young, on *Ragged Glory* by Neil Young and Crazy Horse (Reprise, 1990). Published by Silver Fiddle Music.

CHAPTER TWENTY-EIGHT

257 *"I once went down"* Available online: http://hyperrust.org/General/NeilSpeaks.html.

259 *"Aurora borealis"* From "Pocahontas" by Neil Young, on *Rust Never Sleeps* by Neil Young and Crazy Horse (Reprise, 1979). Published by Silver Fiddle Music.

260 *"more synthetic–Neil Young"* McDonough, p. 663.

260 *"When the dream came"* From "On the Way Home" by Neil Young, from *Last Time Around* by Buffalo Springfield (Atco, 1968). Published by Springalo Toones—Warner Tamerlane.

261 *"This is a song I wrote"* Rogan, p. 187.

261 *"I come down from"* From "Human Highway," on *Comes a Time* by Neil Young (Reprise, 1978). Published by Silver Fiddle Music.

261 *"Four strong winds"* From "Four Strong Winds" by Ian Tyson, on *Comes a Time* by Neil Young (Reprise, 1978). Published by Warner Bros. Inc.

SELECTED

DISCOGRAPHY

THE SQUIRES
"The Sultan/Aurora," V Records · Released: September 1963.

BUFFALO SPRINGFIELD
Buffalo Springfield, Atco · Released: December 1966.
Go and Say Goodbye; Sit Down I Think I Love You; Leave; Nowadays Clancy Can't
Even Sing; Hot Dusty Roads; Everybody's Wrong; Flying on the Ground Is Wrong;
Burned; Do I Have to Come Right Out and Say It; Baby Don't Scold Me; Out of My Mind;
Pay the Price.

Buffalo Springfield Again, Atco · Released: December 1967.
Mr. Soul; A Child's Claim to Fame; Everydays; Expecting to Fly; Bluebird; Hung Upside
Down; Sad Memory; Good Time Boy; Rock & Roll Woman; Broken Arrow.

Last Time Around, Atco · Released: July 1968.
On the Way Home; It's So Hard to Wait; Pretty Girl Why; Four Days Gone; Carefree
Country Day; Special Care; The Hour of Not Quite Rain; Questions; I Am a Child;
Merry-Go-Round; Uno Mundo; Kind Woman.

CROSBY, STILLS, NASH, & YOUNG
Déjà Vu, Atlantic · Released: March 1970.
Carry On; Teach Your Children; Almost Cut My Hair; Helpless; Woodstock; Déjà Vu;
Our House; 4+20; Country Girl: A) Whiskey Boot Hill, B) Down, Down, Down,
C) "Country Girl" (I Think You're Pretty); Everybody I Love You.

4 Way Street, Atlantic · Released: February 1971.
Suite: Judy Blue Eyes; On the Way Home; Teach Your Children; Triad; The Lee Shore;
Chicago; Right Between the Eyes; Cowgirl in the Sand; Don't Let It Bring You Down;
49 Bye Byes/America's Children; Love the One You're With. (CD bonus tracks: King
Midas In Reverse; Laughing; Black Queen; Medley: The Loner, Cinnamon Girl, Down by
the River; Pre-Road Downs; Long Time Gone; Southern Man; Ohio; Carry On; Find the
Cost of Freedom.)

American Dream, Atlantic · Released: November 1988.
American Dream; Got It Made; Name of Love; Don't Say Goodbye; This Old House;
Nighttime for Generals; Shadowland; Drivin' Thunder; Clear Blue Skies; That Girl;
Compass; Soldiers of Peace; Feel Your Love; Night Song.

Looking Forward, Reprise · Released: October 1999.
Faith in Me; Looking Forward; Stand and Be Counted; Heartland; Seen Enough;
Slowpoke; Dream for Him; No Tears Left; Out of Control; Someday Soon; Queen of
Them All; Sanibel.

THE STILLS-YOUNG BAND

Long May You Run, Reprise · Released: November 1976.
Long May You Run; Make Love to You; Midnight on the Bay; Black Coral; Ocean Girl;
Let It Shine; 12/8 Blues (All the Same); Fontainebleau; Guardian Angel.

NEIL YOUNG (INCLUDES NEIL YOUNG AND CRAZY HORSE)

Neil Young, Reprise · Released: January 1969.
The Emperor of Wyoming; The Loner; If I Could Have Her Tonight; I've Been Waiting for
You; The Old Laughing Lady; String Quartet from Whiskey Boot Hill; Here We Are in the
Years; What Did You Do to My Life?; I've Loved Her So Long; The Last Trip to Tulsa.

Everybody Knows This Is Nowhere, Reprise · Released: July 1969.
Cinnamon Girl; Everybody Knows This Is Nowhere; Round & Round (It Won't Be Long);
Down by the River; The Losing End (When You're On); Running Dry (Requiem for the
Rockets); Cowgirl in the Sand.

After the Gold Rush, Reprise · Released: July 1970.
Tell Me Why; After the Gold Rush; Only Love Can Break Your Heart; Southern Man;
Till the Morning Comes; Oh, Lonesome Me; Don't Let It Bring You Down; Birds; When
You Dance I Can Really Love; I Believe in You; Cripple Creek Ferry.

Harvest, Reprise · Released: February 1972.
Out on the Weekend; Harvest; A Man Needs a Maid; Heart of Gold; Are You Ready
for the Country?; Old Man; There's a World; Alabama; The Needle and the Damage
Done; Words (Between the Lines of Age).

Journey through the Past, Reprise · Released: December 1972.
For What It's Worth/Mr. Soul; Rock & Roll Woman; Find the Cost of Freedom; Ohio; Southern Man; Are You Ready for the Country; Let Me Call You Sweetheart; Alabama; Words; Relativity Invitation; Handel's Messiah; King of Kings; Soldier; Let's Go Away for Awhile.

Time Fades Away, Reprise · Released: September 1973.
Time Fades Away; Journey through the Past; Yonder Stands the Sinner; L.A.; Love in Mind; Don't Be Denied; The Bridge; Last Dance.

On the Beach, Reprise · Released: September 1974.
Walk On; See the Sky about to Rain; Revolution Blues; For the Turnstiles; Vampire Blues; On the Beach; Motion Pictures (For Carrie); Ambulance Blues.

Tonight's the Night, Reprise · Released: June 1975.
Tonight's the Night; Speakin' Out; World on a String; Borrowed Tune; Come on Baby Let's Go Downtown; Mellow My Mind; Roll Another Number (For the Road); Albuquerque; New Mama; Lookout Joe; Tired Eyes; Tonight's the Night—Part II.

Zuma, Reprise · Released: November 1975.
Don't Cry No Tears; Danger Bird; Pardon My Heart; Lookin' for a Love; Barstool Blues; Stupid Girl; Drive Back; Cortez the Killer; Through My Sails.

American Stars 'n' Bars, Reprise · Released: June 1977.
The Old Country Waltz; Saddle up the Palomino; Hey Babe; Hold Back the Tears; Bite the Bullet; Star of Bethlehem; Will to Love; Like a Hurricane; Homegrown.

Decade, Reprise · Released: October 1977.
Down to the Wire; Burned; Mr. Soul; Broken Arrow; Expecting to Fly; Sugar Mountain; I Am a Child; The Loner; The Old Laughing Lady; Cinnamon Girl; Down by the River; Cowgirl in the Sand; I Believe in You; After the Gold Rush; Southern Man; Helpless; Ohio; Soldier; Old Man; A Man Needs a Maid; Harvest; Heart of Gold; Star of Bethlehem; The Needle and the Damage Done; Tonight's the Night—Part I; Tired Eyes; Walk On; For the Turnstiles; Winterlong; Deep Forbidden Lake; Like a Hurricane; Love Is a Rose; Cortez the Killer; Campaigner; Long May You Run.

Comes a Time, Reprise · Released: July 1978.
Goin' Back; Comes a Time; Look Out for My Love; Peace of Mind; Lotta Love; Human Highway; Already One; Field of Opportunity; Motorcycle Mama; Four Strong Winds.

Rust Never Sleeps, Reprise · Released: June 1979.
My My, Hey Hey (Out of the Blue); Thrasher; Ride My Llama; Pocahontas; Sail Away; Powderfinger; Welfare Mothers; Sedan Delivery; Hey Hey, My My (Into the Black).

Live Rust, Reprise · Released: November 1979.
Sugar Mountain; I Am a Child; Comes a Time; After the Goldrush; My My, Hey Hey
(Out of the Blue); When You Dance I Can Really Love; The Loner; The Needle and the
Damage Done; Lotta Love; Sedan Delivery; Powderfinger; Cortez the Killer; Cinnamon
Girl; Like a Hurricane; Hey Hey, My My (Into the Black); Tonight's the Night.

Hawks & Doves, Reprise · Released: November 1980.
Little Wing; The Old Homestead; Lost in Space; Captain Kennedy; Stayin' Power;
Coastline; Union Man; Comin' Apart at Every Nail; Hawks & Doves.

Re*Ac*Tor, Reprise · Released: November 1981.
Opera Star; Surfer Joe and Moe the Sleaze; T-Bone; Get Back On It; Southern Pacific;
Motor City; Rapid Transit; Shots.

Trans, Geffen · Released: December 1982.
Little Thing Called Love; Computer Age; We R In Control; Transformer Man;
Computer Cowboy (aka Syscrusher); Hold On To Your Love; Sample and Hold; Mr. Soul;
Like an Inca.

Everybody's Rockin', Geffen · Released: January 1983.
Betty Lou's Got a New Pair of Shoes; Rainin' in My Heart; Payola Blues; Wonderin';
Kinda Fonda Wanda; Jellyroll Man; Bright Lights, Big City; Cry, Cry, Cry; Mystery
Train; Everybody's Rockin'.

Old Ways, Geffen · Released: August 1985.
The Wayward Wind; Get Back to the Country; Are There Any More Real Cowboys?;
Once an Angel; Misfits; California Sunset; Old Ways; My Boy; Bound for Glory;
Where Is the Highway Tonight?

Landing On Water, Geffen · Released: July 1986.
Weight of the World; Violent Side; Hippie Dream; Bad News Beat; Touch the Night;
People on the Street; Hard Luck Stories; I Got a Problem; Pressure; Drifter.

Life, Geffen · Released: July 1987.
Mideast Vacation; Long Walk Home; Around the World; Inca Queen; Too Lonely;
Prisoners of Rock 'n' Roll; Cryin' Eyes; When Your Lonely Heart Breaks;
We Never Danced.

This Note's for You, Reprise · Released: April 1988.
Ten Men Workin'; This Note's For You; Coupe de Ville; Life in the City; Twilight;
Married Man; Sunny Inside; Can't Believe Your Lyin'; Hey Hey; One Thing.

Eldorado, Reprise · Release: April 1989.
Cocaine Eyes; Don't Cry; Heavy Love; On Broadway; Eldorado.
[Note: this EP was released only in Japan and Australia.]

Freedom, Reprise · Released: October 1989.
Rockin' in the Free World; Crime in the City (Sixty to Zero Part One); Don't Cry; Hangin' on a Limb; Eldorado; The Ways of Love; Someday; On Broadway; Wrecking Ball; No More; Too Far Gone; Rockin' in the Free World.

Ragged Glory, Reprise · Released: September 1990.
Country Home; White Line; F*!#in' Up; Over and Over; Love to Burn; Farmer John; Mansion on the Hill; Days That Used to Be; Love and Only Love; Mother Earth (Natural Anthem).

Weld, Reprise · Released: October 1991.
Hey Hey, My My (Into the Black); Crime in the City; Blowin' in the Wind; Welfare Mothers; Love to Burn; Cinnamon Girl; Mansion on the Hill; F*!#in' Up; Cortez the Killer; Powderfinger; Love and Only Love; Rockin' in the Free World; Like a Hurricane; Farmer John; Tonight's the Night; Roll Another Number.

Arc, Reprise · Released: November 1991.
Arc.

Harvest Moon, Reprise · Released: October 1992.
Unknown Legend; From Hank to Hendrix; You and Me; Harvest Moon; War of Man; One of These Days; Such a Woman; Old King; Dreamin' Man; Natural Beauty.

Lucky Thirteen, Geffen ·Released: January 1993.
Sample and Hold; Transformer Man; Depression Blues; Get Gone; Don't Take Your Love Away from Me; Once an Angel; Where Is the Highway Tonight?; Hippie Dream; Pressure; Around the World; Mideast Vacation; Ain't It the Truth; This Note's for You.

Unplugged, Reprise · Released: June 1993.
The Old Laughing Lady; Mr. Soul; World on a String; Pocahontas; Stringman; Like a Hurricane; The Needle and the Damage Done; Helpless; Harvest Moon; Transformer Man; Unknown Legend; Look Out for My Love; Long May You Run; From Hank to Hendrix.

Sleeps With Angels, Reprise · Released: August 1994.
My Heart; Prime of Life; Driveby; Sleeps with Angels; Western Hero; Change Your Mind; Blue Eden; Safeway Cart; Train of Love; Trans Am; Piece of Crap; A Dream That Can Last.

Mirror Ball, Reprise · Released: June 1995.
Song X; Act of Love; I'm the Ocean; Big Green Country; Truth Be Known; Downtown; What Happened Yesterday; Peace and Love; Throw Your Hatred Down; Scenery; Fallen Angel.

Broken Arrow, Reprise · Released: July 1996.
Big Time; Loose Change; Slip Away; Changing Highways; Scattered (Let's Think about Livin'); This Town; Music Arcade; Baby What You Want Me to Do.

Year of the Horse, Reprise · Released: June 1997.
When You Dance I Can Really Love; Barstool Blues; When Your Lonely Heart Breaks; Mr. Soul; Big Time; Pocahontas; Human Highway; Slip Away; Scattered (Let's Think about Livin'); Danger Bird; Prisoners; Sedan Delivery.

Silver & Gold, Reprise · Released: April 2000.
Good To See You; Silver & Gold; Daddy Went Walkin'; Buffalo Springfield Again; The Great Divide; Horseshoe Man; Red Sun; Distant Camera; Razor Love; Without Rings.

Road Rock Vol. 1, Reprise · Released: December 2000.
Cowgirl in the Sand; Walk On; Fool for Your Love; Peace of Mind; Words; Motorcycle Mama; Tonight's the Night; All Along the Watchtower.

Are You Passionate?, Vapor · Released: March 2002.
You're My Girl; Mr. Disappointment; Differently; Quit (Don't Say You Love Me); Let's Roll; Are You Passionate?; Goin' Home; When I Hold You in My Arms; Be with You; Two Old Friends; She's a Healer.

Greendale, Vapor · Released: August 2003.
Falling from Above; Double E; Devil's Sidewalk; Leave the Driving; Carmichael; Bandit; Grandpa's Interview; Bringin' Down the Dinner; Sun Green; Be the Rain.

Greatest Hits, Reprise · Released: November 2004.
Down by the River; Cowgirl in the Sand; Cinnamon Girl; Helpless; After the Gold Rush; Only Love Can Break Your Heart; Southern Man; Ohio; The Needle and the Damage Done; Old Man; Heart of Gold; Like a Hurricane; Comes a Time; Hey Hey, My My (Into the Black); Rockin' in the Free World; Harvest Moon.

ACKNOWLEDGMENTS

I'D LIKE to thank:

My interview subjects (roughly in order of appearance): Nardwuar the Human Serviette, Bev Davies, Jim Fitzgerald, John and Barb Yellowlees, Fran Gebhard, John Einarson, Miriam Toews, Vice-Principal Furtado, John K. Samson, Carmine LaRosa, Brian Moniz, Nicholas Jennings, Jeanine Hollingshead, Sharry Wilson, Stephen Cross, Bill Neuschulz, Joost Groen, Denis Stephan, Curt Vigg and Ragged Glory, Kris Bournay, Deb Navickas, Ian Rosen, Bob Lee, Mike Heinz, Jim Dickie, Paul Tomita, Cosmo Spada, and Cathy Harris.

The people who let us stay in their yards, motor homes, and motels: Ian and Donna Stevenson, Karen and Brian Moniz, Gary in Cleveland, Barb from Amherst Township, and Mike Heinz.

The big-hearted people at Greystone Books: Rob Sanders, Chris Labonte, Belinda Bruce, Scott McIntyre, and Peter Cocking.

Yvonne Gall at the CBC (the best radio producer in the world).

My editor, Barbara Pulling, and my copy-editor, Pam Robertson.

Sharry Wilson, my fact-checker and bootleg pusher, whom I can't thank enough.

And for additional encouragement and advice: Will Ferguson, Claudia Casper, John Einarson, Nicholas Jennings, Rick Maddocks, Sara Frank Bristow, Susan Serran and Toronto Artscape, Selina Martin, Roel van Dijk (for last-minute bootleg assistance), everyone at the Sidebar, and my brother Dan (for walking the dog).

ABOUT
THE AUTHOR

KEVIN CHONG spent his adolescence noodling on the guitar, playing in garage bands, and listening to a lot of Neil Young. His first published piece as a teenager was a song-by-song review of a Young concert for the official fanzine, *Broken Arrow*.

Kevin Chong studied at the University of British Columbia and at Columbia University, where he received an MFA in writing. His first novel, *Baroque-a-Nova,* was published in Canada, the U.S., and France. He lives in Vancouver, B.C., where he is working on his second novel.